D1475170

RENEWALS 458-4574

DATE DUE

ʳ

WITHDRAWN
UTSA LIBRARIES

THE UNSINKABLE FLEET

THE UNSINKABLE FLEET

The Politics of U.S. Navy Expansion in World War II

JOEL R. DAVIDSON

Naval Institute Press   Annapolis, Maryland

© 1996 by Joel Robert Davidson

All rights reserved. No part of this book may be reproduced without written permission from the publisher.

Library of Congress Cataloging-in-Publication Data

Davidson, Joel Robert, 1959–
    The unsinkable fleet: the politics of the U.S. navy expansion in World War II / Joel R. Davidson.
        p.   cm.
    Includes bibliographical references and index.
    ISBN 1-55750-156-4 (alk. paper)
    1. World War, 1939–1945—Naval operations, American. 2. United States. Navy—History—World War, 1939–1945. I. Title.
D769.45D38   1996
940.54'5973—dc20   96-13714

Printed in the United States of America on acid-free paper ∞
03 02 01 00 99 98 97 96   9 8 7 6 5 4 3 2
First printing

Library
University of Texas
at San Antonio

All photographs are from the U.S. Navy Collection of the National Archives unless indicated otherwise.

To my parents,
Lt. Irene Belzer, Army Nurse Corps,
and Sgt. Jerome K. Davidson, Army Air Forces,
two of the millions of ordinary Americans
who risked everything from 1941 to 1945
so their children could live in freedom

CONTENTS

PREFACE

On reading various histories of the United States in World War II, I was struck by how little was said about the process of deciding what naval forces the country should create to fight the war. Only two conclusions seemed possible; either the issue was so obvious that historians felt no explanation was necessary, or no one had really studied the questions that arose and how they were resolved.

Further research revealed the latter explanation to be correct, leaving an important gap in any understanding of how the United States fought the greatest war in its history. I have attempted to close part of that gap with this book. My aim is to examine wartime navy growth as a product of naval policy, broadly construed. By this I mean policy on the national level, from its origins in the minds of naval planners and leaders, as it is filtered through the political and bureaucratic machinery of state, to its implementation in the imperfect world of men, machines, and money.

ACKNOWLEDGMENTS

Many dedicated and generous individuals have contributed invaluable assistance to this project out of a sense of professionalism and a love of learning. Those mentioned here gave me all the help for which I asked and more; this book would not have been possible without them. Yet despite their expertise and knowledge, I am responsible for selecting and analyzing the historical materials and for any faults or errors that this volume contains.

I have been privileged to have been helped by several accomplished historians. The sage advice and invaluable insights of Alex Roland of Duke University guided my research from its earliest stages through its completion; John Sumida of the University of Maryland encouraged me to pursue this topic and gave unswerving support to my efforts in a non-traditional field of naval history; and I. B. Holley of Duke University oversaw the beginnings of my work and helped me develop the research skills I relied upon for this project.

Numerous individuals and organizations have also provided invaluable assistance in day-to-day research, giving me guidance and informed access to the documents that make up the heart of this book. I received particularly generous help from Kathleen Lloyd and the staff at the Naval Historical Center. At the National Archives, Barry Zerby and his

Acknowledgments

colleagues in the Naval History Branch provided assistance above and beyond the call of duty, as did Wil Mahoney and the staff of the Modern Military Branch.

Historical research and writing is largely a solitary endeavor. I was fortunate to have nearly limitless moral support from my friends, who knew little of the topic but were happy to encourage me if I believed the work was worthwhile. Finally, I thank Mark Gatlin at the Naval Institute for his unwavering faith in this project.

THE UNSINKABLE FLEET

INTRODUCTION

When the USS *Missouri* sailed into Tokyo Bay in September 1945 to accept Japan's surrender, the massive battleship with its imposing heavy guns perfectly embodied American determination, industrial muscle, and technological ingenuity. Jolted into frenetic action by the Pearl Harbor attack, the United States used its colossal productive powers to create air and naval forces that won control of the world's oceans and reduced Japan's once-mighty Imperial Fleet to a pale shadow of its former strength. More than a symbol of American will, the *Missouri* expressed the overwhelming power and newfound global presence of the greatest battle fleet that has ever sailed.

World War II marked a watershed in the development of the U.S. Navy, as that service experienced a period of rapid growth unparalleled in its history. The navy's wartime expansion program was conceived in the dark days of semi-neutrality following the fall of France and rapidly accelerated after the disasters of 1941. By 1945 it had given this country a battle fleet greater than the rest of the world's navies combined. Not since the early nineteenth century had a single maritime power so completely dominated the oceans. Only Britain's Royal Navy, part of which steamed in American-built ships, possessed a battle fleet worthy of the name. So great had American naval power become that huge

THE UNSINKABLE FLEET

"task forces" could reach out across five thousand miles of ocean, sailing regularly within sight of the enemy's homeland and threatening Japan with aerial attack and amphibious invasion on a scale never before imagined.

The U.S. Navy reached this pinnacle of power partly through the destruction of its enemies, but mainly through a stupendous shipbuilding effort. In a sense, the *Missouri* was at the head of a long column of ships that stretched back beyond the advanced operating base at Ulithi Atoll, beyond Pearl Harbor, all the way to shipyards in Philadelphia and New York, and to the corridors of the Pentagon and the halls of Congress. Reacting in 1940 to the possibility that the United States might have to fight alone against the combined forces of all three Axis powers, the still-neutral United States had begun the difficult and time-consuming program of naval construction that aimed at creating a navy capable of taking on the rest of the world with a good chance of winning.

While progress was slow at first, the combatant shipbuilding program soon gained such momentum that by late in the war ships were entering service at a rate that taxed the nation's ability to provide adequate numbers of crewmen and support personnel. By the end of the war, naval leaders could report that over the previous five years, using massive amounts of material, facilities, and labor, U.S. shipyards had completed nearly two hundred battleships, aircraft carriers, and cruisers, plus more than a thousand destroyers, submarines, and destroyer escorts.

American shipbuilding prowess not only affected the superiority of force with which the United States fought the war, but it also shaped the political posture of America's armed services as they entered the cold war era. The naval preponderance achieved during World War II had global repercussions, for ships built to defeat the Axis powers continued to influence U.S. military and foreign policy during the following decade. In addition, the process of building a vast fleet produced powerful industrial and naval support interests that favored continuing the nation's newly achieved naval dominance.

Although the appearance of a huge U.S. fleet in Japanese home waters was portrayed as a major national triumph, like most great victories it came at a price. A war as fierce and all-consuming as World War II taxed to the limit the economies and societies of all participants. Although the economic potential and industrial capacity of America seemed limitless to many observers, they were in many cases barely suf-

Introduction

ficient to meet the needs of U.S. and Allied forces in global conflict. In this light, each navy ship that left the building ways represented a conscious decision to devote resources to expanding the battle fleet in lieu of using those same resources, be they quantities of steel plate, petroleum, or men, for what were arguably equally important ends.

That these decisions about allocations of scarce resources were often hotly contested should come as no surprise, given the powerful constituencies that were competing for a share of the nation's war-making capacity. Among its many attributes, the combat fleet construction program consumed material and human resources at a prodigious rate. The shipbuilding yards and the factories that fed them steel plate and various finished parts used a significant portion of America's industrial capacity. The millions of men and women who worked on building up and maintaining the navy could have applied their skills to other war projects or, in the case of the able-bodied males, could have entered the armed forces.

As ships entered service and the fleet grew to unprecedented size, navy operating forces began to absorb ever-greater amounts of fuel, ammunition, and, most important, men. By the war's second year, U.S. leaders had begun to suspect that the nation simply lacked enough able-bodied men to do all the fighting and building that the war effort required. At best, manpower would remain tight until the fighting ended.

Although the typical description of a modern combat fleet is usually couched in terms of machines—that is, the ships—a navy of the size built by the United States during World War II employed a surprising share of available military manpower. If in August 1945 the entire U.S. fleet had rendezvoused at a particular point at sea, the crews of those thousands of vessels would have numbered more than one million men. Add to this the shore stations, training facilities, and other miscellaneous support establishments, and total navy strength amounted to between a quarter and a third of the men in America's armed forces.

Since the war, the American public and even most historians have been content to view the U.S. Navy in World War II as a fighting force and judge it by its accomplishments. However, those responsible for allocating the nation's resources during the war saw the navy as one of several constituencies competing for an ever-larger share of an enormous but ultimately limited pool of material and personnel. This competition forced naval leaders to advocate the needs of their service in a manner calculated to obtain the resources that would enable them to build and operate a fleet of the magnitude they thought necessary to win the war.

Because the nation's resources appeared inadequate to meet the stated requirements of all claimants, especially in terms of manpower, a struggle soon ensued among the armed services and key civilian war agencies. The leaders of these organizations attempted to obtain priority in the distribution of resources by criticizing the claims and plans of other services and defending their own programs from similar attacks. For reasons partly strategic, partly political, and partly inherent in the nature of naval expansion planning, U.S. Navy leaders succeeded in defeating critics who charged that fleet growth had outstripped the needs and abilities of a nation committed to fighting a global war. All outside attempts to curb naval expansion in the name of economy or to divert resources elsewhere met with failure at the hands of a formidable navy staff led by Chief of Naval Operations Adm. Ernest J. King.

As the war dragged on, growing shortages at home and strategic successes abroad made influential civilian leaders within the Navy Department question the sheer magnitude of planned fleet expansion. King and his staff were ready with justifications for continued shipbuilding and even with proposals to expand the program further. Navy planners thereby preserved their program intact despite the misgivings of the country's highest civilian officials. Their success suggests that wartime military leaders in the United States were able to force their views about resource allocation upon civilian officials who were at least nominally responsible for vital decisions regarding procurement levels and production targets.

The navy staff won the contest for resources and preserved the fleet expansion program, but to what end? As the *Missouri* entered Tokyo Bay, her sister battleship, the *Kentucky*, was still only partially completed. The *Kentucky* was one of scores of combatant ships that were still on the ways when Japan capitulated. The material and effort expended on such vessels contributed nothing to the war effort, and many unfinished ships, the *Kentucky* included, were scrapped without ever joining the fleet. In effect, these never-to-be-completed ships made no contribution to national security except as a very expensive form of insurance against some unforeseen military catastrophe.

Introduction

In the midst of a great naval war with all its uncertainties, such insurance has a significant value that would not apply in peacetime. Leaders cannot assume that the enemy will oblige them by acting as they expect him to, and a single severe reverse can undo months or even years of preparation. Faced with the onslaught of waves of fanatical suicide pilots, navy leaders were naturally careful to guard against unexpected losses or defeats. In that respect, the unfinished "insurance" ships can be viewed as an unavoidable cost of making war.

In light of this fact, the key question raised by the debates over navy expansion is not whether a rational strategist might insist on building more warships even after Allied forces had almost totally destroyed the enemy fleets; the answer is almost certainly yes. To the more difficult question of whether the United States wisely spent the resources used to build up the wartime fleet, this study can give no certain answer but can only offer a range of issues for consideration.

This book primarily focuses on the process by which U.S. leaders determined the scale of fleet expansion and the navy's priority in the overall war effort. Given the growing shortages in men and materiel, U.S. leaders had to accept some risks in order to maximize the yield in fighting power from limited war-making assets. By determining the allocation of resources for building military and naval forces, the nation's war leaders decided where risks would fall. Unfortunately, such vital choices depended upon a planning system ill-adapted to produce rational decisions that would optimize the results in terms of national interest. The planning organizations charged with resource allocation were unsuitable and their methods flawed, casting doubt on the essential rightness of the choices that were made.

The decisive victory achieved by the United States and her allies has tended to obscure the difficulty that American leaders faced when allocating seemingly insufficient resources among the various claimants. The U.S. Navy, by dint of its success in garnering men and materiel to support its expansion program, became arguably the key player in this essentially competitive process. The means by which the navy achieved a level of dominance in resource allocation planning is thus a historical question of some importance. The navy's success owed at least as much to naval leaders' bureaucratic skills and ability to manipulate a highly politicized planning system as to the unassailable logic of their arguments. In addition, the navy's long-term building schedule and the industrial infrastructure created to build the fleet generated a momentum of their own, giving naval leaders an inherent advantage over their rivals in the allocation debates.

In advocating the navy's position, Admiral King and his colleagues did what the existing military planning system expected of them. If at times their zeal overrode their logic, leading to requests for war assets that almost certainly were needed more elsewhere, they were only playing their assigned role within the national war planning apparatus. Unfortunately, the country as a whole may have been better served by leaders who could rise above parochial interests and by a system that encouraged them to determine objectively the optimum mix of armed forces with which they could successfully prosecute the war. In this regard, the course and final outcome of the interservice competition over resources cast doubt on the generally positive reputation that the nation's multiservice, or "joint," planning system acquired during the war.

The attacks on and spirited defense of the navy program suggest that parochial service concerns often overshadowed any cooperative search for objective criteria by which U.S. leaders might decide how to allocate scarce strategic resources. Unfortunately, the joint planning organizations created to help military leaders make these crucial choices could not adequately deal with the inevitable effects of service self-interest. The failure of joint agencies to transcend insular viewpoints of single-service planning staffs, at least in the area of resource allocation, undoubtedly hampered overall the U.S. war effort.

Through their defense of the fleet expansion program, naval leaders sought not only the means to win the war but also the ability to remain the world's preeminent naval power long after the fighting ended. In the later stages of the war Admiral King and his staff realized and openly stated that any diminution of naval construction would have a substantial negative impact upon America's position in the postwar world. Unlike the army, whose units would soon disband, and the Air Force, whose equipment would rapidly become obsolete, the navy could use wartime access to resources to ensure its postwar material and political health. This consideration spurred navy leaders to insist not just on having enough ships, but on having new ships through continued building after operational demands for new construction had all but disappeared.

Introduction

The controversy over combat shipbuilding has been largely ignored in literature on the navy's World War II accomplishments. Postwar official and semiofficial histories tend to treat fleet expansion as an unqualified success, noting only that production goals were influenced by the progress of the war. Recent biographies of the principal participants touch on the roles they played in building the navy but contain little analysis of the rationale behind procurement decisions. Those few books that do discuss particular episodes of controversy regarding shipbuilding fail to place such events in the context of an ongoing struggle for resources.

The story of navy wartime fleet expansion policy is a vital link in any understanding of the nation's experience in World War II. It provides us with an example of farsighted, determined leadership at its best and also of parochialism and narrow-mindedness that arguably put service interests before the national good. Through the efforts of millions of ordinary citizens and the determination of a few powerful individuals, a fighting force was created that permanently altered the balance of world power and brought the United States awesome opportunities and responsibilities that are with us to this day.

· 1 ·

A TWO-OCEAN FLEET
The Prewar Origins of Navy Expansion Policy

When World War II began in September 1939 with the Nazi invasion of Poland, the U.S. Navy was enjoying a modest renaissance after a prolonged period of decline. Shackled by tight budgets and disarmament treaties after World War I, by 1932 the combat fleet had shrunk to under a million tons aggregate strength.[1] The navy's maximum authorized strength was based on the international naval disarmament treaties: the Washington Treaty of 1922 and the London Treaty of 1930, which established fixed ratios of forces among the signatories in an effort to stabilize the relative strength of the world's major naval powers. The participating nations had agreed to limit ship construction in hopes of avoiding a naval arms race of the type that many believed had contributed to the outbreak of World War I. In an effort to save money and set an example by voluntary disarmament, the United States had chosen not to build the navy to the full strength allowed under these treaties.

From the low point reached in the early 1930s, several factors created a period of limited navy expansion after 1933. Rising international tensions and the beginnings of rearmament undercut the great powers' desire for naval limitations treaties, which were perceived as unfairly restricting some nations in an attempt to preserve the status quo. At the same time, the continuing depression in the United States made naval

THE UNSINKABLE FLEET

ship construction attractive as a federally funded employment program. Finally, the election of Franklin D. Roosevelt as president placed executive power in the hands of a former assistant secretary of the navy and enthusiastic naval booster.

The first step toward naval rearmament took place in 1933, when the National Industrial Recovery Act authorized the president to allocate funds for building naval vessels allowed under the terms of existing treaty limitations.[2] This act resulted in navy contracts for thirty-two combatants, including two aircraft carriers, four cruisers, and twenty destroyers.[3] Although these orders were motivated more by the need for public works projects than by any strategic calculation, they nevertheless marked the end of a long building drought.

In Congress the push for new naval legislation was led by Rep. Carl Vinson of Georgia, since 1932 chair of the House Naval Affairs Committee and a self-proclaimed "big Navy" man. Vinson and President Roosevelt worked together in 1934 to pass a bill authorizing the navy to build up to the maximum strength that existing naval limitations treaties permitted, or about 1.2 million tons of underage combatants. About three hundred thousand of the navy's existing 1 million tons of combatant ships were overage by the treaty's definitions and thus did not count against building limits.[4] Vinson's bill permitted the navy to replace older vessels as they became overage, thereby automatically maintaining full treaty strength with modern vessels.[5] As enacted, the 1934 naval authorization act (the Vinson-Trammel Act) provided for ninety-four ships, including most of those previously authorized in the 1933 naval bill. Together, the 1933 and 1934 acts helped revive navy shipbuilding in time for the program to make some impact before war broke out in Europe. In the six years preceding the attack on Poland, the navy built sixty-nine major combatants (submarine or larger), along with thirty-seven minor craft.[6]

In late 1935 and early 1936, existing limitations treaties expired, negotiators failed to reach a new agreement on naval expansion, and the United States thus became free to build a fleet that fit its strategic needs.[7] In 1938 the German occupation of Austria and rumblings over the possible partition of Czechoslovakia suggested that Britain and Germany might again be slipping toward war. Both Britain and Japan had been building their navies above the expired treaty limits since

A Two-Ocean Fleet

1936, as the United States continued to observe the limits voluntarily and fell further and further behind.

Alarmed by events in Europe and Asia, in 1938 Chief of Naval Operations Adm. William D. Leahy recommended legislation that authorized building the fleet beyond treaty limits.[8] A special message from the president, together with Japan's apparent attempt to reach naval parity with the United States, helped ease passage of another Vinson-sponsored bill authorizing a 20 percent increase in the U.S. fleet.[9] This bill met with vigorous resistance from those who saw further naval expansion as a war measure rather than a method of deterring war, but Vinson defended it as the best method to protect against attack from the sea. Despite opposition in the Senate, especially from midwestern senators, the bill became law in May 1938.

Using authority granted in the 1934 and 1938 acts, the navy adopted a ten-year building and expansion program that would produce fourteen battleships, five carriers, twenty-seven cruisers, seventy-eight destroyers, and forty-nine submarines through 1948.[10] As with most peacetime military programs, it would turn out ships at a rather leisurely rate, with only eighty-five combatants projected to come off the ways from 1941 through 1945.[11] The last prewar plan for operating forces indicates that during fiscal year 1940 (1 July 1939–30 June 1940) the navy planned to add forty ships of all types and approximately six thousand men.[12]

For several reasons, the outbreak of war in Europe did not lead to immediate plans for fleet expansion. So long as the war remained confined to the Continent, navy leaders could work with some assurance that the Atlantic approaches to the United States would be covered by Britain's Royal Navy. This left U.S. Navy planners free to concentrate most of their attention on Japan, whose growing international assertiveness was backed by an increasingly large and capable battle fleet. The U.S. fleet had numerical superiority over the Imperial Japanese Navy, however, and the incremental increase Congress approved in 1938 promised to at least maintain this advantage. Under the replacement and expansion provisions of the 1934 and 1938 authorization bills, by September 1939 the navy had under construction eighty-nine ships, including eight battleships, two carriers, five cruisers, and nearly forty destroyers.[13]

THE UNSINKABLE FLEET

Political considerations limited any possibility that the outbreak of war would change the expansion program. The recent passage of a major naval expansion act combined with the isolationist tendencies of Congress and the public would make any new naval legislation a difficult proposition. In terms of ship tonnage, the size of the fleet was strictly limited by law; Congress and the president would have to approve any increases. Public opinion in the United States remained divided on the question of U.S. intervention in European affairs, and many would view increased naval construction as a prelude to war.

In addition, many observers believed the navy and its building program were entirely adequate for a country still at peace. Despite the lean years of the 1930s, the new decade found the navy in possession of an aging but still formidable fleet. On 1 January 1940, it had on hand 14 battleships, 5 carriers, 33 cruisers, 170 destroyers, and 27 modern submarines, and U.S. shipyards were building nearly half a million tons of additional combatant ships.[14]

Although the outbreak of war in Europe failed to stimulate an outpouring of new naval appropriations, top-level navy planning organizations were already exploring the possibility of an all-out expansion program to meet Axis aggression. One source of such planning studies was the General Board, the senior advisory body to the secretary of the navy. The board consisted of ten senior officers, usually admirals serving in their last assignment before retirement. As elder statesmen, board members were expected to provide the secretary with impartial advice on policy. Although the board's duties had been increasingly circumscribed since its creation in 1900, it was still charged with reviewing ship construction programs and characteristics.[15]

The other navy organization charged with planning fleet growth operated under the chief of naval operations (CNO), the senior naval officer directly responsible for the operations of the fleet and the preparation of war plans. The CNO's War Plans Division, code-named Op-12, supervised war planning, including not only plans for operations but also estimates of requirements in ships and personnel.[16] Op-12 also had responsibility for collaborating with the War Department in preparing joint army-navy war plans. During the months leading up to Pearl Harbor, the General Board and Op-12 would collaborate on new plans for future navy growth.

A Two-Ocean Fleet

During the 1920s and 1930s, navy war plans centered on a war in the Pacific between the United States and Japan. These plans, code-named Orange, provided the rationale for force structure, because naval leaders had long considered a Pacific offensive the navy's key mission.[17] However, the Orange plans were primarily short-term operational studies and since the mid-1930s had not included any details beyond an initial offensive designed to seize bases in the central Pacific.[18] The navy needed more far-reaching plans that covered the long-term strategy and force requirements for an all-out war.

In late 1938 the Munich crisis convinced American leaders that U.S. policies conflicted with those of Germany and Italy, two potential allies for Japan. If France and England failed to stop German expansion, the United States might find itself alone at war against Japan and both European fascist powers, and in November 1938 the Joint Board began taking steps to plan for such a contingency. As the senior army-navy advisory body assigned to improve coordination between the services, the Joint Board relied on the Joint Planning Committee (JPC) to prepare detailed strategic studies. The board directed the JPC to begin work on a series of joint war plans that envisioned possible operations against a German-Italian-Japanese coalition.[19]

In particular, the Joint Board wanted a study that addressed what the United States could do if Germany and Italy attempted to penetrate the Western Hemisphere in conjunction with a Japanese push into the Philippines.[20] During work on this project, the JPC turned to navy planners for estimates of the combatant forces the U.S. fleet would need for a war against the combined navies of Germany, Italy, and Japan. Thus, even before the European war began, the navy was preparing outlines of a two-ocean navy, a fleet strong enough to single-handedly secure the Western Hemisphere against any likely combination of potential enemies.

In late 1938 and early 1939 such studies were extremely conjectural, for a war as postulated would probably come about only after the military defeat or political collapse of Britain and France. However, war plans in peacetime are by their nature speculative, and any good staff will give at least some consideration to a worst-case scenario. Few of these officers could have guessed that their seemingly academic estimates would eventually form the basis for the navy's wartime expansion plans.

THE UNSINKABLE FLEET

In a December 1938 study, navy planners concluded that to operate offensively in both the Atlantic and Pacific against a German-Japanese-Italian coalition, the navy would need 40 battleships, 18 aircraft carriers, 108 cruisers, 399 destroyers, 162 submarines, and an appropriate number of auxiliary ships.[21] For offensive action in one ocean and defensive operations in the other, somewhat smaller forces were necessary, with an offensive strategy in the Pacific requiring more units than an Atlantic offensive.

These figures were incorporated into the Joint Planning Committee's April 1939 report on a possible war pitting the United States against all three Axis powers.[22] As the JPC report explained, in order to secure the Western Hemisphere and protect America's Pacific outposts, the navy would have to build and maintain a fleet sufficient to provide a favorable ratio of forces with respect to potential enemy fleets. The actual ratio of forces needed would vary as the political and strategic factors changed, but some rough estimates were possible.

In the Pacific, the JPC reported that the U.S. fleet should have numerical parity with the Japanese fleet at all times. As the aggressors, the Japanese could choose the moment to attack and presumably would move in full force. Thus, the U.S. fleet would require a 4:3 ratio of combatants in order to allow for 25 percent of the fleet that would be under repair or on detached duty at any one time. Additional ships would be needed to support planned amphibious operations, where planners calculated requirements at one-third the strength of the enemy fleet. Thus, the overall ratio of forces needed rose to 5:3, or even as high as 6:3 if American offensive operations extended west of Guam.

Navy planners expected no major amphibious operations in the Atlantic, where the navy's primary mission would be to protect army expeditionary forces and deny naval support to Axis troops in South America. In this theater the Pacific equation would be reversed, with U.S. units operating close to their bases and enjoying a fair amount of land-based air support. Thus, a 4:3 overall force ratio would suffice, again allowing for a 25 percent repair and replenishment rate. Taken together, the naval units needed to achieve a 5:3 ratio in the Pacific and a 4:3 ratio in the Atlantic, plus those required for unspecified special missions, equaled the figures reached in the navy study in December 1938.

A Two-Ocean Fleet

Navy planners quickly adopted and expanded upon the figures in the JPC report, adding additional factors that could alter the force ratios required for success. For example, in a May 1939 memorandum, the General Board reported that a minimum of 2:1 superiority would be needed to conduct operations against Japan in the western Pacific under adverse conditions. If certain (unstated) favorable conditions prevailed, the ratio might be reduced to 5:3, which would also suffice to assure protection of U.S. interests as far west as Guam.[23] If the Pacific force ratio dropped to 4:3, the U.S. Navy could protect the Aleutians and Wake Island but could not assure the successful defense of Guam.

In the Atlantic, a 4:3 ratio of forces would allow the United States effective freedom of action, while a rough parity would suffice to control the western Atlantic and dispute Axis movements into South America. As a minimum, the board recommended a 5:3 advantage in the Pacific and a 4:3 advantage in the Atlantic, which would require roughly the number of ships set forth in the JPC study. Such a fleet would have about 3.7 million tons of combatant ships, more than double the tonnage authorized by existing laws.

Although early estimates of combatant ship requirements were based on simple strength comparisons of the opposing fleets, naval planners did cite other factors that might change the ratio of forces needed. For instance, they favored developing and fortifying Guam as a major base. The General Board suggested that a fortified Guam base would make a 5:3 superiority of forces in the Pacific as effective as a 6:3 superiority without a major base at Guam, and a 4:3 ratio as good as a 5:3 ratio.[24] Because the cost of fortifying Guam would be far lower than the cost of building additional ships, the General Board suggested that this estimate presented a good argument for proceeding with fortification plans. Yet plans to fortify Guam ran into stiff opposition from isolationist elements in Congress, and the idea of a major naval base there was dropped in 1939.[25]

When war broke out in Europe, navy planners began giving more consideration to the makeup of a two-ocean battle fleet. In 1939 aircraft carriers had yet to prove themselves in actual combat operations. Most naval leaders still believed that big-gun battleships would be the decisive element in naval warfare. Traditional naval thought held that dominance over an ocean area required superiority, or at least parity, in the battle line of heavy capital ships. Using the number of enemy capital ships as a starting point, the CNO's War Plans Division noted that fleet expansion plans could be based on battleship construction, with other types to be built in sufficient numbers to support the battle line and carry out necessary operations away from the main fleet.[26] No matter how the planners turned the problem around, the numbers remained roughly the same because their estimates were based on known and projected enemy strength, be it in battleships or all combatant types. As a result, the proposed figures being discussed for a two-ocean navy in late 1939 were little different from those of 1938.

After the defeat of Poland, the European combatants settled into a six-month period of relative inactivity known as the "Phony War." So long as the relative balance in Europe lasted, proposals for mammoth navy building programs were mere phantoms. The naval expansion legislation passed in 1938 allowed for building and maintaining a fleet of just over 1.5 million tons of underage combatants, with the status of a ship as underage or overage still regulated by the now-expired treaty terms. About 80 percent of this tonnage was already built or on order by 1940, with just over 300,000 tons of building authority available before 1941. Vessels authorized under existing legislation, together with about half a million tons of overage ships still in service, put the maximum legal limit on naval strength at just over 2 million tons.

Despite the political obstacles and dangers of doing so, Roosevelt, navy leaders, and their legislative supporters believed the outbreak of war justified at least some expansion. Representative Vinson had been the primary force behind the 1934 and 1938 expansion acts; at his suggestion, in the autumn of 1939 the navy drafted a proposal for a further 25 percent increase in the combat fleet.[27] The proposed increase would provide the navy with authority to build approximately seventy additional combatant ships, mostly cruisers and destroyers, at a cost of nearly $2 billion.[28] Under this legislation combatant authority would increase from approximately 1.56 million tons to approximately 1.95 million tons, and available building tonnage would rise from 174,000 tons to 563,000 tons.[29] While battleship construction would hold steady at two ships per year, the navy expected to complete the additional half-million tons of smaller combatants within four years.

Vinson introduced the bill (HR 7665) in November 1939 but quickly ran into serious opposition. In the Senate, leaders asked why a new expansion bill was needed when construction had not yet begun on ships authorized in the 1938 bill.[30] Testifying before the House Naval Affairs Committee in January 1940, Chief of Naval Operations Adm. Harold Stark defended the request for new tonnage authorization, which amounted to nearly 400,000 tons of combatant ships.

Stark noted that an Allied defeat was possible and that the navy must be measured against the strength of the potential enemies that might then combine against America. He also pointed out that the United States, due to aggressive building programs by Britain and Japan, had fallen well below the ratios established in the now-defunct arms control treaties.[31] Drawing from the General Board's study on a two-ocean navy for a war against the German, Italian, and Japanese fleets, Stark noted, "Theoretically, again, to insure victory, we should have say, a 5:3 superiority available for the Pacific and a 4:3 superiority available for the Atlantic."[32] The CNO estimated that such a fleet would ideally require 2 million tons of combatant ships beyond the 1.5 million tons already built or authorized. Stark cited the practical limitations of time, money, and resources (though he did not mention political expediency) to explain why the navy was asking for an increase of only 400,000 tons.

Stark's arguments apparently failed to sway the House members; after a month of testimony, the Naval Affairs Committee trimmed the navy's request to a net increase of 167,000 tons, or about 11 percent of existing authorized strength.[33] Essentially, the 11 percent bill (HR 8026) represented the first two years of the original 25 percent bill's four-year building program. Stark and the navy bureau chiefs would have preferred the 25 percent bill because it would have allowed them to plan four years ahead, but Vinson decided that the smaller measure was the best that he could do politically.[34]

Under either version the navy would lay down twenty-five new combatants in 1941 and thirty-eight in 1942. Although these numbers seem modest in retrospect, Admiral Stark testified that they were the maximum possible with yards operating on a peacetime basis.[35] These same ships could be built much faster if the yards used multiple work shifts, but such an effort would require far greater expenditures than a peacetime Congress was willing to make.

Even the scaled-back 11 percent version of Vinson's naval bill languished in Congress for months, stalled by opponents of rapid military expansion. As late as 7 May 1940, Secretary of the Navy Charles Edison appeared before the Senate's Naval Affairs Committee to explain why the navy needed additional authorizations. Senators were particularly curious to learn why, if the crisis was really so great, navy leaders had not rushed to obtain immediate funding for the nearly 200,000 tons of current authorization remaining from the 1934 and 1938 acts.[36]

Three days after the hearing, the German blitz across France and Belgium changed the history of warfare. Its political ramifications were even more far-reaching. The stunning defeat of the Allied armies dramatically altered the U.S. public's perception of the European war and provided fresh impetus for army and navy growth. Suddenly, with the panzers everywhere triumphant, a war that had seemed far away just a few weeks earlier now threatened the Atlantic Coast. In these crucial weeks, an attitude of caution and indifference gave way to a concerted effort to prepare for the worst. Although isolationists did not disappear entirely, they were more muted, and the voices calling for preparedness were ascendant. Under the rubric of defense, money was suddenly available for training camps, munitions factories, airfields, and fortifications; within a few months a draft law was debated and eventually passed. In this atmosphere of uncertainty the fleet that had seemed adequate just a few months earlier now appeared dangerously weak.

The navy's wartime construction program had its origins in this hectic period immediately following the fall of France. Although navy leaders had counted on the French and British navies to protect the Atlantic approaches before 1940, now they had to consider the strong possibility that their worst-case scenario would be realized. The U.S. fleet might fight alone against the combined navies of the Axis powers. The loss of the French fleet and the possible invasion of England undercut assumptions on which a decade's worth of navy planning had been based. Worse yet, the Axis fleets were likely to be augmented by French and British ships captured during Germany's conquests.

In May and June of 1940, the possible fates of the French and British navies dominated American strategic thinking. In the desperate days following the German breakthrough, Roosevelt tried to ensure through diplomatic channels that the French fleet would not fall into German hands. He repeatedly urged French leaders to move their navy to North Africa or to their overseas colonies.[37] During this period British Prime Minister Winston Churchill was not above using the possible surrender of Royal Navy units to press his demands for more American aid, suggesting that the ships might otherwise be used as bargaining chips by an appeasement-minded government in London.[38]

In 1939 the Joint Planning Committee had begun work on a series of Rainbow war plans that explored the possible involvement of the United States in various coalition wars. Priority had been given to Rainbow Plan 3, which posited minimal American involvement in a European conflict and concentration of the U.S. fleet against Japan. With a French and possibly British surrender imminent, planners gave top priority to Rainbow 4, which dealt with a war pitting the United States alone against all three Axis powers.

Completed on the last day of May 1940, the Rainbow 4 war plan marked the most pessimistic point of U.S. strategic thinking during World War II. The plan envisioned the same basic strategic scenario as set forth in the JPC study of early 1939, with German-Italian penetration of South America and Japanese advances in the Pacific. Also added was the assumption that Great Britain and France had fallen and that the Axis powers had captured their fleets.[39] Although Germany and Italy would need at least six months to integrate these captured ships into their own navies, such surrendered units would give the European Axis fleets numerical parity with the U.S. Navy. Forced to fight in two oceans and outnumbered in both, the navy could hope only to protect Hawaii and the West Coast while warding off incursions into Brazil. Military victory against such a coalition would require drastic changes in U.S. naval policy.

In light of the gloomy strategic situation, a major reassessment of the navy program was in order. Admiral Stark therefore asked the General Board for a revised estimate of navy requirements, and the board fell back on naval planners' prewar worst-case estimates of the combatant strength needed for a war against the combined Axis fleets (table 1). The board's estimate, which became the blueprint for navy expansion until Pearl Harbor, was essentially a rehash of the two-ocean fleet studies of late 1938 and early 1939.

The board began by pointing out that a true two-ocean navy was beyond America's capabilities; the country simply could not afford a fleet strong enough to guarantee freedom of action in both oceans simultaneously. The next best option was a navy that could act offensively in one ocean while successfully defending the Western Hemisphere in the other. The board estimated that such a fleet would require 32 battle-

TABLE 1. Prewar Estimates of Fleet Requirements, 1938–41

	Battleships	Aircraft Carriers	Cruisers	Destroyers	Submarines
General Board two-ocean fleet of late 1938	40	18	108	399	162
General Board program of May 1940, approved July 1940	32	15	87	373	185
Suggested program in Navy Victory Plan study, 1941	32	24	111 (including 10 battle cruisers)	444	238

ships, 15 aircraft carriers, 87 cruisers, nearly 350 destroyers, and nearly 200 submarines.[40]

Within a month, this estimate evolved into the navy's official building program. As the extent of the French disaster became clear, Congress rapidly passed the 11 percent expansion bill that had been lying dormant for months. With Vinson's aid, navy leaders presented Congress with another request for even more tonnage. Events moved so swiftly that on the night before hearings began on the new bill the proposed authorization was increased from 400,000 to 1.25 million tons, or about 200 combatant ships.[41]

Not all of the players were in such a hurry. When Vinson sought Roosevelt's support for this drastic measure, the president demurred. He favored further navy expansion but wanted any radical and potentially unpopular moves put off until after the November presidential elections. Vinson, however, felt that the situation demanded immediate action and brought the bill before Congress without the president's consent.[42]

Introducing the new navy bill in the House, Representative Vinson warned his colleagues that the Axis navies totaled more than 2.5 million tons of combatants against 1.9 million for the U.S. Navy. If, as seemed possible, the French and British navies fell into German hands, within a year or two the United States could well be under attack by a combined force totaling more than 5 million tons.[43] Although Vinson's figures were calculated to alarm, they did have at least some basis in fact. By July 1940 the victory over France had encouraged the German high command to restart a large naval building program aimed at challenging the U.S. fleet in Atlantic waters.[44] The Royal Navy had attacked its erstwhile French ally for fear that the Axis would gain control of French ships, and the Luftwaffe was preparing to beat down any opposition to a cross-Channel assault.

In short order, Vinson and navy representatives were able to persuade Congress to pass the bill, which authorized an additional 70 percent increase in the existing fleet. Counting 100,000 tons of auxiliary ships, the bill provided authority for 1.35 million tons of new construction. Faced with Vinson's numbers and spurred on by editorials calling for all measures short of war, Congress pushed through the 70 percent expansion bill with astonishing speed. Principal debate in the Senate revolved around whether to substitute aircraft carriers for some of the proposed new battleships.[45] Overall debate on the measure lasted just two hours in the House on 22 June and an hour in the Senate on 11 July, passing without a single negative vote.[46]

Together, the 11 percent expansion bill and the 70 percent bill had pushed the navy's authorized underage combat strength from just over 1.5 million tons on 1 June 1940 to just under 3 million tons less than two months later.[47] In addition, the fleet would retain the services of approximately 700,000 tons of overage combatants, mostly destroyers. The navy quickly translated this new tonnage authorization into construction orders, delaying only long enough for a supplemental appropriation bill to pass Congress in early September.

On 9 September the navy placed contracts for 199 ships, enough to bring fleet strength eventually up to the levels the General Board had recommended in June. The growing number of ships under construction reflects the massive impact of this legislation. On 1 June 1940 the navy was building 52 combatant ships and 62 other types; by February of the following year construction totals had risen to 368 combatants and 338 others.[48]

Along with new building authority, the navy had new leadership to oversee the expansion program. On 11 July, Republican newspaperman Frank Knox replaced Edison as secretary of the navy. Whatever his other merits, Knox was a staunch big-navy man who would provide Roosevelt's war cabinet with a bipartisan flavor. In an editorial on 11 May, he had called upon the United States to meet the Axis threat by building "the most powerful fleet in the world as soon as is humanly possible."[49] An able manager, Knox knew almost nothing about technical or strategic issues and would have to rely heavily on the advice of military professionals.

With legislation, leadership, and funding in place, the navy's new expansion program rapidly took shape. By the summer of 1941 the projected combatant fleet for the end of 1945 approximated the force estimates that the General Board report of June 1940 had provided.[50] The requirements were originally based on speculative forecasts of enemy fleet strength, yet in the rush to prepare for war the two-ocean navy estimates had acquired a life of their own. Between June 1940 and July 1941 the world military situation had changed drastically. Germany had invaded Russia, the Italians were defeated in Egypt, Vichy France remained neutral, and Great Britain showed a surprising ability to survive and strike back at her foes. In the United States, the doomsday-scenario Rainbow 4 war plan had been superseded by Rainbow 5, which envisioned American participation in the war as part of a grand coalition that included Britain, Russia, and China along with unconquered territories of France and the Netherlands.

Despite the changing strategic picture navy planners, having attained a large portion—although not all—of the fleet they believed was needed, began to search out opportunities for further growth. In June 1940 the General Board had asserted that a navy capable of offensive action in both oceans was unobtainable and that the fleet it proposed represented the best the nation could produce. That same body now suggested that the planned fleet could yet be augmented by further construction.

During the summer of 1941 Secretary Knox asked the General Board to review the approved building program. After a series of hearings and studies, the board suggested that further fleet growth could be achieved by extending the program, currently scheduled for completion in 1945, for an additional year. Although a shortage of armor plate would prevent construction of battleships beyond those currently planned, seven additional aircraft carriers, thirty cruisers, and hundreds of smaller ships could be built during 1946.[51]

Other navy leaders weighed in, intent on shaping long-term fleet growth. In June 1941 Adm. R. K. Turner, director of the Navy War Plans Division, testified before the General Board in special hearings on the issue. Turner explained that the navy's strategic planners felt that the current program should be enlarged, based on the possibility that Great Britain would eventually surrender. Should this occur, he believed that the Axis powers would then pause for several years to augment their fleets before attempting to bring the war into American waters. Thus, both sides would engage in a massive naval building race, and the United States would be wise to get a head start. Turner noted that the entire program was premised on the loss of Great Britain and the Royal Navy: "If there is always to be a United Kingdom and a strong British fleet, we wouldn't need any such program as we have laid out for ourselves. It would be unnecessarily large. However, we cannot now be sure that there will be a British fleet two years from now, and we certainly ought to take steps to build a Navy that will be able to enforce our policy when the United Kingdom is no longer in existence."[52] Turner eventually proposed expanding the building program by an additional four carriers, twenty cruisers, and fifty-four submarines.[53]

Adm. Ernest J. King, commander in chief of the Atlantic Fleet, also spoke out on the subject. He had served on the General Board from August 1939 to September 1940 and was undoubtedly familiar with its studies on force requirements for a two-ocean war.[54] In July 1941 he presented the board with a fairly detailed outline of his views on navy requirements for a war against Germany, Italy, and Japan. As the General Board had done in its prewar studies, King expressed navy requirements in terms of force ratios to be achieved in each ocean.

In the Pacific, King reasoned, the decisive theater was the South China Sea. Because U.S. Navy supply lines to that area would be nearly two thousand miles longer than Japanese supply lines, King considered that a 2:1 ratio in the Pacific would be necessary to achieve actual parity in terms of fighting strength.[55] In the western Atlantic, the U.S. Navy would have the advantage of fighting closer to its bases and would be arrayed against a somewhat suspect German-Italian coalition fleet, whose effectiveness would be undermined by its heterogeneous nature. Thus, U.S. forces could achieve parity with only a 2:3 ratio of combatant units. Using these figures, King arrived at the minimum requirements for a two-ocean U.S. Navy but warned that these numbers would increase as the Axis fleets pursued their own building schemes.

In light of these various appeals Admiral Stark decided in September 1941 to request legislation authorizing additional combat ships.[56] These additions would include six aircraft carriers, twenty cruisers (including four "large cruisers," the navy's term for battle cruiser capital ships), eighty destroyers, and more than fifty submarines. If Congress and the president approved these additional units, authorized navy strength would rise to 32 battleships, 24 carriers, 111 cruisers, 444 destroyers, and 240 submarines. Except for battleships, which were limited by armor production, this proposed force was actually larger than the General Board's 1938 estimated requirements for a fleet strong enough to operate offensively in both oceans.

Even as Admiral Stark contemplated further additions to the planned fleet, his staff was preparing a report to the president that set out the navy's "ultimate" combat ship needs. The report, part of an army-navy study prepared under the auspices of the Joint Board, marked the transition of U.S. Navy force structure planning from a single-service to a joint endeavor. From this point forward, navy leaders would be continuously and acutely aware that their service needs would be balanced against the rest of the national war effort.

The Victory Program report, as the study was later called, is significant as the last major prewar attempt to determine what resources the armed forces ultimately would require in order to win the expected war. Less than three months before Pearl Harbor, the army, navy, and Army Air Forces (AAF) each estimated the equipment and personnel necessary for a war against the Axis powers. This three-part report is widely regarded as the blueprint for the military machine that the United States actually created when war came.

The Victory Program study is also important because of what it reveals about the attitudes and practices of the military staffs when they participated in multiservice force planning. Many of these practices would carry forward into the war years, significantly affecting the force structure planning process. A brief review of this early attempt to estimate U.S. military requirements provides a glimpse of how the navy, army, and Army Air Forces approached cooperative planning for resource distribution and production requirements. It also highlights some of the problems military planners would face when their services' expansion plans eventually ran up against limitations in the amount of resources that the nation could make available for military mobilization.

The need for an overall estimate of military requirements had become acute by the summer of 1941 as the United States steadily abandoned its position of neutrality for one of nonbelligerence. American war materiel was flowing across the Atlantic, often with U.S. escort, and the nation was well into a vast program of peacetime mobilization. At military staff talks in early 1941, Great Britain and the United States reached understandings on basic war aims, many of which were incorporated into U.S. strategic plans.[57]

Unlike the navy, the army had developed no expansion program geared to providing the forces needed to defeat the Axis. In April 1941, Under Secretary of War Robert P. Patterson, in charge of army procurement, suggested to Secretary of War Henry L. Stimson that the army, navy, maritime commission, and civilian production agencies meet to determine the U.S. production effort that would be necessary to achieve victory.[58] Patterson was concerned by the seemingly haphazard allocation of military equipment to U.S. forces and friendly powers and the possible repercussions should the United States enter the war without an overall plan for meeting national military requirements. At Patterson's request, Army Chief of Staff Gen. George C. Marshall ordered the War Plans Division (WPD), the army's principal strategic planning organization, to estimate the army's ultimate munitions requirements in the event of war.[59]

This initial single-service study was soon superseded by a multiservice investigation along the same lines that the president had ordered. On 22 June, Germany invaded the Soviet Union, giving the United States a new potential ally and another claimant for military assistance. On 9 July, President Roosevelt directed the secretaries of war and the navy to draw up an estimate of the over-all production requirements that would be needed to defeat potential enemies.[60] Roosevelt acknowledged that the study would require "appropriate assumptions" about the nation's probable friends and enemies; the planners were therefore guided by their respective services' views of what constituted major threats to U.S. security.

Although Roosevelt's directive was framed in terms of items of equipment, the resulting studies also included estimates of the military units and manpower necessary to achieve victory. The Victory Program report of September 1941 consisted of three separate studies: navy planners reported their estimates of the fleet's ultimate requirements, the Army War Plans Division prepared an estimate of ground units needed, and the planning staff of the AAF created a study estimating the forces necessary to wage a successful campaign of strategic bombing. The three reports provided ample evidence of the incomplete coordination in force structure planning between the ground army and the AAF and the nearly total lack of cooperative force planning between the army and the navy.

The circumstances surrounding the Victory Program report indicate that the army and the navy pursued separate approaches in their requirements studies. The two services evidently failed to consult or collaborate while preparing their estimates; only at what was literally the last hour did they compare their findings in an effort to coordinate their presentation to the president. As late as the last week of August, while Roosevelt impatiently awaited his military leaders' estimates, army officers in the WPD were unaware of the status of the navy report.[61]

Soon thereafter, the president told the secretary of war that he wanted the report by 10 September at the latest. A week before the deadline, army and navy planners had still not met to coordinate their proposals.[62] Late in the afternoon of 10 September, General Marshall told Secretary of War Stimson that army and navy representatives were meeting "at this hour" to discuss their presentations.[63] This lack of cooperation would result in reports that lacked consistency in their basic strategic assumptions and contained conflicting views of how the nation's resources should be allocated for the upcoming war.

The task of estimating army ground force requirements fell to Maj. Albert Wedemeyer, an able but relatively junior staff officer. He first had to determine America's military goals, most of which were easily gleaned from strategic understandings that existed between the U.S. and British high commands. In general, the United States would try to defend the Western Hemisphere, deter Japanese aggression, and defeat the European Axis powers.

The army estimated that offensive ground operations would not be possible until mid-1943. Intelligence reports suggested that Russia would be defeated by July 1942; by July 1943, Germany would have recovered from its losses in the Russian campaign and reoriented its forces (more than four hundred divisions) toward the West.[64] Wedemeyer decided that an all-out effort would be needed, limited only by how many men the United States could divert from its civilian work force into the armed services. His studies suggested that 10 percent of the population (135 million in 1941) was the maximum that could enter military service without destroying the nation's economy.

Armed with AAF and navy estimates regarding the number of men necessary to prosecute their war plans, Wedemeyer could set a reasonable figure for the manpower available to army ground forces.[65] He believed that the men left over after navy and AAF needs were met would produce a ground force of more than 6 million, comprising some 215 divisions of about 15,000 men each.[66] The proposed ground forces were highly mechanized, with many armored and motorized divisions suitable for the mobile warfare that the Germans had practiced so successfully in Poland, France, and Russia. Including the AAF, army strength would be approximately 8.8 million men.[67] The proposed ground army would be divided into task forces that would operate in overseas theaters from South America to the Mideast.

THE UNSINKABLE FLEET

A report compiled by the AAF staff's Air War Plans Division (AWPD) complemented Wedemeyer's. Reflecting the prevailing view among AAF leaders that heavy, long-range bombers were the key to defeating Germany, the plan, known as AWPD-1, detailed the method for destroying a large number of selected industrial targets in Germany and occupied Europe, thereby permitting and supporting the final invasion of Germany by Allied ground forces.[68] Although AWPD-1 allowed for a number of ground support aircraft units, its emphasis was heavily and unequivocally on strategic bombing. Air Forces planners hoped that a bombing campaign would "virtually break down the capacity of the German nation to wage war."[69] They saw the primary mission of the ground forces as securing air bases from which bombing raids could be launched.

In contrast to these two reports, the navy staff's estimates broke no new ground and presented no detailed strategic rationale for the proposed force structure. Navy planners simply reiterated the established construction program that had been approved in 1940, augmented by the additions that Admiral Stark had proposed a few days earlier. However, the rationale given for the planned forces changed. The initial General Board plan of June 1940 supposedly provided enough ships for freedom of action in one ocean and defensive purposes in the other. The report to the president indicated that the forces already approved, plus the additions the CNO had suggested for completion by 1947, were sufficient to launch strong offensives in the eastern Atlantic and the central and western Pacific.[70] In short, the navy requirements study proposed the creation of a true two-ocean fleet.

The three separate Victory Program studies provide an early illustration of the often nebulous relationship between strategy and force structure planning. Although the navy's estimate of its combatant ship requirements produced numbers that were essentially equivalent to the two-ocean navy proposed in late 1938, that earlier report had based its recommendations on simple force ratios with respect to Axis powers. Such forces were deemed to guarantee "superiority" but rested on no overall plan of operations. To state that the fleet proposed in the Victory Program report could launch offensives in both oceans ignored the logistic and political realities of the times. For example, if the Axis overran all of Europe, including Great Britain, as navy leaders feared, what sort of "offensive" could the navy undertake in the eastern Atlantic? As

A Two-Ocean Fleet

Admiral Turner had explained in his testimony before the General Board some two months earlier, a U.S. Navy offensive in the Atlantic would be virtually impossible without European allies. Yet Great Britain, the only remaining ally in Western Europe, was the nation whose anticipated destruction provided the underlying rationale for the naval forces proposed.

Had the navy report spelled out more clearly its underlying strategic background, its incompatibility with the army and AAF plans would have become all too apparent. The absence of interservice consultation had resulted in requirements studies that made fundamentally different assumptions about how the war would be fought. Would the army begin offensive operations in Europe by 1943, as Wedemeyer suggested, or would the decisive phase of the conflict come only after Germany, Italy, and the United States spent several years building transoceanic navies? Would England and the British possessions in North Africa serve as the major bases for a strategic bombing campaign along the lines of the AAF plan, or would Great Britain fall, leaving the U.S. fleet alone to face the Axis navies? If the principal U.S. effort were to be oriented toward Europe, as the army and AAF plans assumed, why was almost all navy strategic planning concentrated on a Pacific war? Without any thorough multiservice examination of the three plans, such questions would remain unanswered for the present.

The lack of planning coordination also affected army and navy estimates of the amount of merchant shipping that would be needed to implement U.S. military strategy. These estimates covered an area where army and navy interests intersected, and the conflicting views on this subject quickly led to a clash between the service planning staffs. Even so, army and navy leaders preferred to gloss over their differences for the time being rather than risk an open split in their report to the president.

The scale of the U.S. merchant marine construction program was naturally of vital importance to both the army and the navy. The army would need significant numbers of cargo ships to transport equipment for the large mechanized forces it planned to deploy overseas. However, the same steel, shipyards, machinery, and personnel needed to build and man navy combatant ships would also be essential to any rapid expansion of the merchant marine service. The potential conflict between the two programs was obvious.

THE UNSINKABLE FLEET

Navy planners proposed only incremental growth in the U.S. merchant fleet. In an effort to limit anticipated merchant ship construction, the navy plan allocated just 2.4 million tons of shipping for transporting and supplying army forces overseas as of the end of 1944. Navy planners estimated that this would be enough to move and support an expeditionary force of 1.5 million men.[71] The latter figure was at odds with Wedemeyer's report, which called for overseas task forces of nearly 2.2 million ready for action by July 1943 and another 3 million troops in reserve. Clearly, the small expeditionary force envisioned in the navy report was incompatible with the army's goal of defeating Germany by invading Western Europe.

When army planners became aware of the navy's suggested allocation of merchant shipping, they protested to General Marshall that the navy was meddling in army affairs. The acting head of the Army War Plans Division warned the chief of staff that the navy appeared to be overemphasizing its role at the expense of the army. Although the navy program called for a "tremendous superiority at sea," its plans for merchant ship construction would place army forces in the European theater at an estimated ratio of 1:5 against Axis ground forces.[72]

War Department estimates called for a much more ambitious merchant ship construction program than that the navy suggested. The army portion of the Victory Program study had recommended the maximum possible construction of merchant shipping over the next several years. While the navy proposed expanding the existing construction program by 9.6 million tons by the end of 1944, the army wanted increases of 12.6 million tons by the end of 1943.[73] Army planners apparently failed to inquire about or investigate the effects, if any, of this increase on navy combatant ship construction.

General Marshall's reaction to the navy's report is indicative of his prewar views on interservice cooperative planning. The chief of staff evidently felt that each service should be responsible for determining its own force structure and requirements; attempts by one service to influence another's requirements plans were little more than unwelcome meddling. Marshall told Admiral Stark that the navy's statements pertaining to army forces were "somewhat unacceptable." He insisted that the War Department alone was responsible for studying army deployment requirements, suggesting that the two services respect each other's conclusions in the area of force planning. He also proposed that "in the matter of Army forces the navy should accept the Army studies to the extent that we accept the navy statement of requirements, recognizing that the navy is the expert as far as naval matters are concerned."[74]

The issue of ship construction priorities and the potential conflict between navy growth and army deployment capabilities were real and important problems, yet Marshall's approach was hardly conducive to realistic planning for joint resource allocation. In a world of finite resources, his live-and-let-live philosophy would only postpone the difficult choices, perhaps beyond the point where such choices could be made in an efficient manner. The question of merchant marine versus combat ship construction would inevitably return to plague military planners in the coming years.

Taken together, the three sections of the Victory Program study reveal no agreed interservice approach to setting production priorities or allocating manpower and other crucial resources. Each report was the product of a different planning staff that usually worked without interservice coordination. At the time the Victory Program was written, the nation's ability to provide men and materiel to its armed forces had yet to be tested. The planners' belief that American manpower and production capabilities could meet all the nation's military needs prevented any immediate major disagreements among the services about the figures that appeared in requirements estimates. Unfortunately, the uncertain limits of productive capacity and the generous estimate of available manpower encouraged the services to gloss over potential conflicts rather than address them. More important, the planners' optimistic estimates also hid serious flaws in the national war planning system, including a nearly total lack of cooperative requirements planning. These shortcomings would assume greater importance when war brought home the reality that service expansion goals might outstrip America's finite war-making capacity.

· 2 ·

THE IMPACT OF

PEARL HARBOR

1942

The attack on Pearl Harbor caught the navy poorly prepared for an all-out war. The Victory Program study and the General Board's recommendations had produced no real changes in the combatant building program, which still reflected the military outlook of July 1940. In fact, no new combatant ships had been ordered for the navy since September 1940.[1] The battleships and other vessels lost on 7 December 1941, and the immediate need to begin fighting a two-front war, posed problems for the navy beyond any imagined in prewar planning papers.

New proposals flowed in quickly. Four days after the attack, Admiral Stark presented the president with a plan to increase the existing program by 8 carriers, 24 cruisers, 102 destroyers, and 54 submarines totaling 900,000 tons, all of which could be laid down by the end of 1944.[2] The following month, the General Board recommended building a fleet of immense proportions to meet the emergency. As the board envisioned it, the wartime fleet ultimately would include 34 battleships, 24 carriers, 12 battle cruisers, 104 other cruisers, 379 destroyers, and 207 submarines.[3] Although notable for increase of carrier versus battleship strength and the addition of more than twenty cruisers, the board's recommendations broke new ground with the call for hundreds of "escort ships" and the proposal to build additional combatant units on a yearly basis as loss replacements.

Both Admiral Stark's and the General Board's proposals, however, were unrealistic. The prewar expansion program already in place occupied almost all of the existing shipbuilding facilities. Therefore, no major additions to the program could be made until increased labor and material allocations appreciably shortened construction time or until new facilities were completed. Just after the attack Congress passed a small expansion bill (150,000 tons), after which the navy placed contracts for two carriers, two cruisers, seventeen destroyers, and twenty-three submarines.[4] These ships represented all the additional tonnage that could be laid down before 1943.[5] Except for this relatively minor authorization, the fleet expansion program remained unaltered until late spring of 1942.

By that time, Admiral King in his new role as chief of naval operations began to make an impact on navy planning. In March 1942 Roosevelt appointed King, already commander in chief, U.S. Fleet (COMINCH), to replace Stark as CNO. Thus, King simultaneously held the navy's two top military posts. As COMINCH, King was in command of the navy's operating forces; as CNO, he began to place his imprint on his new areas of responsibility for fleet readiness, preparation, and logistics.[6] He was uniquely positioned to determine the size and makeup of the navy building program.

Both Admiral King and the General Board realized the vital importance of determining the optimum mix of ships for the fleet. Given the limited resources available, tough choices had to be made to maximize the fighting power of the fleet that could actually be built. Although the navy had access to additional building facilities, shortages of battleship armor, experienced shipyard workers, and ship machinery, especially pumps, valves, and turbines, would limit the number of ships that could be added to the program.[7] Debates that had been going on for years about the relative advantages of particular ships were intensified by the sudden rush toward massive expansion of the combatant forces.

With the nation turning its full economic and human resources to the prosecution of the war, King needed a quick outline of how the building program should be expanded. That April he and Adm. Chester W. Nimitz, commander in chief of the Pacific Fleet, agreed on a target ratio of two cruisers per aircraft carrier and one per battleship, decided to push ahead with battle cruiser construction, and reduced the number of destroyer and destroyer escort types from four to two.[8]

This formula ran counter to the recommendations of the more tradition-bound officers on the General Board. Although the board spoke of maximizing the number of aircraft carriers in the fleet, its members were apparently still wedded to the idea of battleship supremacy. The board opposed converting light cruiser hulls into small carriers and suggested a program that would lay down only nine additional carriers through 1944.[9]

King strongly disapproved of this proposal. As a former carrier commander, the CNO's attachment to the big-gun ship was probably weaker than that of the board members. In early May he unilaterally modified the board's recommendations, indefinitely deferring five battleships and replacing them with five carriers and ten cruisers.[10] The deferred battleships included the entire 60,000-ton *Montana* class, which King had opposed building during his tenure on the General Board, in part because the ships would not fit through the Panama Canal.[11] He must have taken some pleasure in forcing his views on his former colleagues. The secretary approved King's version, and from that point forward the CNO took the lead on expansion policy. The board's role diminished accordingly, and its members eventually were reduced to conducting special studies and commenting on plans that King's staff presented.

During the early stages of the war, the president became actively involved in the debates over fleet composition. In May 1942, Roosevelt demanded information on the types of ships that the CNO planned to include in the navy's first major wartime expansion program.[12] The president had specific suggestions for reducing the size of aircraft carriers and cruisers and for building smaller carriers with the tonnage saved thereby. Admiral King pointed out that because smaller carriers would require an entirely new design, the yards could not complete them any faster than the proposed repeat ships of the *Essex*-class fleet carriers now on the ways. In addition, the smaller carriers would use the same number of building ways as the *Essex* follow-ons and have much less resistance to torpedo or bomb damage.[13]

Even after he approved a new building program based on King's recommendations, Roosevelt continued to dabble in naval force structure planning. In August and September 1942 he questioned whether the navy should be building cruisers as elements of carrier task forces. Because most sea battles were now air battles, he reasoned, why not replace expensive, difficult-to-build cruisers with a larger number of smaller destroyers loaded with antiaircraft guns?[14] The General Board studied the question and determined that task force composition should be left to commanders on the scene. Given the large variety of missions assigned to surface units attached to carrier task forces, the board concluded that the navy would need even more cruisers as the number of aircraft carriers increased.[15] Armed with these findings, Secretary Knox tactfully persuaded Roosevelt that a "balanced" fleet required cruisers as well as destroyers.[16]

Roosevelt especially opposed the navy's plans to build a series of 45,000-ton "large" carriers (the *Midway* class). These four ships were the only portion of the navy's 1942 expansion proposal that failed to win his approval. In an eerily prescient memo written on 12 August, the president argued that the enormous ships used too much steel and would take far too long to build, concluding that "in light of history, and on the doctrine of probability, this war may well be over before the lapse of three years."[17] In fact, he was correct almost to the day, and none of the *Midway* class was completed in time to see action.

Roosevelt believed that navy leaders tended to favor smaller numbers of larger ships over large numbers of standardized designs. Although he felt this was a "historic" and "thoroughly understandable" tendency, he wanted the navy to keep tonnage down in favor of more units.[18] Not until December 1942, after much prodding, did Roosevelt approve construction of the first two *Midway*-class carriers.[19]

Top navy leaders had their hands full with the president's intervention in expansion planning, but no such problems were encountered in their dealings with Congress. Two bills passed in early 1942 added to the navy's combatant building authority. A February act for 1,799 vessels included provision for more than three hundred destroyer escorts, although these ships were intended for lend-lease. In May, Congress voted for 200,000 additional tons of submarines to harass Japanese shipping.

The first major wartime naval expansion act appeared in June, when Representative Vinson introduced a bill (HR 7184) authorizing construction of 1.9 million tons of carriers, cruisers, and destroyers but no additional battleships. Vinson, a naval air enthusiast, explained that he considered existing authorizations for battleships adequate and that losses were likely to be higher in the ship types that the new legislation provided.[20] Increasing numbers of navy leaders shared his view. When the chief of the Bureau of Ships testified about the bill before the House Naval Affairs Committee, he echoed Vinson's position that new construction should stress carriers, cruisers, and escort ships, and he omitted any mention of battleship construction.[21] As submitted by Vinson, the bill reflected the shortage of battleship armor and the realization that battleships had been supplanted by aircraft carriers as the backbone of the fighting fleet.

The legislation was revolutionary in several ways. It included a provision allowing the navy to shift tonnage between types, thereby giving navy leaders flexibility in building the types of ships they needed most. The bill also provided for automatic replacement of losses, but not necessarily of the same type as the ship lost.[22] Therefore, a sunken battleship could be replaced by a carrier of the same tonnage or by a mix of cruisers and destroyers. In addition, the bill retroactively applied these provisions to the ships authorized under previous expansion acts.

That July, with little debate, both houses unanimously passed the new act authorizing an additional 1.9 million tons of combatant ship construction and 800 small patrol craft, along with a companion bill providing for 1.2 million tons of auxiliaries.[23] Almost all of these ships would be laid down in 1943 and 1944, with completion scheduled by the end of 1946. The act made no provision for submarine construction, because authorizations in the May 1942 act would keep the building yards busy until the end of 1944.

The 1942 navy expansion act went well beyond anything envisioned before the war. It authorized the navy to maintain a fleet of underage combatant vessels at more than five and a quarter million tons, or about the strength of the combined Axis fleets potentially augmented with captured French and British vessels—the nightmare scenario of 1940–41.[24] In addition, just over half a million tons of overage combatants, mostly cruisers and destroyers, would remain in service for the foreseeable future. With nearly 2 million tons of additional building authority, in July 1942 the secretary of the navy requested Roosevelt's permission to place orders for 14 carriers, 33 cruisers, 100 destroyers, and 420 destroyer escorts.[25]

This legislation proved to be the last naval expansion act passed during the war. So great were the forces authorized that no further similar acts were necessary, especially because Congress had included a provision allowing automatic replacement of losses. Even after accounting for the 570 combatant ships that the navy proposed to build under this act, nearly a quarter of a million tons of construction authority remained unallocated. From the date the act passed until mid-1945, navy leaders could adjust their massive building program with little formal congressional oversight, ordering new ships, canceling others, and transferring tonnage among types. Of course, the navy would still have to ask Congress for funding on a yearly basis, giving lawmakers a chance to review the program during appropriations hearings.

As a result of these authorizations and the nation's all-out effort to mobilize production for the war effort, by summer's end the navy had under way a building program of unprecedented size. As of November 1942 this program would bring fleet strength by late 1946, barring losses, to 39 carriers (including four 45,000-tonners pending authorization), 36 battleships and battle cruisers (work on 10 of these was already suspended, however), 108 heavy and light cruisers, 500 destroyers, 114 escort carriers, 314 submarines, and 750 escort ships.[26] The program also included several thousand mine, patrol, and auxiliary vessels totaling more than 4 million tons.

An effort of this scope required vast amounts of material and labor, to say nothing of money. However, the demands of total war mandated that such an enormous program be part of a carefully coordinated whole, lest the nation's resources be expended in a haphazard and ultimately wasteful fashion. While numerous civilian agencies sprang up to oversee the economic aspects of war-fighting, military responsibility for synthesizing the disparate demands of the armed services rested squarely with the U.S. Joint Chiefs of Staff.

From its beginnings as an ad hoc body of service leaders who met to present a united front in interallied discussions, the Joint Chiefs rapidly evolved into a full-blown interservice planning agency. Not a true general staff in the classic sense, the Joint Chiefs and their subordinate staffs created a hybrid system in which joint and single-service responsibilities, duties, and authorities often overlapped and conflicted.

No full understanding of decisions on U.S. military force structure and resource allocation during World War II is possible without a picture of the army, navy, and joint organizations responsible for performing the actual studies and estimating military requirements. Although the composition and functions of these organizations have been the subject of numerous detailed studies, a brief description of some attributes common to many of the agencies should provide some insight into the force structure planning process.

Several organizations that participated in the Victory Program study continued to perform similar functions throughout the war. The Army War Plans Division, renamed the Operations Division (OPD), remained the War Department's principal strategic planning agency. A reorganization of the War Department in early 1942 enhanced OPD's authority at the expense of, among others, the Organization and Training Division (G-3). Until 1942, G-3 had primary responsibility for preparing the army's troop basis, which was essentially a blueprint of the men and units that the army expected to field at a given date. The 1942 reorganization also placed the Army Air Forces on an equal basis with the army ground forces and provided for AAF representation on various interservice and interallied planning committees.[27]

Navy planning evolved as responsibility for force structure gradually shifted from the Office of the Chief of Naval Operations to the Plans Divisions of the Headquarters of the Commander in Chief, U.S. Fleet. Both staffs fell under the authority of Admiral King after early 1942, but the COMINCH staff remained small and presumably elite. In January 1942 the navy reorganized COMINCH, transferring a portion of the CNO's War Plans Division, or Op-12, to the COMINCH headquarters staff. The Op-12 office retained its Policy and Projects Section, which had planning responsibility for the building program. However, it lost the Op-12 Plans Section, which provided King with strategic estimates on which building programs would be based.[28] This section formed the nucleus of the COMINCH Plans Division (F-1), which had responsibility for determining the number of ships needed for future operations. In July 1942 the COMINCH Plans Division added the Future Plans Section (F-126), specifically tasked with planning production of ships and equipment for future operations.

Within the Office of the Chief of Naval Operations, Vice CNO Adm. Frederick Horne took primary responsibility for seeing to the fleet's need for ships. In fact, King was so busy with his duties as COMINCH and as a member of the Joint Chiefs that Horne had virtual control over the logistic side of the navy's war effort. The functions of the Op-12 group included implementing the plans that F-1 created, especially checking on their material practicability and coordinating the various navy bureaus that would provide the logistic means to carry out operational plans.[29]

These and other single-service planning organizations were supplemented and to some extent supplanted by the planning agencies subordinate to the Joint Chiefs of Staff. The U.S. entry into the war at the end of 1941 quickly demonstrated the need for a more integrated national military planning system, which the Joint Chiefs were supposed to provide. The Joint Chiefs formed the U.S. half of the Anglo-American Combined Chiefs of Staff, the principal coordinating and planning organization for the U.S.–British war effort. The various subordinate agencies that served these groups were designated as "combined" if they involved both U.S. and British members and "joint" if they were purely American. Like the Joint Chiefs, many subordinate joint organizations had combined counterparts; usually the same American members served in both.

From mid-1942 until the end of the war, the Joint Chiefs consisted of General Marshall, Gen. Henry H. "Hap" Arnold of the AAF, Admiral King, and Adm. William D. Leahy, who was chief of staff to the president. Collectively, these four men formed the most powerful military decision-making body in the country. They were the single most important source of military advice to the president, who had the ultimate responsibility for setting military policy as commander in chief of all U.S. forces.

Although the joint planning organizations often had antecedents in prewar agencies, the Joint Chiefs system was effectively a brand new operation, with the shortcomings of any hastily assembled complex organization. In addition to the indefinite and often overlapping spheres of authority, problems included uncertain procedural methods and inappropriate staffing. In many cases these problems alone were enough to delay projects or otherwise degrade the quality of joint planning.

To make matters worse, joint planning agencies often operated under bureaucratic and political imperatives that at times overshadowed the national goal of ensuring the most efficient allocation of resources to the military services. Before the war, individual services necessarily used their own staffs to determine their requirements for personnel and equipment; the three sections of the supposedly "joint" Victory Program study indicated that this habit still prevailed up to the time of Pearl Harbor.

THE UNSINKABLE FLEET

The rapid creation of a nominally joint system failed to effect a cure for this problem. Ideally, the joint and single-service organizations formed a network of complementary planning groups, each adding its contribution to the whole. In reality, planners from different services often worked at cross-purposes; conflicting interests and ill-defined duties fostered delays and disagreements that hampered force planning throughout the war. In questions dealing with resource allocation, conflicts among services were supposed to be worked out within the joint system. Unfortunately, the subordinate agencies were created and staffed in such a way that a true interservice approach to such problems was rare.

The primary joint planning agency during the war was the Joint Staff Planners (JPS), which reported directly to the Joint Chiefs. Although membership on the JPS varied over time, the two senior members were ordinarily the chief of the Strategy and Policy Group of OPD and the assistant chief of staff for plans (F-1) from COMINCH Headquarters.[30] Service on the JPS was strictly part-time, but this agency had a full-time subordinate planning group known as the Joint U.S. Strategic Committee (JUSSC). The JUSSC did the actual working up of plans under the direction of the JPS and was staffed with less senior officers drawn from the army and navy planning staffs.[31]

Throughout the war the JPS remained the principal centralized source of multiservice military planning information for the Joint Chiefs. Although the JPS took on almost all major joint planning tasks, some specialized studies were performed by joint agencies that had expertise in a particular aspect of the war effort; for example, the Joint Military Transportation Committee (JMTC) dealt with questions involving shipping and convoy scheduling.[32] Because JPS members served only part-time and had pressing duties within their own services, they could do little planning themselves. The eight full-time planners on the JUSSC could do only a fraction of the work required, so the JPS routinely appointed ad hoc special committees to carry out specific planning studies.[33]

These ad hoc committees were generally made up of officers appointed by the senior army and navy JPS representatives, usually from their service planning staffs. Through these ad hoc arrangements a large number of officers participated in joint planning while they continued to serve on the planning staffs of their respective services. The appointees functioned as joint planners only for the duration of the particular appointment; thus, they had even less practical experience in joint planning than their full-time counterparts.

On the positive side, temporary appointments ensured that the ad hoc joint planning groups would always have access to the latest viewpoints and decisions of the service staffs. Unfortunately, this staffing system also created situations where the officers appointed to these groups tended to spend much of their time and energy zealously debating the positions of their respective services, positions usually drawn up by service staffs before the joint committees even began discussing the issue.[34] These junior officers ordinarily reflected the attitude of the senior JPS members and routinely viewed themselves as advocates for their service first and participants in a joint planning system second.

By their very nature these ad hoc arrangements encouraged compromise solutions to the issues being studied. Most of the planning groups consisted of committees of several officers; each service would have a senior member, but no single leader had ultimate responsibility for decisions. Conflicts tended to develop along service lines, and often bargaining among service representatives was the only way to resolve these disagreements. When the members were unable to agree on a compromise, they often sent a split report to the next-higher echelon, hoping that the more senior officers could sort things out. In the alternative, they might produce a report that simply skirted the tough issues.

A good staff tries to provide its commanders with a plan, not an argument. The JPS members knew their superiors were extremely busy trying to run their respective services while dealing with momentous national and interallied decisions. Consequently, the JPS diligently tried to reach unanimous decisions on all matters before it.[35] Issues involving resource allocation proved particularly intractable, however. Each service felt uniquely qualified to gauge its own requirements, but the growing competition for scarce resources soon turned the joint force planning into an essentially zero-sum process. Compromise naturally became more difficult when cherished goals ran up against the demands of other services. Staff officers, no matter how experienced, were loath to retreat on issues of service priorities; as a result, usually only the service chiefs could break impasses that involved resource distribution.

By early 1943 the inadequacies of American joint planning had become obvious to almost all concerned and sparked an attempt to reform the joint staff system. Several studies produced by the joint planning agencies suggested that radical changes were necessary to speed work and improve its quality. While the service chiefs attended the Casablanca Conference, their deputies began the process of trying to improve and rationalize the organization and methods of the Joint Chiefs' supporting agencies.

Marshall's deputy chief of staff, Gen. Joseph McNarney, recommended that the JPS study the entire joint planning system in order to reorganize it along more efficient lines. McNarney believed that the JPS had not performed adequately, in part because it was required to study a variety of miscellaneous matters not directly related to strategic planning. He also criticized JPS planners for their habit of splitting into factions along service lines, a practice dictated by the members entering into deliberations with fixed instructions from their respective services.[36]

The other deputy chiefs also favored restructuring the planning apparatus but lacked confidence that the JPS could adequately perform the task of reforming itself. They agreed that a special subcommittee would perform this task better than the JPS, "who, because of their divided interests, would probably reach an impasse."[37] The deputy chiefs therefore appointed a special subcommittee to study the joint planning agencies and recommend changes that would improve the quality of planning.[38]

The special subcommittee found that the JPS, because of its workload, had become little more than a screening agency that evaluated planning papers going from subordinate planning groups to the Joint Chiefs.[39] This special subcommittee recommended creating a coordinate agency to handle these matters, thereby freeing the JPS for actual strategic planning.[40] This recommendation led to the creation in May 1943 of the Joint Administrative Committee (JAdC), later called the Joint Logistic Committee (JLC), to handle problems not directly related to strategic plans, including most issues relating to force structure and resource distribution.

In practice, this change had little impact on joint planning for allocation of resources to the services. A few weeks after the reorganization took effect, the Joint Chiefs had decided to order a new joint study on manpower requirements. The question was whether to give the project to the JPS, which had handled such issues in the past, or to the newly created JAdC. A senior naval planner pointed out that it made no difference which agency did the report; the practice of assigning ad hoc subcommittees to such projects ensured that the same group of staff officers would perform the study whether it was assigned to the JPS or the JAdC.[41]

The reorganization of JCS war planning agencies also affected the JUSSC, which was expanded to handle a greater portion of the planning work. At the same time, the agency was renamed the Joint War Plans Committee (JWPC). The charter for the JWPC, as approved in May 1943, included special provisions designed to prevent the splits along service lines that had become common features of joint studies. Committee members were enjoined to enter upon all deliberations with instructions from no source other than the JPS as a body, thereby hopefully preventing planners from having to defend predetermined service positions.[42]

The practical impact of these changes appears to have been fairly limited. The JWPC consisted of eight full-time members, but most of the actual work was still performed by ad hoc committees or "teams" of part-time planners. Given that these part-time members were still appointed by senior members of their service staffs, simple organizational realignments could not significantly diminish the influence of F-1 and OPD on multiservice planning.

In sum, U.S. force structure planning during World War II was carried out by an amalgam of single-service and joint planning agencies, generally dominated by the views of the service staffs. Not surprisingly, as resources became scarce the process became more competitive than cooperative. Under such conditions, the outcome of this essentially political process would be heavily influenced by the political and bureaucratic skills of the service representatives and the personalities of the service chiefs.

The early efforts to coordinate army and navy growth did not provide much reason for optimism. From the time of the Victory Program study until the summer of 1942, both General Marshall and Admiral King were too busy dealing with immediate crises to examine closely the long-term implications of the other service's burgeoning mobilization programs. Within a few months after Pearl Harbor, however, the CNO realized that the rush of war orders from various agencies had created serious material shortages that might cause delays in navy shipbuilding. Simply put, the nation as a whole was trying to expand production faster than the economy would allow. Federal war agencies, chief among them the War Production Board (WPB), quickly instituted a system of priorities for scarce goods. The priorities system effectively rationed a large number of items vital to defense production with the hope that they would go where they could most benefit the war effort.

Admiral King's problem as CNO was to see that the priorities system did not unduly dislocate the grand scheme of naval construction that he and his staff had pushed through Congress. He had no hesitation in taking his case directly to the president if he perceived a direct threat to navy expansion. Even before the navy completed plans for the 1942 expansion program, Admiral King had occasion to seek relief from impending shortages that threatened ship construction.

As early as February 1942, before he became CNO, King had advised Secretary Knox that the WPB's priorities system was dangerously skewed against the navy program. Arguing that shortages of shipping and escorts were the major limiting factors on the U.S. war effort, King noted that the program allotted material to army production when naval building should have priority. He concluded that allocating steel and labor for the all-out production of tanks was "of little use" if the navy lacked ships to bring those tanks to the fighting fronts.[43]

The following month the new CNO and Secretary Knox went to the president on the issue of resource priorities. King complained that the WPB had not given the navy program a sufficiently high-priority rating. Noting that the navy was already having trouble meeting its building schedule, he urged Roosevelt not to allow the nation to create tanks and aircraft that available shipping could not move to the overseas fighting fronts.[44] The CNO noted that the navy program was also in competition with industrial development schemes, and stressed the need to balance long-term growth in industrial production with short-term increases in fighting strength.

In May 1942 Roosevelt issued a directive to the War Production Board, setting out production goals for the rest of the year. This directive assigned top priority to navy combatants that would be completed by 1 July 1943, and lower priority to ships scheduled for completion after that date.[45] Vice CNO Horne informed King that the president's priority system would result in indefinite delays for nine battleships, ten carriers, thirty-three cruisers, and 50 percent of the auxiliary program. The priority schedule would rob the navy of new ships during 1944, King wrote to Roosevelt, a time when the United States would presumably be engaged in a costly all-out offensive. Eventually, King's arguments prevailed, and the precedence list was retracted.[46]

While naval leaders formulated proposals for further fleet growth and defended their access to resources in the first six months of 1942, possible changes in U.S. strategy threatened the delicate calculations underlying military expansion plans. U.S. global strategy was uncertain through the early summer of 1942 as military leaders were kept busy reacting to Axis initiatives. By June and July the situation finally began to clarify when defensive victories at Midway and in New Guinea made offensive action possible in the Pacific. The Pacific option became even more attractive when the British vetoed any plans for a landing in Europe during 1942, throwing into question the army's plans for a rapid buildup in the United Kingdom.[47] Placing strategic emphasis on the Pacific front would sharply curtail army deployment, perhaps even obviating the need to raise a large ground force during 1943.

In late July, Roosevelt chose a third option, an invasion of North Africa, even at the cost of reducing army movement to England.[48] This decision promised to delay the all-out offensive in Europe and would release additional army forces—mainly AAF bombers—for the Pacific. King requested redeployments of air units to support navy initiatives, but the army was unwilling to send all the air units the navy wanted to support its offensive in the Solomons.

In light of the strategic decisions taken in late July 1942, Admiral King took a keen interest when in August the army announced its plans for growth during calendar year 1943. With competition for resources growing more serious by the hour, the CNO actively questioned the army's new mobilization schedule, which threatened to accelerate what he saw as the "senseless" production of tanks and other equipment for ground forces. The mobilization plan that General Marshall approved called for an enlisted strength of 7.5 million by 1 January 1944. Including officers and nurses, army strength would be about 8.2 million, which the War Department believed would produce about 111 ground divisions and 224 air groups.[49]

The army predicated its mobilization plan on an estimate that the Selective Service could induct ten million men for all of the armed services by the end of 1943. As of mid-1942 War Department planners had seen nothing to shake their confidence in Wedemeyer's Victory Plan estimate that the United States could eventually put 13.5 million men in uniform. Allowing for a sizable navy, an army of 8.2 million men seemed manageable in light of the military-age manpower then thought to be available.

The proposed increases were not based on induction possibilities alone. General Marshall told the Joint Chiefs of Staff that the army's plan was "designed to provide trained units at a rate that will conform to the shipping capacity that present estimates indicate will be available through calendar year 1944 for the movement of troops to theaters where operations are projected."[50] In short, army growth was to be geared to Allied shipping capabilities. Because War Department policy required divisions to have a year's training before entering combat, the 111 divisions proposed for 1943 were roughly the number (plus a reserve) that planners then estimated could be shipped overseas by the end of 1944.[51]

Final authority to approve the army's mobilization schedule lay with the president, who initially indicated that he favored the plan. However, acting Budget Bureau Director Wayne Coy argued for further analysis. He urged Roosevelt not to approve Marshall's proposed increase until it had been studied by the Joint Chiefs and correlated with the rest of the military program. Coy also suggested that the army proposals be sent to the British-American Combined Chiefs of Staff for approval.[52]

Perhaps as a result of Coy's memorandum, on 24 August the president directed General Marshall and Admiral King to produce a joint report on overall 1943 requirements for U.S. armed forces.[53] Roosevelt was being bombarded by all sorts of requests for civilian and military material and wanted a "fresh and realistic" look at overall 1943 military requirements from a strategic point of view.

Faced with the requirement that he seek joint approval for the army's 1943 mobilization plan, the chief of staff asked Admiral King to approve the army proposal as quickly as possible. Marshall stated that mobilization planning had been held up until the president decided on a strategic emphasis for 1943: "The trouble has been that until we determined our strategical program—whether the Pacific with long turnarounds for troop convoys and therefore less tonnage available and fewer troops that could be moved overseas—or Bolero [the buildup in Great Britain] or Africa we could not reach a decision as to the number of troops that should be built up or in process of being conditioned in the calendar year 1943."[54] Marshall also opposed Coy's idea of allowing the British members of the Combined Chiefs of Staff to pass judgment on the army augmentation program, a point with which King undoubtedly agreed.

If General Marshall had hoped for complete cooperation from King in the live-and-let-live spirit he had urged on Admiral Stark a year earlier, he must have been keenly disappointed. As demonstrated in the Victory Program study, the navy was not above challenging army growth if its leaders believed that such growth threatened naval expansion. Although King's primary concern at this point was material allocations, his response set a pattern that would be followed in future conflicts over manpower.

Admiral King's reply the next day clearly demonstrated that he did not share Marshall's views on the nature of joint force structure planning. King noted that because of unexpectedly large losses of merchant ships the shipping available for army deployment had actually decreased since April.[55] He suggested that the army reexamine its estimates of the number of men who could be moved and supported overseas and then base its planned 1943 troop basis on the results of those studies. Sounding like a man who would take advantage of his new veto power to scrutinize army mobilization rates closely, King refused to sign off on the army's plans.

Yet Admiral King apparently had few concerns at this point about the overall availability of manpower for the armed services. He told Marshall that ten million men would be sufficient to support the planned army and leave approximately two million to fill the navy's needs. The CNO was concerned, however, that war production targets would have to be curtailed because of material shortages, an accurate appraisal of the situation. He suggested that Allied production should be adjusted to provide maximum impact against the enemy during 1943; by this he undoubtedly meant the United States should build more ships and fewer tanks and artillery pieces.[56] King strongly believed that the proposed army program would require equipment for troops who would not be in action during 1943 and tie up war production that might otherwise be allocated more efficiently. He therefore recommended to Marshall that they direct the Joint Staff Planners to reexamine all service expansion plans and prepare joint army and navy troop bases using the latest shipping information available.

In fact, the JPS was already putting together military deployment estimates based on future shipping capabilities and failing to agree on just how large an army the available cargo shipping was capable of moving and supporting overseas. In response to Roosevelt's memo of 24 August, General Marshall informed the president that the Combined Chiefs of Staff had already ordered an estimate of the forces that the Allies would require by 1 April 1944.[57] The purpose of this estimate was to provide Allied production officials with long-range projections of military equipment requirements. In order to determine American unit and equipment needs, the JPS had to estimate what U.S. forces would be in action overseas by the date in question.

In the ensuing discussions of future U.S. military deployments, navy and army planners espoused different standards for determining the optimal rate of growth for the army. Navy planners favored using conservative estimates of shipping capacity to set the maximum limits on army expansion. They questioned the army's own deployment estimates and suggested that more realistic figures would provide ample reason to slow the mobilization process. Their army counterparts argued that long-range estimates of shipping capacity were too unreliable to be used as limiting factors for army mobilization.

For the purposes of the Allied force requirements study, the JPS directed the Joint U.S. Strategic Committee to prepare an estimate of the strength of U.S. forces as of 1 April 1944.[58] In keeping with standard joint staff procedure at this stage of the war, the army and navy portions of the study were prepared separately. The senior army member of the JUSSC asked the Operations Division to determine the number of U.S. troops that could be moved and maintained overseas by the target date.[59] The army's Services of Supply (SOS) estimated that by using all available cargo shipping, the army could have 3.5 million troops overseas at that time, assuming that the bulk of them went to Europe.[60]

These deployment figures formed the basis for the estimate of army troop strength in the report on military requirements. This estimate was combined with the navy's mobilization plans and passed on to the JPS in early September in a report entitled JPS 53.[61] Because a total deployment picture included both forces abroad and those still in the United States, JPS 53 was essentially an early attempt to predict the strength of the armed forces some eighteen months into the future.

The army figures must have stunned navy planners. Out of an armed forces strength of 11.5 million, by April 1944 the army would have 8.5 million soldiers, comprising no less than 160 divisions. Almost half of these divisions, nearly five million men, would still be in the United States awaiting shipment overseas. Army planners explained this apparent excess by claiming that troops would need at least one, and perhaps two years of training before facing battle-seasoned German and Japanese forces. In addition, OPD argued that a large reservoir of trained manpower created a strategic asset that "would be available for use in any unexpected situation."[62] This explanation failed to satisfy Admiral King and his staff, who could see no reason for arming and equipping a force of almost eighty divisions to sit idly by while the war was fought overseas.

The study reveals that the navy also planned to stockpile men, although to a lesser extent. Out of the roughly 2.5 million the navy staff believed were needed by April 1944, nearly nine hundred thousand were to be stationed in the United States. The navy report acknowledged that many of those personnel were in training to man ships and aircraft that would be joining the fleet at a later date.[63] The navy's planned strength for 30 June 1943 had been set at just over one million, so the proposal in JPS 53 provided for an increase of more than a million men in just nine months. Army planners criticized the proposal, which the navy staff had not supported with detailed deployment estimates. One army staff member recommended forcing the navy to justify the increase "to prevent the navy ear-marking a large portion of the available manpower for no specified purpose."[64]

At a JPS meeting in late August, army and navy representatives debated what was to become a recurring theme in joint force planning. The navy members thought that the army should grow only to the extent it could move overseas, whereas OPD planners replied that the army should create sufficient forces to win the war, regardless of shipping limitations.[65] The AAF weighed in with a separate memo that questioned whether the armed forces could really reach their manpower goals because the maximum available for April 1944 was estimated at ten million. The memo argued that planned ground and naval surface forces should be cut, receiving only the men not needed by the AAF and navy air arm.[66]

Thus, by early September 1942, the JPS had to sort out no less than three versions of how the nation's armed forces should expand. In addition, at least some planners now believed that the ultimate supply of military manpower would turn out to be smaller than earlier studies had suggested. Due to the surprising increase in projected army and navy strength for April 1944, planners were faced for the first time with the question of how the military should handle possible manpower short-ages. If available manpower was insufficient to carry out the mobiliza-tion plans in JPS 53, how were the deficits to be distributed among the services?

Army planners proposed that the shortages should fall equally on the AAF, the army, and the navy.[67] This proposal favored the ground army, which as the largest service would lose a smaller percentage of its planned strength should shortfalls be distributed evenly. Although such a solution might have been politically expedient, it demonstrates a lack of serious attention to the problem of long-term mobilization priorities. The failure to address this problem and others like it would continue to hamper joint resource allocation planning throughout the coming year.

The attempts at joint military expansion planning in July and August of 1942 demonstrated two things clearly. First, in terms of coordinat-ing their mobilization policies to ensure an efficient distribution of resour-ces, the services had made little progress in the year since the Victory Program studies. Second, in addition to possible production shortages, the armed forces faced the possibility that insufficient personnel would be available to meet their needs during coming months.

Interservice debates over JPS 53 were cut short in early September when the Joint Chiefs ordered planners to prepare a study recommend-ing military manpower levels for all services for calendar year 1943.[68] This directive almost certainly arose out of the correspondence among the president, General Marshall, and Admiral King regarding the army's proposed 1943 mobilization plan. The new study effectively superseded JPS 53, which was quietly dropped from the planners' agenda. The Joint Chiefs ordered the study completed by 1 October and specified that the recommended troop bases be coordinated with the best information on available manpower, shipping, and production capacity.

For this study, military leaders for the first time sought outside advice on the number of men that the nation actually could make available for military service during the next few years. The Joint Chiefs first asked the director of the Selective Service System for the number of men that could be inducted without jeopardizing war production. Separate esti-mates were requested for the years 1943, 1944, and 1945.[69] The Selec-tive Service replied in mid-September that it was unable to provide the

The Impact of Pearl Harbor

requested information at that time. The director had ordered his staff to undertake studies on the question and promised that the data would become available as soon as those studies were completed.[70] Because of the complex nature of the issue, completing the studies would take a considerable amount of time.

Pressed for time, the Joint Chiefs next turned to the War Manpower Commission (WMC), a civilian agency created by the president in April 1942 to plan the maximum utilization of the nation's manpower in the prosecution of the war and ensure that manpower demands from any one area did not interfere with the overall war effort.[71] In September 1942 the WMC still functioned as a coordinating agency that had little real power over military or civilian manpower distribution; it competed with the autonomous Selective Service for the role of lead executive agency on manpower issues.[72] The Joint Chiefs asked WMC chair Paul McNutt for the same information that they had requested of the Selective Service, plus an estimate of the maximum personnel available for military duty once the nation was fully mobilized.[73]

This request proved to be the beginning of a long and often uncomfortable relationship between the military planners and the civilian leader most directly concerned with manpower issues. Having invited McNutt to participate in setting troop bases, the Joint Chiefs soon found themselves trying either to refute or to ignore the WMC's conclusions regarding military manpower limits. In this case, McNutt's reply must have caused consternation among the planners, for it threatened to undermine the reassuring existing assumptions about manpower.

McNutt told the JCS that any estimates would be only rough approximations, subject to change as more information became available.[74] However, preliminary figures showed that by the end of 1943 approximately nine million men could be spared for military service, with a margin of error of 5 percent in either direction. For the future, the WMC estimated that a maximum of 10.5 million men, give or take 5 percent, was the maximum number that could enter service without compromising war production. McNutt also suggested that armed forces representatives hold staff conferences with the WMC and other civilian war agencies to coordinate future manpower planning on a national level.

McNutt's figures were far lower than the manpower estimates that military planners had been using and completely inadequate to meet existing expansion goals for 1943 and following years. General Marshall had recently quoted an estimate of ten million men in service by the end of 1943 and had based his recommendations for 1943 army mobilization rates on this estimate. As late as 9 September General Wedemeyer had assured the JPS that 13.5 million men would ultimately be available to the armed forces and had confidently predicted that manpower would not be a limiting factor in setting joint troop bases for 1943.[75] If McNutt's figures proved correct, the armed forces would have to revise their mobilization schedules radically downward.

The JPS subcommittee assigned to the military manpower study dealt with the WMC's estimates by ignoring them in favor of more generous figures that the Selective Service finally provided, an estimate that 10.5 million men would be available by the end of 1943 and 13.5 million at some unspecified later date. Even this figure was too low for the planners, who felt that civilian agencies failed to envisage the realities of a maximum war effort.

Consequently, the subcommittee sent the JPS a report (JPS 57/3) proposing that military strength reach approximately 10.9 million in 1943, with the navy's share set at 2.15 million.[76] The army would grow to 8.2 million, even though shipping estimates suggested that fewer than half of the troops would be overseas by the end of 1944. At least for the purposes of this report, army planners had prevailed with their arguments that "capabilities for the transportation of military forces overseas are not alone a proper basis for determining the personnel strength of the Army." The planners noted that to create and support armed forces of the size they proposed, the nation would have to increase the work week drastically, cut civilian production, and increase employment of women and children.

A brief of JPS 57/3 was presented to the Joint Chiefs in late September, the full report of more than forty pages being considered too voluminous for the busy service leaders.[77] Despite the fact that the proposed joint troop levels exceeded the number of men that the most optimistic manpower estimates indicated would be available by the end of 1943, the Joint Chiefs approved the figures in the report. The president approved the recommendations for planning purposes only, with actual funding for personnel increases to be approved as necessary.[78]

With the president's approval in hand, by mid-October 1942 the Joint Chiefs had apparently settled the issue of military expansion programs for 1943. Beneath the surface, however, serious problems remained. The planners had ignored the findings of two different manpower agencies, which suggested that the 1943 troop bases demanded more men than the nation could provide. The army and navy still disagreed over whether shipping estimates should limit army troop levels or whether the army should expand in the hope that the shipping situation would improve. No concrete steps had been taken toward a joint decision on how any manpower shortfalls should be distributed, and the services continued to pursue essentially independent policies on expansion.

All of these problems would quickly reappear when the services attempted to extend their planning beyond 1943. Just two days after receiving the condensed version of JPS 57/3, the Joint Chiefs directed the JPS to begin work on a similar report covering military growth for 1944 and beyond. The Joint Chiefs intended that this study would be the final word on maximum service strengths, directing the planners to "allocate the ultimate military manpower which the nation can reasonably be expected to sustain."[79] Work on the new study would soon disrupt the delicate consensus on 1943 service strengths, as planners realized that planned expansion during the coming year might exhaust the supply of military manpower.

Thus, by late fall of 1942 the stage had been set for more severe interservice conflicts over priorities for growth and each service's ultimate force requirements. With resources becoming more scarce, the relative merits of each service's expansion plans became a major point of contention among the army, navy, and AAF staffs. In the short run, Admiral King and his subordinates would continue to challenge any program that threatened to disrupt navy growth. Longer-term trends suggested, however, that competition for resources would grow in intensity as mobilization hit its stride. Within a year navy leaders would find themselves on the defensive, as other claimants argued that their expansion program unduly encumbered the national war effort. Before meeting that challenge, the navy leadership would have to concentrate on sustaining and managing the immense productive machinery that had been put in place to build the fleet.

· 3 ·

THE APPARATUS OF GROWTH

The naval expansion bills enacted from 1940 to 1942 posed a daunting challenge for the Navy Department and the nation's shipbuilding industry. Through this legislation Congress had mandated levels of ship construction and material procurement far beyond the experience of anyone involved. To meet the targets for fleet growth set during this period of frantic planning, the navy's administrative organization and the fleet's supporting industrial base would have to undergo far-reaching changes.

The first step would involve reversing a decade of decline in the nation's major shipyards. In the twenty years following World War I, shipbuilding in navy-controlled yards had been a closely regulated and rather leisurely activity. Only six of the nation's eight navy yards existing in 1940 continued to build ships. Private shipbuilding had also contracted dramatically since World War I. During the lean years following the first naval limitation treaties the industry shrank to the point where only six private yards still built navy vessels.[1]

The main problem was lack of contracts. From 1927 through 1933, the nation's shipbuilding industry completed only twenty-six ships for the navy.[2] As orders for new construction dried up, the skilled design and drafting teams necessary for construction of large combatant ships began to break apart. These essential specialists had become so scarce by the mid-1930s that major shipbuilding firms had to pool their design and drafting resources to handle the few contracts that became available.

In an effort to control costs and prevent the private monopoly of shipbuilding, Congress mandated in the prewar expansion bills that half of the ships built for the fleet be constructed in the Navy Department's own yards.[3] As the navy began rapidly adding construction programs in 1940, navy yards could not begin to handle the increasing burden of construction and repair that the new legislation would bring. All eight navy yards were located in heavily developed areas, and most had been in place for many years. The potential for their physical expansion was therefore usually restricted by surrounding buildings or by property lines.[4] Nevertheless, these facilities had to be improved to maximize possible output.

Navy leaders consistently included requests for shipyard improvements in their proposals to augment fleet strength. The 1940 proposal for an 11 percent increase included a request for a modest appropriation to permit yard expansion. The 70 percent expansion act of 1940 contained a provision for $150 million to be spent on new shipbuilding facilities, along with $100 million more on new ordnance and armor plants.[5] These appropriations soon proved inadequate, and within six months the navy was back with a request for $315 million more for yard improvements and $194 million for ordnance plant expansion.[6] This money also went rapidly; by July 1941 the navy had obligated approximately $223 million for navy yards, $141 million for private yards, and $100 million for feeder plants. Still lacking the facilities needed to meet production targets, navy leaders went back before Congress to seek another $300 million for shipbuilding yards and $160 million for repair facilities.[7]

Between 1938 and 1945, expenditures for improvements to or expansion of navy shipyards totaled approximately $590 million.[8] In addition, the navy acquired two West Coast repair yards and built new dry docks at several bases; nearly one and a quarter billion dollars was spent on navy shipbuilding and repair facilities.[9] In addition, the navy gained ownership over several privately run yards and controlled manufacturing facilities at many nongovernment plants.

Strategic and technological considerations played a large part in the pattern of navy yard growth. Because the fleet might be forced to commit its full strength into one ocean or the other, shore establishments on both coasts required expansion to provide repair facilities adequate to service the entire fleet. The trend toward ever-larger combatants necessitated construction of new building facilities, and eventually several special dry docks were built to handle the planned class of super-battleships.[10]

Wherever possible, new facilities were crammed into existing navy yards to increase productive capacity. For example, the submarine building yard at Portsmouth, New Hampshire, added a building basin that could handle three boats at a time, a dry dock, and a steel ship house with five ship ways.[11] Philadelphia Navy Yard, already one of the world's largest shipyards, received new facilities worth more than $100 million, including two new dry docks for building capital ships, a turbine-testing laboratory, storage buildings, docks, cranes, and associated infrastructure improvements.[12]

In an effort to maximize production within the physical limitations that hampered expansion, the navy contracted for various ship subassemblies to be fabricated off-site. This system of farming out work ordinarily done in the yards sped production of standardized types such as escort vessels by conserving scarce yard space and cutting the time each unit spent on the building ways. For instance, the Mare Island Navy Yard in San Francisco Bay built destroyer escorts with hull sections and other subassemblies prefabricated by a firm in Denver and shipped to the yard by rail.[13] In some cases, yards expanded by creating off-site annexes in convenient nearby areas. The Norfolk, Virginia, facility, for example, grew from 352 to 746 acres during the war, in part by adding an eighty-acre annex across the river.[14]

In the effort to increase shipbuilding capacity, however, the physical constraints on navy yard expansion proved decisive. From July 1940 through the end of the war the navy added only twelve new shipbuilding ways and thirty-two dry docks to existing yards, and most of the dry docks were slated to perform repair work rather than new construction.[15] By way of contrast, the number of building ways that the Maritime Commission controlled rose from 51 in January 1941 to a wartime peak of 267.[16] Overall, between 1939 and 1944 private shipyard facilities in the United States added 437 building ways and 19 dry docks of 200 feet or more in length.[17]

Despite the investments in navy-owned facilities and innovative subcontracting techniques, the overwhelming bulk of new construction would have to be handled in private yards. Although the expansion acts of 1934 and 1938 had mandated that navy ship construction be divided equally between navy yards and private concerns, the acceleration of shipbuilding after September 1940 made this policy impossible to continue. In his testimony on the 70 percent expansion act, Secretary Knox estimated that the proportion of navy combatants built in navy yards would drop from 50 percent to 15 or 20 percent.[18]

The pattern of construction contracts proved the accuracy of Knox's prediction, and the spread of navy work to private yards accelerated dramatically after the two-ocean navy acts passed. Of the 368 combatants under construction or on order by February 1941, 88 were in navy yards and 280 had been assigned to private facilities.[19] In June 1940 six private yards were working on navy orders; by early 1941 fourteen held contracts for combatant ships and an additional fifty-four were building other types.[20] By December 1941 the number of yards doing navy work had grown to 156 and by the end of 1942 reached 322.[21]

The majority of these yards did not build major combatants but were engaged in manufacturing the thousands of small boats and landing craft needed to guard harbors, assault enemy-held beaches, and perform myriad other tasks. Most work on major combatants was done by the existing eight navy yards and twenty-eight major private yards. Of the latter, ten were "emergency" yards built from the ground up to meet the sudden demand for new ships.[22]

Navy leaders found that they could improve or create private yards more easily than they could expand navy facilities. Many existing private yards had not been fully developed and had more room available for additional plant. Yards that had gone out of business during the depression could be reopened and reequipped. For example, the Cramp Shipyard in Philadelphia had closed in 1927 but was rehabilitated and reopened beginning in July 1940. By August 1942 more than ten thousand Cramp employees built cruisers and submarines for the fleet.[23]

Greater availability of financing also encouraged a heavy reliance on private yards. The government had created several different funding schemes that allowed some private plants to expand without direct expenditure from navy appropriations. The most significant of these schemes in the shipbuilding industry provided for accelerated tax amortization for plant owners who made capital investments on facilities deemed essential to the war effort. If the armed service involved certified that the facility was necessary for defense production, the owner could deduct the cost over five years rather than the usual twenty.[24] The Bureau of Ships issued certificates of necessity for $400 million for construction of private yards and related facilities, and almost $700 million more for private yard expansion came directly from navy coffers.[25]

In contrast, the Bureau of Ships made little use of the Defense Plant Corporation (DPC), a special branch of the Reconstruction Finance Corporation set up to help finance the building of defense factories. Under a DPC contract, the contractor would purchase or build the plant, be reimbursed by the DPC, and then rent and run the plant. The DPC form of financing proved popular in the aircraft and metals industries, but the Bureau of Ships and Bureau of Ordnance together contracted for only about $60 million of facilities in this manner.[26]

Although the DPC invested only $20 million in actual shipyard expansion, it was more active in the industries that built ship parts, financing construction of eighteen plants worth $90 million.[27] Overall, DPC financing worked best where the plant in question turned out products that more than one government agency would need. Direct Bureau of Ships financing and continued supervision over certificates of necessity allowed the navy to maintain more control over the highly specialized shipyards.

Additions to private building facilities and the creation of new emergency yards vastly increased the navy's ability to meet its ambitious building schedule. At the New York Shipbuilding Corporation's established yard in Camden, New Jersey, for example, the expansion program brought orders for forty-two new cruisers between 1940 and 1943. A new wing was added to the yard's turret shops, and the five existing building ways were lengthened by 250 feet to accommodate the larger new designs.[28] In Bath, Maine, the famous Bath Iron Works had new orders for destroyers and specific instructions from the secretary of the navy to expand its facilities. Bath constructed two new building ways and an entirely new steel shaping plant to meet war orders. Using private and public funding in roughly equal amounts, the company quintupled the value of its yard in just four years.[29]

While established plants handled construction of major combatants, emergency yards were created specifically to mass-produce the smaller combat types (destroyers, destroyer-escorts, and submarines) that soon entered the fleet in record numbers. In Groton, Connecticut, Electric Boat

The Apparatus of Growth

Company built a new "victory yard" half a mile from its existing submarine plant, thereby increasing output by nine boats per year.[30] To increase destroyer escort production, the navy funded construction of yards in Hingham, Massachusetts; Houston, Texas; Newark, New Jersey; and Orange, Texas.[31] All four were operated by shipbuilding subsidiaries of large private corporations, including U.S. Steel and Bethlehem Steel.

Starting from nothing, the emergency yards went into operation in an impressively short time. For example, construction work began on the Newark yard, which was assigned contracts for thirty-six destroyer escorts, in January 1942 with $21 million from the Bureau of Ships.[32] The first destroyer escort left the ways in March 1943, and by the end of that year the yard had launched thirty-four ships.[33]

The navy also had ships built in yards not under its control. Maritime Commission facilities built landing craft, small escorts, and various auxiliaries for the fleet, thus freeing navy-controlled yards to concentrate on combatants. Once the conversion of merchantmen to escort aircraft carriers proved feasible, the navy could use Maritime Commission yards for construction of larger combatants as well. In mid-1942 industrialist Henry Kaiser proposed that one of his merchant shipyards be used to build escort carriers. Despite naval leaders' initial reluctance, Kaiser managed to convince the president that he could convert his yard to mass-produce escort carriers the way it mass-produced liberty cargo ships. Thus, the Maritime Commission found that one of the shipyards under its control was entirely occupied in building fifty of these carriers for navy use.[34] Navy demands on merchant shipyards continued to grow, and by 1944 nearly a quarter of the Maritime Commission's production consisted of military types, although most were not combatants.[35]

The net effect of appropriations, private investment, and the use of Maritime Commission yards was to create a gigantic shipbuilding industry dedicated to meeting the fleet's needs. By 1944 yards working on navy contracts had available approximately 205 ship ways and building dry docks that were more than 400 feet long and another 650 between 100 and 400 feet—ample to complete the planned construction program.[36]

These building yards required an uninterrupted flow of raw and finished material, parts, and fuel to operate at full capacity. To meet the needs of fleet expansion, the navy took steps to augment various ancillary industries, especially those supplying metals and finished metal ship parts. Other users also demanded more of these products, access to which eventually would be determined through the political give-and-take among various competing claimants (chapter 4).

The relative scarcity of heavy armor plate constituted a special case because the nation's small production capacity placed an absolute ceiling on capital ship construction. Even before the emergency building program began, navy planners recognized that limited armor production capacity was the chief bottleneck in any fleet expansion program.[37] When shipbuilding accelerated in 1940, the deficit in armor output forced naval leaders to give lighter ships priority and accept delays in battleship construction in order to get the most units out of the limited armor available.[38] Although construction of other types could be increased by adding new yards or workers, the output of armor put a definite cap on the number of battleships that the navy could build before 1948.[39] Naval leaders did take steps to remedy this shortage and by early 1941 had plans in place to quadruple armor production capacity, but this would take time.[40] In the end, the shortage may have proved a blessing, preventing the navy from laying down too many battleships and encouraging planners to place greater reliance on aircraft carriers.

Accelerated ship construction placed a serious strain on naval ordnance plants. Before the buildup, most naval weapons had been manufactured in a few government-owned plants. Private manufacturers either seized upon generous amortization schedules and the chance for more business to expand with their own money or contracted with the DPC for plant expansion. In addition, the navy built five new factories from the ground up. By early 1943 ordnance plant expansion was virtually complete after expenditures of approximately $700 million.[41]

The ability to harness human resources played an even greater role than the expansion of facilities in accelerating ship construction. By extending work hours, yards could maximize their productive capacity and move ships off the ways more quickly. In May 1940 the CNO promised to switch navy yards to an eighteen-hour day.[42] By early 1941 the yards were all operating multiple shifts and workers were on a forty-eight-hour week, but private firms were slower to use these expensive procedures.[43]

The outbreak of war removed many restrictions on employment hours and mobilized millions who entered defense industries, often migrating to factory sites from thousands of miles away. Previously unacceptable

The Apparatus of Growth

workers, such as minorities and women, hired on in large numbers, and most yards established on-site training programs to teach novices the basics of shipbuilding. As a result, the number of shipyard workers engaged in building and repairing navy ships doubled during 1942 and continued to grow until it reached nearly a million in 1944.[44]

Labor forces at individual yards jumped dramatically as three shifts kept construction work going around the clock. At the Boston Navy Yard, for example, employment rose from 8,700 in June 1940 to just over 50,000 three years later.[45] By 1943, women made up between 15 and 20 percent of the work force at the yard, not unusual for the industry as a whole. At Mare Island Navy Yard the number of workers increased from 6,000 in 1939 to 40,000 in 1944, straining the housing and social services in nearby towns such as Vallejo, which also had to accommodate workers from Maritime Commission yards.[46] Even with these increases there were never enough hands, and labor shortages continued to plague the program throughout the war.

Yards working on navy contracts had to compete with other industries and with the Maritime Commission for labor, often within the same urban areas. Maritime Commission yards created the most problems because they absorbed workers with the same skills and interests as the navy needed for its building program. The number of shipyard workers assigned to Maritime Commission contracts rose from fewer than 50,000 in early 1941 to more than 650,000 in mid-1943.[47] Although only a small portion could be classified as skilled shipbuilders, merchant shipbuilding obviously placed a severe strain on the available supply of yard labor.

By early 1944, the 966,000 workers allocated to naval shipbuilding and the fleet maintenance program accounted for just over half of shipyard employment in the United States. About a third of these worked in navy yards or in ship repair facilities at navy bases, the rest in private yards. Geographically, 55 percent of the workers were located on the Atlantic Coast, 27 on the Pacific Coast, 9 percent on the Gulf Coast, and 9 percent were at inland yards and at the Great Lakes.[48]

In addition to shipyard labor, the navy program relied on workers in hundreds of plants that fed material into the yards. A 1944 congressional investigation found that between two and three workers were needed in collateral industries for every yard worker engaged in ship construction and repair.[49] It is likely that more than three million civilians were devoted to building and maintaining the fleet.

THE UNSINKABLE FLEET

The chief impediment to production was the high rate of turnover at all shipyards as workers either were drafted or quit to seek higher pay in a booming job market. Despite pleas from both services, Congress was never willing to pass "work or fight" legislation that would have made defense work mandatory or to enforce rigorously the laws that prohibited workers from leaving one war job for another with higher pay.

Fortunately for the navy, the reliance on mass production of standard designs drastically reduced the number of man-hours needed to complete most types. As builders perfected methods and workers (those who stayed) developed their skills, astonishing gains were made. By 1944 the New York Shipbuilding Corporation had cut the man-hours needed to build a light cruiser from 7.7 million to 5.5 million.[50] At Bath Iron Works, the man-hours per destroyer dropped from 1.35 million in 1941 to 677,262 by late 1944, even though the ships had increased in size and complexity.[51] The repetition of tasks, the use and reuse of jibs, dies, and templates, and the workers' increasing familiarity with the layout of complex internal systems all contributed to increased efficiency.[52] Although Bath was an extreme example, the average time to build destroyers dropped from 1.7 million man-hours to approximately one million, and significant although less spectacular reductions were achieved in the construction of other combatant types.[53]

By the time production peaked in 1944, navy leaders worried less about building ships than about maintaining the ones they already had. After early 1943 naval facilities expansion virtually ceased, with the major exception of West Coast repair yards.[54] These yards received priority as the strategic direction of the naval war became clear in early 1942 and planners realized that an overwhelming majority of the fleet would operate in the Pacific. Most fighting would occur in that theater, and therefore most overhauls and damage repair work would be performed on the West Coast.

Unfortunately, the West Coast was also home to a significant portion of the aircraft industry and a large number of Maritime Commission building yards. The navy therefore found that shipyard laborers were particularly scarce exactly where they were needed most. By late 1944 manpower shortages in West Coast yards were causing harmful delays in the overhaul and repair of combatant ships.[55] This problem was exacerbated by the widespread feeling of complacency that set in after the Allies liberated most of Western Europe and workers began positioning themselves for the postwar market. Shortages of shipyard labor continued into 1945, even after some yards began reducing work forces as building programs wound down.[56]

The navy dealt with the repair yard bottleneck in two ways. Beginning in 1943, contracts for new construction were awarded wherever possible to Atlantic or Gulf Coast yards, thereby freeing western facilities and workers for repair operations.[57] When the navy awarded contracts for its final wartime expansion program in early 1945, almost all ships were scheduled to be built on the East Coast, save for a dozen escort carriers at the converted West Coast yards.[58]

The navy also undertook to provide the fleet with mobile repair facilities by building a number of large floating dry docks. Towed or moved under their own power to advanced bases in the Pacific, these units performed many of the repair and maintenance tasks that would otherwise have fallen to shore stations. The largest of the docks were marvels of engineering, and once assembled on site had enough lifting capacity to service even battleships and large aircraft carriers.[59]

At enormous expense and with great effort, the navy forged a vast industrial complex adequate to build and support the huge fleet envisioned by naval planners and authorized by an anxious Congress. This endeavor made possible the rapid growth of American naval power on a scale that would have been unbelievable twenty years earlier. However, the human and material resources dedicated to expanding the navy's industrial base must be included in any assessment of what the nation sacrificed to build the battle fleet.

The massive wartime increases in facilities, manpower, and appropriations mandated corresponding growth in bureaucratic agencies charged with overseeing these assets. As the building program expanded so did the bureaucracy; between June 1940 and February 1941 the number of civilian employees in the bureaus and offices of the Navy Department climbed from 3,800 to 6,200.[60] In late 1942 Congress passed legislation giving the Bureau of the Budget authority to determine the number of civilian employees permitted to various executive departments. By 1943, Budget had formally limited Navy Department white-collar workers to 19,400 in Washington and 125,000 in the field.[61]

The stresses of expansion also forced organizational changes as the navy struggled to adapt to its new environment. One of the most significant changes occurred in June 1940, when Congress amalgamated the navy's Bureau of Construction and Repair and Bureau of Engineering into the Bureau of Ships. This new organization had primary responsibility for designing, building, and repairing vessels for the fleet and carried out the day-to-day procurement of most shipbuilding materials.[62]

The flood of defense production that began in 1940 quickly showed that the navy's old decentralized procurement practices would not suffice during national mobilization. Before the war emergency, responsibility for material procurement had shifted from place to place within the navy hierarchy; with naval construction proceeding at a snail's pace in the 1930s, the question of who controlled industrial mobilization had not seemed urgent. After World War I, the Material Division under the CNO had responsibility in this area; when it was abolished in 1934, industrial planning functions went to a subordinate section of the Fleet Maintenance Division while the Bureau of Supplies and Accounts handled procurement.[63]

None of these agencies was equipped to deal with the massive management challenges that the 1940 expansion legislation posed. Overall, the CNO's staff was weak in the area of procurement and tended to rely on technical advice from the several bureaus—Ordnance, Ships, Navigation (later Personnel), and others—charged with various aspects of administration.[64] Worse yet, each bureau functioned as an independent procurement agency within its sphere of authority, contracting directly for material or labor to meet its particular needs.[65]

Into this situation stepped James Forrestal, a Wall Street investment banker appointed to the newly created post of under secretary of the navy. Secretary Knox gave Forrestal the difficult task of coordinating and directing the navy procurement effort. As mobilization accelerated, Forrestal found himself overwhelmed by contracts for construction of ships and shore facilities and for procurement of material of all sorts. His staff grew gradually, often taking over responsibility on an ad hoc basis for matters that the offices of the CNO or the various bureaus had dealt with previously. For example, Forrestal created within his office the Procurement Legal Division when the navy's judge advocate general proved unable to handle efficiently the mass of legal problems involved in fleet expansion.[66]

By late 1941, the navy still had no centralized organization to coordinate procurement. With other claimants making increasing demands on many scarce and vital resources, the navy would have to compete for the material it needed to continue expansion, and the lack of a single navy authority in the procurement area was a distinct disadvantage.[67] The under secretary became convinced that the Office of the CNO and the bureaus simply could not adequately plan and schedule production on the scale that now seemed necessary.

Forrestal and Secretary Knox therefore decided to create an office under Forrestal's control that would serve as a central coordinating organization for the entire navy procurement program. The attack on Pearl Harbor lent urgency to this reorganization, and the Office of Procurement and Material (OP&M) was officially established in January 1942. OP&M had responsibility for translating production goals into actual material requirements, for overseeing contract negotiations, for controlling utilization of facilities, and for coordinating navy production with the rest of the war effort.[68] The bureaus continued as the navy's purchasing agents, but overall policy coordination became the responsibility of Forrestal's office, with the power to disapprove contracts that failed to comply with coordinating directives.[69]

With the administrative bureaucracy in place, Forrestal's office became the central clearinghouse for all navy procurement. The CNO and his staff would transmit their needs in terms of end-use items to the bureaus, which in turn would break these requirements down into materials and components. This information would go to OP&M, which would then establish a schedule for purchase and delivery of each item.[70] Because OP&M was the navy's principal liaison with civilian war production agencies it could use its centralized position in the department to adjust navy procurement to mesh with the overall output of military items.

Unfortunately, the navy's civilian and military leaders had never reached an understanding over how to divide control over these important administrative aspects of fleet expansion. At hearings before the House Appropriations Committee in January 1942, several members of Congress expressed misgivings about the new procurement arrangements and suggested that the navy's military leadership should control production for the fleet. Among those present was Admiral King, appearing in his new role as commander in chief of the fleet (COMINCH).

Responding to questions from committee members, King put forth the commonly held view that only military leaders with actual responsibility for fleet operations were competent to set procurement requirements and establish priorities among different production items. The representatives agreed, but wanted to know King's views on who should have administrative control over the actual production apparatus.[71] Because Admiral Stark was still CNO, King had little responsibility for overseeing procurement and quite correctly replied that the issue was out of his sphere, but the hearing may have stimulated him to consider placing procurement under military control when he became CNO some two months later.

King's deferential attitude evaporated once he became CNO and took over responsibility for the fleet's logistic support. The executive order placing the two jobs of COMINCH and CNO under a single man gave King authority to direct the semiautonomous bureaus and charged him with the preparation, readiness, and logistic support of fleet operating forces.[72] The order also provided that the CNO would control the offices within the Navy Department that Knox did not specifically reserve for civilian authority.

In mid-March, even before he was officially sworn in as CNO, Admiral King took aim against Forrestal's consolidation of navy procurement authority in the Office of Procurement and Material. The new CNO notified his senior subordinates that the president had ordered him to "streamline" naval administration. King therefore put forth a plan that would have placed responsibility for material procurement directly under the CNO. He proposed organizing the CNO's office into four grand divisions, including Materials, Personnel, Readiness, and Operations.[73] Each division would have its own planning section and be responsible for coordinating a distinct sector of the navy's war effort. Operations would determine requirements, Materials and Personnel would feed adequate supplies of both into the fleet, and Readiness would see to organization and tactical training.

Admiral King's proposal to create a new Materials Division threatened to dismember the administrative apparatus that Forrestal and Knox had created in the preceding months. Specifically, King desired that the Materials Division would absorb many of the administrative and planning functions regarding procurement that were currently assigned to the Office of Procurement and Material.

Adm. S. M. Robinson, the current chief of OP&M and King's choice as head of the proposed Materials Division, recommended against splitting OP&M functions between the under secretary's office and the CNO.[74] King, however, had no such intention. As his organization plan crystallized, he made it plain that the new Materials Division would absorb OP&M and almost all of the procurement functions currently performed by Forrestal's office. The division would also take over the administrative responsibility for shore establishments that Secretary Knox had assigned to the assistant secretary of the navy.[75]

The plan raised serious questions for it essentially gutted the two most prominent administrative divisions that Secretary Knox had established during the preceding year. As Adm. Walter R. Sexton of the General Board pointed out, such a sweeping arrogation of power by the CNO at the expense of the under and assistant navy secretaries was likely to be controversial: "While military functions have rightly been removed from these offices, the result is that little has been left for them. Whether opposition to the general plan of reorganization will result should be carefully considered."[76]

Sexton had correctly anticipated civilian reaction to King's scheme. Perhaps overimpressed with the executive order making him CNO, King had misjudged the president's determination to maintain civilian control in the Navy Department. Roosevelt adamantly opposed any sweeping reorganization of the Department during the war and summarily rejected King's formula. The CNO only increased the president's ire by promulgating an order putting his plan into effect without first getting clearance from the White House.[77] This blatant disregard of protocol strengthened Roosevelt's determination not to increase the CNO's powers, and he directed King to issue an order canceling implementation of the reorganization plan.

This presidential directive killed King's attempt to control procurement, but the CNO remained dissatisfied with existing arrangements. In May 1943 he proposed a slightly altered version of his original plan, with four deputy CNOs assigned to handle Operations, Personnel, Materials, and Aviation.[78] Once again King suggested that the functions of OP&M be absorbed by the office of the CNO, in this case by the deputy CNO for material, who would coordinate all material procurement activities of the Navy Department. In essence, the new plan would allow King to control not only the what and when of procurement but the how as well. The plan would effectively isolate Forrestal's office from the coordinating function that it had been performing for the past year, leaving the under secretary with vague powers of administrative supervision over the procurement process.[79]

Once again resistance from the navy's civilian leaders and from the bureaus themselves proved decisive; the second reorganization plan went the way of the first. Nevertheless, the CNO persisted with reorganization schemes, creating a deputy CNO for air and proposing in August 1943 to transform the navy yards into naval bases. Knox approved the deputy CNO for air position in order to please naval aviators, and the navy base reorganization plan eventually succeeded in modified form after the war, but the cost to civil-military relations within the navy had been high.

By 1943 Knox had come to resent King's efforts to diminish civilian influence within the navy.[80] After he helped thwart the second attempt to obtain control over procurement, Knox suggested to the president that King should relocate to the Pacific to oversee operations there.[81] King successfully parried this attack but ultimately blamed Forrestal for the defeat of his reorganization scheme and for Knox's attempt to remove him from Washington.

Knox then asked Roosevelt to consider separating the offices of COMINCH and CNO, leaving King in command of the fleet and promoting Vice CNO Frederick Horne to CNO.[82] This would remove King entirely from the area of procurement policy and presumably destroy any ambition he might still have to absorb Forrestal's office. Roosevelt, Knox, and Vinson all agreed that the CNO's logistical duties logically should be separate from those of the fleet commander.[83] King and his staff resisted this change, suggesting alternative organizational schemes that would retain King's authority in both operational and logistic spheres.

Ultimately, Knox's sudden death in early 1944 put an end to the plan for separating King from procurement policy. Although Forrestal had backed the proposal and supported Knox, he was determined not to have an open break with the fleet commander during a critical phase of the war effort. The defeat of the CNO's earlier proposals had also cemented civilian control over procurement to the extent that removing King now would provide relief more in form than in substance.[84] In the end, the status quo prevailed.

All the disagreements over who would control procurement should not obscure the navy's accomplishment in establishing a strong and centralized administrative apparatus for meeting the fleet's material needs. Even as the top leaders quarreled over lines of authority, the organization already in place went about the massive task of ordering goods, supervising construction, and inspecting the finished product. Successful creation of administrative bodies to handle naval procurement put navy leaders in position to compete with other claimants for the materials and services needed for fleet expansion. As national mobilization efforts skyrocketed after Pearl Harbor, the increasing competition for resources would test the navy's ability to maintain the momentum of expansion.

· 4 ·

HOLDING THE LINE ON
RESOURCE ALLOCATIONS
1942–1943

The hectic planning and legislative maneuvering during the summer of 1942 had provided the navy with sufficient appropriations and authorizations for an all-out building program. At the same time, the navy had made significant progress in assembling the logistic, administrative, and industrial apparatus needed to carry out its approved wartime expansion plans. Unfortunately, by late 1942 naval leaders, along with the rest of the nation's top decision makers, had failed to solve the problem of integrating navy growth with the rest of the war effort.

In late 1942 and early 1943 the conflicting demands of various war programs threatened to deprive the navy of the men and equipment necessary to carry out the vast fleet expansion program approved the previous summer. In response to these threats, Admiral King and his staff waged an often-bitter bureaucratic struggle to ensure that shortages of vital resources did not disrupt navy mobilization. Over the course of these planning debates navy leaders demonstrated that they could aggressively use the Joint Chiefs of Staff system to ensure their needs were met.

During the fall and winter of 1942 and throughout the early spring of 1943 three non-navy war programs emerged as rival claimants to vital resources needed for scheduled fleet expansion. Two of those—the Maritime Commission's shipbuilding program and the aircraft industry's massive production upsurge—increased demands for many of the same materials, parts, and tools that the naval shipbuilding industry relied upon. The third claimant, the ground army, appeared ready to absorb the remainder of America's dwindling military manpower pool, leaving an insufficient number of men to support and operate the great fleet now under construction. In each case navy leaders within the joint planning system used political connections, bureaucratic acumen, and plain stubbornness to ensure that the progress of naval expansion suffered no major disruptions. The resulting reaffirmation of existing expansion plans directly and dramatically affected the type of military forces with which the nation would fight World War II.

In essence, all of the struggles revolved around the issue of priorities. As the demands of all-out war production and mobilization grew ever higher, U.S. leaders had to decide which segments of the national war effort should have priority access to the limited resources available for continued expansion and operation. The question had been implicit in several early planning disputes but first broke to the surface in October 1942, when studies revealed that American industrial capacity would not be sufficient to complete all planned military items during 1943. The Joint Chiefs therefore began considering where to make possible cuts in national war production goals for the coming year. The ensuing debates revealed a continuing lack of coordination at the highest levels and an alarming inability of the joint staff system to produce solutions where service interests clashed.

On 19 October 1942 Donald Nelson, chair of the War Production Board, informed the Joint Chiefs that, measured in dollar terms, war production scheduled for 1943 was about $97 billion. Nelson's organization had determined that U.S. production capacity for 1943 was about $75 billion, just over three-quarters of planned requirements. Leaving aside "must" items such as aircraft, merchant ships, escorts, and aid to allies, Nelson figured that approximately 40 percent of the remaining 1943 production program would have to be deferred until 1944. He therefore asked the Joint Chiefs to provide guidance about what military items could safely be deleted from the 1943 production schedule.[1]

The WPB possessed all the president's powers over industry and technically could act in Roosevelt's place to determine industrial resource allocation to the various services, but Nelson wisely left that decision to the Joint Chiefs.[2] In order to comply with his request, military leaders would have to participate to an unusual if not unprecedented degree in national economic planning.

The Joint Chiefs readily agreed, however, that their duties included advising the president about what they believed would be the best distribution of America's productive capacity.[3] Their efforts were complicated by his insistence on building 107,000 aircraft during 1943.[4] The Joint Chiefs had previously told the president that 107,000 airplanes were the most that U.S. industry could possibly produce during 1943, and Roosevelt now insisted that this number actually be built. This enormous effort, placed in the "must" category, threatened to derail other military expansion programs, including fleet construction.

Prior experience did not bode well for cooperation on the airplane issue. After failing to cooperate at all in the Victory Program study of 1941, navy and Army Air Forces planners had never agreed about the relative priorities to be accorded aircraft production and the navy's planned combatant shipbuilding program. AAF leaders had consistently claimed that aircraft production, especially heavy bombers, should enjoy the highest priority of all U.S. industrial efforts. Their argument rested on the claim that U.S. operational strategy required air supremacy to weaken enemy defenses before a ground invasion. If production were to be correlated to strategy, air units should be produced first, even at the expense of other military equipment.[5]

Navy planners had never accepted this scenario. With its own preapproved building program, the navy had refused to discuss modifying the production goals that the original Victory Program set forth, which the building authorizations of the summer of 1942 later augmented.[6] Navy planners worried that if the aircraft program received overriding priority in material allocation, the aircraft industry would deplete the supply of machine tools and other items necessary to build combatant ships. Even before Pearl Harbor, Admiral Stark had insisted that the airplane program should have no higher priority than the ship construction programs.[7]

At the time of Chairman Nelson's request, these issues were still unresolved, and the potential for disagreement remained undiminished. Now forced to revise their production goals, the Joint Chiefs directed the JPS to determine the relative priority of various items required for the war effort. The Joint Planners assigned this task to their subordinate planning arm, the Joint U.S. Strategic Committee (JUSSC).

Holding the Line on Resource Allocations

In late October the JUSSC reported that aircraft, munitions for active war theaters, and the maritime (merchant shipping) program were the most vital components of the current production effort.[8] The navy members on the Joint Planners were alarmed that the JUSSC had omitted the naval program from the highest-priority category and refused to approve the report. They then drafted an alternative priorities list that put the aircraft program and the bulk of the navy combat ship program, along with fleet tankers, in a special category with higher priority than other war production programs.[9]

At the next Joint Staff Planners meeting the navy representatives argued that without the changes they recommended the aircraft program would divert so many machine tools and other materials that the navy would not reach its ship construction targets.[10] Their position was supported by Adm. Samuel M. Robinson, chief of Forrestal's Office of Procurement and Material. Just before the meeting Robinson had warned Admiral King that an acute shortage in machine tools would result if the aircraft program were given top priority. Without these tools, the navy ship construction program would have to cut six or seven carriers, two cruisers, eight to ten submarines, sixteen destroyers, and hundreds of smaller craft.[11]

After some debate the JPS was unable to reach a consensus on the priorities list and in November 1942 gave the Joint Chiefs a report that was split along service lines. The matter would have to be settled by the Joint Chiefs themselves, but the service leaders also failed to reach an agreement on the relative priority of the airplane production program and the navy's shipbuilding effort. When the Joint Chiefs met to discuss the split JPS report, General Arnold repeated the AAF argument that building airplanes was the single most important military production task and should have priority over other items.[12] Navy representatives replied that the aircraft would sit idle if the nation failed to produce sufficient aircraft carriers from which to operate them as well as supporting vessels and tankers needed to supply overseas air bases. Using this argument, navy planners apparently hoped to bootstrap the bulk of the shipbuilding program into the highest-priority category.

The Joint Chiefs avoided an open split over production priorities by returning the report to the JPS for further clarification. The Joint Planners were to amend the report to include a list of the critical items essential to the war effort in the coming year, a list to be as restricted as possible. Once again the JPS proved unable to make hard choices that would favor one service over another. The revised report gave top priority to nearly all of the major military production programs, including navy combatant shipbuilding.[13]

Although this outcome satisfied navy planners, Gen. Bennett E. Meyers of the Army Air Forces was highly critical of the new report. He complained that the list of essential items was no more "restricted" than the broad directives currently in place and warned that aircraft production goals could only be met if aircraft were given top priority.[14] Meyers especially objected to the list of essential navy and Marine Corps items, which, he claimed, allowed the navy to proceed with its building plan "without regard to the resulting effect on the programs of other agencies."

The JPS report was indeed useless in terms of supplying the War Production Board with what it had requested; Chairman Nelson had asked for a trimmed down proposal of absolute necessities, and had been given a virtual wish list. Predictably, in early December the WPB warned the Joint Chiefs that the nation simply could not produce all of the items listed in the highest-priority category in the JPS report.[15]

Planners now recognized that they were deadlocked on the priorities issue. When General Arnold suggested that the JPS re-draft the priorities schedule to give aircraft production top rating, his plan was criticized within the Army Operations Division as potentially divisive. The OPD staff worried that Arnold's suggestion would exacerbate interservice tensions and noted that "discussions of this subject in the JCS Meeting will only antagonize the navy who have opposed the program from the start, which antagonism will cause further delay and indecision."[16]

King's chief of staff, Adm. R. S. Edwards, warned the CNO that implementation of Arnold's proposal probably would cripple destroyer escort production and possibly retard the remainder of the navy program. Edwards recommended that King take the position that the navy could not support the army overseas until it knew what forces it would be getting in coming years. He argued that the AAF should be informed that Arnold's plan would make such planning (and, by implication, naval support of the army) impossible.[17]

Once again, the planners were hampered not only by interservice rivalries but also by the lack of a clearly defined strategic program beyond the current campaigns. In late November a JUSSC report on war production complained that there was no overall strategy on which to base production priorities or other resource allocation decisions:

> Production programs are now geared to the equipment and employment of forces for which no general strategic plan has been enunciated. The size and composition of forces which result may not be adequate or suitable for successful conduct of the war. In the early part of this war, such production planning was justified. However, the time has now arrived when this type of planning is dangerous and unsound. It is vital that broad strategic plans be developed which will determine objectives, troop strength, shipping and advanced bases necessary. Until such plans are developed and promulgated, our production planning is on an unsound basis.[18]

In late 1942 Allied strategy had again drifted into indecision. The North African and Solomons landings had succeeded, but the campaigns there dragged on and drew in more and more resources. No one knew what the next step in Europe would be, and army movement into England had been greatly retarded by the demands of North African and Pacific operations.[19] Not until the Casablanca Conference of January 1943 would Allied leaders agree on a firm direction for the coming year.

In the absence of strategic guidance and intervention from above, the stalemate over production priorities continued throughout the last months of 1942. The failure to reach a consensus on vital materiel requirements demonstrated that joint resources planning could not produce results if the Joint Chiefs themselves were unable to agree on the relative merits of various programs. Without direction from their service chiefs, the subordinate planning agencies lacked the authority to work out allocation of resources where they believed service interests collided.

By early 1943 planners from both services realized that the issue could be resolved only at the highest level. On 4 January the senior logistics officers of the army and navy urged the Joint Chiefs to meet with Donald Nelson and make a final decision on priorities of military production.[20] OPD supported this course of action, noting that "lesser committees in the past have only introduced confusion and delayed decisions" on the production issue.[21]

The debate dragged on well into 1943 as the Army Air Forces continued to resist cuts in the aircraft program. The issue was not so much aircraft as the ability of joint staff agencies to cooperate and arrive at national goals for war production. In early March the JPS once again delivered a split report on priorities, a prime example of just how persistent interstaff conflict over the navy program had become. Army planners divided war production into three priority categories, with Category I being the highest and Category III the lowest. The army portion of the report put into Category II patrol and mine craft, auxiliary ships (including some escort carriers), and 25,000 tons of equipment and construction materials for combatant ships scheduled for delivery in 1945.[22] The navy version of the report contained only two priority levels and put almost all of such items in Category I. Navy planners explained that the Category II items in the army version would have to compete for resources on the same priority level as a large portion of the civilian production program. They predicted that the army priorities proposal would delay deliveries of a battleship, four aircraft carriers, three escort carriers, eighteen cruisers, and a large number of destroyers, submarines, and escorts.

The split report did not satisfy the Joint Chiefs, who had been waiting for more than four months for a production priorities proposal to send Chairman Nelson. Admiral King had no more patience with this paper war and ordered his staff to revise the navy portion of the study so priorities for naval production would reflect the rankings that the army staff had established.[23] The resulting joint report to the WPB put the 1945 navy program in Category II, along with a portion of the Maritime Commission program.[24]

Why King gave in remains unclear, but he may have believed that the dire predictions of his planners lacked a solid basis in fact. If so, he soon learned that his confidence had been warranted. Within a month the Joint Chiefs received assurances from WPB Chairman Nelson that production of all three priority groups in the JPS study could be accomplished in 1943.[25]

Nelson's good news had been made possible in part by the unofficial decision to cut the 1943 aircraft program from 107,000 to 95,000 airplanes. Although the Joint Chiefs never actually approved cutting aircraft production goals, General Arnold privately admitted to his staff that even a reduced program would produce more airplanes than could be provided with trained crews.[26] By January 1943 Arnold was more concerned with shortages of manpower than shortages of planes and planned to end AAF expansion in order to reduce the number of men tied up in training establishments.[27] Although the official aircraft production goal remained intact, service leaders proceeded with the tacit understanding that actual production would be lower.

While the debate over the relative priority of aircraft versus naval ships pitted the navy against one rival, the AAF, a related production issue involved possible conflicts with two powerful constituencies. The president had given the War Shipping Administration (WSA), headed by Adm. Emory S. Land, the task of expediting construction of the largest possible number of Maritime Commission cargo ships, transports, and tankers. Allied leaders had discovered in 1941 and 1942 that the shortage of cargo shipping due to sinkings by submarines threatened to cripple, or at least badly retard, all efforts to defeat the Axis. For a time, ships were being sunk faster than they could be built. Until more escorts and better techniques could counter German U-boats effectively, the only way to increase the overseas movement of men and equipment was to build more cargo ships.

In October 1942 Admiral Land made a proposal to the president that had the potential to provide a major boost to Allied fortunes. Land explained that over the previous twelve months American merchant shipbuilding yards had become increasingly proficient at mass-producing standardized EC-2 "liberty" cargo ships with relatively unskilled labor. This increase in efficiency, the result of new techniques and improved yard facilities, had increased the commission's overall building capacity for 1943.[28]

Admiral Land believed that Maritime Commission yards could build ships in excess of the planned production goal for 1943, then set at 16 million deadweight tons (a measure of carrying capacity, not displacement). He estimated that the yards could exceed planned production of liberty ships by just over 2.8 million deadweight tons, or about 20 percent.[29] These additional 275 liberty ships would permit the United States to move and support perhaps as many as 347,000 more troops overseas every quarter. Land therefore asked Roosevelt to allocate the necessary steel (about 1.2 million tons) to build the additional cargo ships.

The availability of cargo ships controlled the army's ability to deploy its forces overseas, and increases in cargo ship production might well accelerate the possible rate of army expansion, which was tied to projected deployment levels. Although ship construction was only one of many factors that determined U.S. shipping capabilities, the Joint Military Transport Committee concluded that the additional ships that Admiral Land proposed, other factors being equal, would increase deployment capabilities significantly.[30] The JMTC concluded that an increased building program would allow the army to move and support 2.87 million troops overseas by the end of 1943, almost four hundred thousand more than previous estimates.

Arising during the debate over production priorities, the question of whether to allocate additional material and machinery to maritime construction further complicated procurement planning. Although all parties agreed that cargo shipping was vital to the war effort, army planners apparently made no special effort to secure approval for Admiral Land's plan. From the Army Services of Supply, the director of the Requirements Division suggested that the army members of the JPS should push for approval. He concluded with more optimism than insight that the additional ships could be given the same priority as the army and navy programs without detriment to either.[31] This prodding produced little activity, in part because War Department staffers may not yet have fully appreciated the implications of impending manpower shortages and the importance of avoiding delays in reaching full army mobilization.

The first issue Land's proposal raised involved the availability of sufficient amounts of steel plate. The Maritime Commission had already curtailed its construction goals for 1942 and 1943 because of the steel plate shortage, and the navy had also modified its program in order to cut its need for steel. In late October, Roosevelt held a meeting about merchant shipbuilding with representatives of the armed services, the Maritime Commission, and the War Production Board. He decided to leave the decision about going ahead with Land's proposal in the hands of the Joint Chiefs.[32]

As they studied the implications of the augmentation Land proposed, the Joint Chiefs reached a tentative conclusion that steel would not be a problem. When they notified Admiral Land that joint planning groups were conducting further studies on the issue of increasing cargo ship production, he responded by raising the stakes and telling Admiral

Holding the Line on Resource Allocations

Leahy that his earlier estimate of yard capacity had been too conservative. With enough steel and other resources, Land claimed, the Maritime Commission could raise 1943 production to 20 million tons, and he urged the Joint Chiefs to approve this new figure.[33] In an earlier letter he made the same proposal directly to Roosevelt.

At this juncture the navy staff planners took the initiative to derail what they saw as a major reallocation of resources that directly threatened fleet expansion. The chief of the Office of Procurement and Material, Admiral Robinson, warned the vice CNO that increased merchant ship production would set up a direct clash with the navy building program. Although Robinson conceded that existing yards would be adequate to meet the proposed increase, he feared that the industrial output of specialized valves, fittings, and other parts common to all seagoing vessels could not keep pace with demand.[34] Robinson suspected that Admiral Land's request for speedy approval of the program was an attempt to enlarge the Maritime Commission's allocation of ship equipment in anticipation of a critical scarcity of such parts. He urged the vice CNO to reject Land's proposal to build cargo ships beyond the currently planned 16 million tons, claiming that the proposed increase would have a serious delaying effect on the navy's own building program.

General Marshall and the army staff apparently agreed with Robinson. With a chance to push through a program that would expedite army deployment and provide some answers to critics of their mobilization scheme, army planners permitted the navy to take the lead on this issue. Before committing to a decision on increased cargo shipbuilding, the Joint Chiefs asked Donald Nelson to determine whether the additional proposed liberty ships would conflict with any military programs.[35] A War Production Board study indicated that accelerated liberty ship construction would not "unduly" dislocate the navy program, but this was not enough to win King's approval. The CNO refused to give the Maritime Commission a green light until he found out exactly what "unduly" meant in that context.[36]

By February 1943 Admiral Land was complaining bitterly to the WPB about a few high-ranking navy officers who were holding up his program even after it had presidential approval.[37] He probably did not help the program's chances when he testified before Congress in early February that increasing output from 16 million to 18.9 million tons in 1943 would require the services of approximately 260,000 additional shipyard workers, thereby highlighting another potential conflict with the navy program during a time of worsening manpower shortages.[38] A series of letters between the Joint Chiefs and the War Production Board confirmed by early January that the service chiefs would approve 2.8 million tons of additional merchant ships only on the condition that the expanded building effort would not interfere with or delay accomplishment of the navy's combat ship program.[39] This Nelson believed possible through the use of better transportation, scheduling, and administration.

In effect, the additional cargo ships were given a lower priority than the bulk of the navy combat ship program. The extra 2.8 million tons of liberty ships for 1943 and combatants scheduled for delivery in 1945 were eventually placed in Category II in the final-priority list that the Joint Chiefs provided to Chairman Nelson. The program thus went forward, but only because industrial output rose to the point where both naval and merchant shipbuilding could be carried out as planned. The Joint Chiefs considered steel supplies too tight to approve even conditionally Land's plan to push production up to 20 million tons.[40]

The debates over aircraft and merchant ship production during late 1942 and early 1943 indicate the degree to which basic questions of how best to use the nation's enormous war potential had a direct impact on navy expansion plans. The service staffs became well aware of how delicately balanced and interdependent were the various programs that formed the national war effort. The ripple effect that such procurement decisions could have on force planning encouraged each planner to focus on his service's goals and requirements. Under these circumstances, the relatively weak joint planning staffs proved totally incapable of making the hard choices that might favor one service over another.

Even proposals to increase industrial facilities that came before the Joint Chiefs and their staffs often elicited a response based on purely service interests. For example, during the debates over the relative position of the air, naval, and merchant marine programs, Chairman Nelson and the WPB had suggested giving certain segments of the synthetic rubber and aviation gas industries a super-priority. All concerned agreed that the proposal would probably create serious delay in the destroyer escort building program because the plants required valves and fittings of the same type as used in escorts, which were scheduled in large numbers for convoy work.[41]

As might be expected, the Joint Planners split along service lines in evaluating the scheme. Army planners supported the super-priority for rubber, which they needed for truck tires, tank tracks, and other items, whereas the AAF moved to protect its vital interest in adequate supplies of high-octane aviation gas. Therefore, the army members of the JPS recommended approval of Nelson's plan, noting that the WPB should take care to minimize harm to the escort ship production effort.[42] Navy planners concurred as far as the rubber program was concerned but opposed any gasoline program that might cause delays in building convoy escorts. They argued that construction of gasoline plants would be futile if the United States lacked sufficient escort ships to convey tankers safely to theaters of operations. Admiral King concurred and suggested that his colleagues tell Nelson that only the Joint Chiefs could authorize a priority that would override the military's current war production program.[43]

Eventually these production disputes were settled to the relative satisfaction of all parties, due to the amazingly successful mobilization of the nation's industrial and construction capacity. As more factories came on line, planners gradually realized that the country's industrial output had soared to the point where the United States would soon produce more military equipment than the armed forces could use effectively. Although persistent shortages remained in some areas, the overall trends pointed to ever greater output of military items, easing the potential for interservice conflict over production planning. The major claimants were able to avoid further disruptive clashes over procurement because increased output promised to meet all service expansion needs.

The real significance of the production priorities disputes lies not in the delays they may have occasioned but in what they reveal about the nature of interservice planning for resource allocation. These debates confirmed the subordinate joint planning agencies' inability to resolve major conflicts of interest among the services. The representatives on these committees usually lacked authority to deviate from service positions, especially where such deviation would involve cutting a service's resource allocation. For this reason, repeated attempts by the Joint Chiefs to solve problems by having their subordinates "re-study" the matter almost always failed.

If the planners refused to compromise, the Joint Chiefs themselves had to decide the issue. They naturally had the authority to make such decisions, but their great and varied responsibilities did not allow them to devote their energies to the detailed investigations necessary to determine the "best" solution. Disagreements among the planners therefore often led to inordinate delays in the planning process, as the Joint Chiefs repeatedly asked subordinate agencies to study issues that only the chiefs could decide. These problems continued to plague the joint planning system as it addressed the more intractable issue of manpower allocation, resulting in wasted time and heightened interservice rivalry and suspicion.

The debates over production during late 1942 also illuminate the services' different approaches to dealing with the challenges of joint force structure planning. Without a doubt, the navy emerged as willing and able to use the system to the utmost in order to protect its interests. Admiral King and his subordinates showed a single-minded determination to resist any plan that threatened the navy's approved building program, and they discovered that they could exercise a virtual veto over any major program that passed through the joint system. The Army Air Forces, in the person of General Arnold, also acted aggressively to protect its prerogatives and push for the top priority that AAF planners felt their branch deserved. The principal difference between these two camps was that, perhaps due to a habitual need to conduct long-term force structure planning, navy planners seemed to see more clearly than the other services how resource allocations would affect service strengths well into the future.

In these debates, the army repeatedly had to respond to initiatives from other branches. Army planning officers were willing to criticize the divisive attitude of their navy counterparts and disavow the self-promotion of the AAF, presumably in the cause of rational and cooperative planning. They were unable, however, to devise means for ensuring that the methods that the other branches employed would not pay dividends, often at the expense of army ground forces. They were handicapped by the fact that although army growth was supposedly geared to a single long-term strategic plan of deployment and operations, Allied strategy and capabilities changed continually in light of strategic considerations.

The apparent disparity in bureaucratic effectiveness between navy and army planners had important consequences once the Joint Chiefs began planning an ultimate military force structure for the war, a plan that necessarily entailed a final division of the nation's finite manpower pool. Although an expanding production base eventually satisfied most of the military's equipment needs, the manpower issue presented an entirely different picture. The same gearing up of yards and factories that eventually produced a massive outpouring of war goods had also soaked up much of the fit male population. Military planners had to balance their requirements for men against the possible disruption of the industrial machine that they needed to supply their own forces and those of U.S. allies.

The process of joint long-term planning for military service strengths had already begun while planners were engaged in debates over production priorities and allocations of materials. Following a directive from the Joint Chiefs, the JPS appointed another special subcommittee of navy and army officers in early October 1942 to recommend joint troop bases to settle the issue of service manpower allocations for 1944 and beyond.[44] After the confusion and disagreements of earlier attempts at joint manpower planning, service representatives apparently came to the table with their own positions already well prepared.

The army members of the subcommittee brought a study on ultimate expansion goals prepared by the War Department Organization and Training Division (G-3) some two weeks earlier. The G-3 staff had assembled a visionary program for total war, basing mobilization on the Selective Service estimate that 13.5 million men would be available for military service, provided that women and unfit men took over many of the jobs now held by men of military age. The G-3 plan included proposed mobilization levels for all the services through 1948; it earmarked 10.5 million men for the ground army and the AAF, leaving three million for the navy, Marine Corps, and Coast Guard.[45] Ultimately, the army would reach a strength of 350 divisions and 12 million personnel, including noncombatant auxiliaries, women, and men unfit for active service.

The G-3 plan was reviewed by the Operations Division (OPD), which concurred in principle. The chief of OPD pointed out, however, that the shipping requirements to move and support such a large ground force were probably beyond Allied capabilities. Based on current and projected availability of shipping, OPD estimated that transporting 350 divisions to overseas theaters would require about ten years and warned G-3 that "the implications attendant upon this fact are obvious."[46] Despite such misgivings, the army members of the subcommittee studying ultimate joint troop bases relied on the G-3 plan, and the subcommittee eventually adopted it with only minor modifications.

The subcommittee's troop basis report, designated JPS 57/6, was completed by the last week of October 1942. The report called for an all-out mobilization of the nation's resources, with the goal of putting 14.5 million able-bodied men in uniform. The armed forces would also take in nearly three million women and "limited service" men to reach a uniformed strength of nearly eighteen million.[47] The projected 1948 army totaled 334 divisions and 10.7 million able-bodied men, with an additional two million women and "physically defective" men. Navy personnel strength would rise from 2.83 million on 31 December 1944, to 3.1 million by the end of 1945, and peak at 3.2 million by late 1946. In addition, the Marine Corps and Coast Guard would together require approximately 700,000 personnel.

The 14.5 million able-bodied men earmarked for the armed forces in JPS 57/6 exceeded by one million even the most optimistic estimates of manpower available to the U.S. military. The subcommittee explained that the joint troop levels were derived from estimated strategic requirements rather than availability of manpower. Navy and Marine Corps strengths were based on the projected progress of the navy shipbuilding program, and proposed army strength was based upon the strategic requirement of defeating Germany and her allies in Western Europe. Army planners estimated that the Axis had approximately 480 divisions, about 200 of which would be occupied on the Russian front. To defeat the remaining 280 Axis divisions the Allies would require 300 U.S. divisions assisted by about 40 British divisions.[48] The report included no strategic plan or timetable of deployment and operations, possibly because the shipping requirements would have been too fantastic. Instead, the planners simply stood by their assertion that the United States would need all of the forces enumerated.

Although JPS 57/6 presented an interesting look at mobilization for a possible doomsday scenario, it provided little guidance to leaders charged with making real-world decisions. In addition, its manpower figures posed a potentially embarrassing problem for the armed forces, especially for the army. Just two weeks before the report was completed, General Marshall and Secretary of War Stimson had testified before Congress in support of a bill that would lower the draft age to eighteen. Evidently, certain congressmen had demanded reassurances because of public anxiety over rumors that the War Department was planning to create a "mass army" of ten to thirteen million men, something Marshall denied vigorously in his Senate appearance.[49] In the House, Secretary Stimson rejected suggestions "that we are building an army out of all relation to our size and ability to get that army into battle overseas."[50]

Now, despite Stimson's and Marshall's denials, the army staff had developed a plan for just such a "mass army" that would almost certainly be far too large to transport overseas within any reasonable period of time. Naturally, senior army staff officers feared the political repercussions should the figures in JPS 57/6 become known to the press and the civilian war agencies. They were justifiably concerned that the unprecedented troop estimates would embarrass the chief of staff and undermine the army's position in the upcoming manpower conferences planned between military representatives and the War Manpower Commission. At the next JPS meeting, General Wedemeyer urged his colleagues not to release JPS 57/6 to anyone outside the war or navy departments.[51] Next to the portion of the report that recommended forwarding a copy to the WMC, a staff officer scribbled, "*Definitely* do not mention to those people at this time."

Under these circumstances, the subcommittee's report failed to garner much support from the Joint Planners. These officers had good reason to believe that the nation simply could not sustain forces of the magnitude envisioned by G-3 and that sending the report to the Joint Chiefs would only create more controversy. In the October congressional hearings on lowering the draft age, military representatives had been subjected to repeated questions about the nation's ability to raise large military forces while simultaneously acting as the Allies' chief source of industrial production. Although the president had approved the services' growth plans through 1943, the influx of men into the armed forces had already caused serious economic dislocation in many parts of the country. With civilian war agencies pressuring the armed forces to limit manpower demands for 1943, the grandiose mobilization scheme for 1944 and beyond seemed utterly indefensible now that the Allies appeared to have gained the strategic initiative over their foes.

In early November the Joint Chiefs met to discuss the manpower issue with the heads of three important civilian agencies: Chairman McNutt of the WMC, Chairman Nelson of the War Production Board, and the secretary of agriculture.[52] McNutt noted that the demand for manpower was reaching a critical stage and required coordinated planning for allocation among agriculture, industry, and the military. He understood that the armed forces would need nine million men by the end of 1943. When General Marshall and Admiral King informed him that the actual number was almost eleven million, McNutt replied that the difference would be vitally important in an increasingly tight labor market. In response, Marshall promised to economize on army manpower, especially on forces stationed in the United States.

Given the widespread concern about manpower shortages, army planners were justifiably concerned that news of a plan to add another two to three million men could be politically disastrous. Deputy Chief of Staff Joseph McNarney believed that there was a concerted drive afoot to take the authority for setting army strength away from the War Department and give it to the WMC.[53] The army's Bureau of Public Relations warned that a campaign had begun in the press against the "mass" army planned for 1943, with editorials charging that the army was too large and could not be deployed to active theaters.[54]

When the Joint Planners next met to review JPS 57/6 they decided that they could not approve the report. Instead, they forwarded JPS 57/6 to the Joint Chiefs as an indication of what overall military manpower requirements might eventually be.[55] The JPS suggested that the report be distributed only to army and navy officers who had a direct interest in the subject. They also recommended that the Joint Chiefs set maximum military manpower requirements for 1944 at eleven million because any increase beyond that number seemed unrealistic.[56]

If approved, the eleven-million-man cap on military personnel would virtually freeze overall service expansion by late 1943 or early 1944. The implications for the navy were ominous; service manpower ceilings would be reached just as the building program began to turn out ever-increasing numbers of ships. The entire expansion program would be threatened, and navy leaders began to lay plans for increasing their share of the personnel pie. For their part, army leaders appeared willing to accept that manpower limitations would prevent any major additions after the coming year. At a War Department General Council meeting in late November, the chief of G-3 stated that army planners should stop talking about any increases beyond the approved 1943 troop basis.[57]

The Joint Planners had no immediate suggestions about how the army and navy should divide this reduced manpower pool should it prove insufficient. This deference is understandable in light of contemporaneous problems with joint allocation of other resources, but with no relief from future shortages in sight some start should have been made toward a rational distribution of manpower among the services. Instead, the planners' uncertainty about how to deal with JPS 57/6 caused the first of many delays that were to plague joint troop basis planning.

Rather than order a restudy of long-term mobilization plans, the JPS simply held the subcommittee's report for more than a month, finally forwarding JPS 57/6 to the Joint Chiefs on 24 November.[58] Unfortunately, the delay provided the planners with no insights into resolving any of the issues involved. The Joint Chiefs reviewed the report, which had been retitled JCS 154, and concluded that its figures were simply too high to be achieved. If nothing else, shipping limitations demanded a thorough restudy of the recommended troop bases.

General Marshall was concerned about the premise of the paper as it related to ultimate army strength. One reason the figures were so high, he suggested, was that army planners had based their ground force estimates on the assumed requirement for numerical parity with Axis ground forces in Western Europe.[59] The chief of staff believed that the planners' estimates could be reduced if they took into account the effects of planned Allied air superiority, the number of Axis forces committed to occupation duties, and the relatively low quality of the Italian and other non-German Axis troops. Although he did not mention them, the Soviet successes around Stalingrad probably contributed to Marshall's optimism, too.

Marshall therefore suggested sending the report to the Joint Strategic Survey Committee (JSSC) for review and comment on how to devise a strategic concept that would enable the JPS to produce an acceptable estimate of ultimate manpower needs. Composed of three senior officers representing the army, navy, and Army Air Forces, the JSSC had been created by the Joint Chiefs the previous month to serve as an advisory board on matters of national strategic policy.[60] Marshall believed that the JSSC could provide the Joint Staff Planners with a revised strategic concept that would not require parity on the ground in Europe, thereby reducing planned army personnel strength without jeopardizing the war effort.

Unfortunately, the Joint Chiefs were asking far too much of the JSSC, which was an advisory committee and not a true planning staff. A three-man committee without significant supporting agencies was unlikely either to produce a detailed plan for future mobilization or to remedy the confusion that typified Allied strategic planning. The Joint Chiefs failed to specify what they meant by asking for a new "strategic concept"; the only requirement seemed to be that the concept not require ground forces of the size that the JPS report suggested.

At this time the Joint Chiefs also had to decide how to handle the upcoming manpower conferences between the armed services and the War Manpower Commission. They decided to go forward with the meetings as planned but to instruct the navy and army representatives to discuss only the 1943 joint troop basis, which was considered settled. If pressed on the issue of military manpower requirements after 1943, they were to tell the WMC only that the original Joint Planners' report was being revised because its figures for military personnel were unacceptably high.[61] Thus, the effects of the planners' indecision over manpower requirements began to ripple outward, preventing any long-term personnel planning on a national basis.

After some three weeks of study the JSSC submitted its findings on service mobilization levels for 1944 and beyond. Other than repeating the points Marshall had made to his fellow service chiefs, the report did little more than note hopefully that Allied production superiority "should be exploited in every practicable way to decrease our requirements for military manpower."[62] Without reaching any other conclusions of note, the JSSC recommended having the Joint Planners restudy troop bases in light of the factors set forth in the report.

After three weeks' further delay, the Joint Chiefs were back to square one. Having rejected the personnel figures the JPS had proposed in November, by late December 1942 the Chiefs had no choice but to order the JPS to try again. The detailed ramifications of the JSSC's insight on manpower savings through production superiority were left to the imagination of the planners, who noted that it was "a sound general statement, but it does not appear possible to resolve it into a formula for determining manpower requirements."[63]

On a practical level, the planners were aware that they would have to arrive at mutually agreeable troop levels that would both satisfy the service staffs and fall within the limits of economic and political feasibility. The JPS instructed the latest manpower subcommittee that the new mobilization plans should specify forces "balanced within themselves and against each other" and in line with the best available estimates of shipping, production capacity, and manpower availability.[64] In a sense this directive marked a watershed in military mobilization planning. It was the first time that a joint committee would endeavor to set expansion goals primarily based on perceived availability of resources rather than on the planners' perceptions of strategic requirements.

By ordering planners to balance proposed army and navy service force levels against each other the JPS tacitly acknowledged that the key limiting factor in one service's growth would be the other service's manpower requirements. With the end of military personnel allocations in sight, the service that most ably justified its needs would not only grow faster but might also lay claim to the last remaining manpower available for expansion. Under these circumstances, reaching a joint agreement on what mix of forces was "balanced" would prove profoundly difficult for any joint planning organization. Such a formula was obviously open to interpretation, and the planners' bargaining skills, political pressure, and bureaucratic maneuvering soon began to play roles that would have been inconceivable twelve months earlier.

Navy planners found themselves in a clearly superior position during the planning and debating process that now ensued. The army was asking for the bulk of the nation's military manpower while at the same time Allied shipping capabilities could bring only a fraction of that manpower to bear against the enemy. The gap between army expansion goals and expected deployment rates created a serious public relations problem for the War Department, one that navy officers were quick to exploit.

By February 1943, Marshall had information from at least three reporters that navy officials had criticized the shipping figures the army used to support its proposed personnel levels for 1943.[65] The leaks came at a damaging time because Congress had just begun hearings on whether the planned 1943 army should be cut to save manpower. When Stimson demanded an explanation from the secretary of the navy, Knox did not bother to deny Marshall's claims. He replied that navy officers had only pointed out imbalances in the production program; they had no objection to army expansion plans but felt that more antisubmarine escorts should be built to protect the army's overseas lifeline.[66] Stimson could only respond that such expansion plans had been approved in joint planning sessions and that War Department leaders "have never considered that we have the right to criticize or attack figures for the Navy and Marine Corps that were arrived at at the same time."[67]

The congressional manpower hearings that began in February confirmed that claims on the national pool of men of military age would almost certainly outstrip supply. War Department leaders had the toughest time at the hearings, largely because even their most optimistic deployment estimates showed that the army would have nearly 3.5 million soldiers in the United States at the end of 1944.[68] Navy representatives experienced fewer problems, asking for just over two million men by the end of the year to operate and maintain the ships and aircraft of the fleet.

Admiral Horne explained that cuts in navy personnel would not solve the basic deployment problem. "Unless you have the navy up to its required strength, there is no use having anybody in the army, because you can't get them where you want to take them," he argued.[69] Although the debates continued, military leaders eventually realized that most elected representatives were unwilling to substitute their judgment for that of the highly respected service chiefs.[70] In the end, Congress simply could not muster the votes or the nerve to reduce the services' approved strengths for 1943. The hearings were not without effect, however. With the threat of future congressional action hanging over them, military planners would have to act carefully in setting personnel levels for 1944.

Although members of the joint subcommittee on troop bases received orders in early January to revise JPS 57/6 and propose new manpower levels for 1944 and beyond, their report was not completed until late April. The delay was caused by the requirement that the revised troop levels be within the limit of maximum available manpower as determined by the best available information. The subcommittee therefore had to wait for the War Manpower Commission's latest study of the national manpower situation, which was not available until early April.[71] To set the limits on military personnel levels for 1944, the subcommittee relied upon the WMC study and an earlier manpower study from the Selective Service.

The subcommittee's report was forwarded to the Joint Chiefs as JCS 154/2, and it represented a significant departure from earlier joint mobilization studies. For the first time, planners agreed that army strength would be frozen during 1944 at the 1943 level of 8.2 million. Although many army officers had accepted since the previous November that the approved 1943 strength represented the maximum that could be expected, the War Department had nevertheless prepared contingency plans that called for the army to grow to nearly nine million men during 1944, an increase of almost 750,000 over 1943 levels.[72] In this sense the agreement on zero army growth for 1944 represented a significant although perhaps inevitable concession by Marshall's staff. By way of contrast, the navy would continue to grow as ship construction accelerated; by the end of 1944 projected strength of the navy, Marines, and Coast Guard was 3.67 million men and 129,000 women. The navy would grow to just over three million, an increase of nearly a million over the authorized 1943 strength. Total strength in the armed forces at the end of 1944 would be just over twelve million, including 11.7 million men.[73]

The troop strengths proposed in JCS 154/2 were derived from two studies of national manpower, one prepared by the WMC and the other by the Selective Service. The two studies reached different conclusions regarding the number of men that the United States could sustain in its armed forces over an extended period. The Selective Service study was the more conservative of the two. It calculated that the national economy could spare indefinitely a maximum of 10.5 million men for military service. In contrast, the WMC estimated maximum military manpower at 11.3 million.

The troop bases subcommittee adopted the mean of the two estimates, concluding that 10.9 million able-bodied men were available for extended military service.[74] Despite this finding the subcommittee proposed troop levels for 1944 (11.73 million men) that exceeded even the relatively optimistic WMC estimate by nearly half a million. The planners relied on a Selective Service finding that, for a short period, the nation could field even larger military forces than the maximum sustainable long-term service strength. The Selective Service report had stated that the United States could sustain armed forces of twelve million men through the first half of 1946, although at a significant cost to the economy.

Based on these figures, the joint subcommittee reported that the troop levels proposed in JCS 154/2 could be maintained through 1946. Allied strategic plans flowing from the Casablanca Conference demanded that maximum forces be mobilized and deployed during 1944 and 1945. The subcommittee therefore recommended temporarily inducting more men than would be available for long-term military service. In effect, planners were willing to gamble that most of the fighting would be over by the end of 1945. If they were wrong, the United States might find that it could no longer adequately support the military forces it had raised.

The subcommittee's decision to suspend army expansion after 1943 failed to satisfy navy members, who still believed the army was asking for too many men. Army members, in turn, complained of continued attempts by navy planners to force cuts in army mobilization levels. A secret War Department memorandum noted the navy's position and warned of a possible interservice split on the manpower issue:

> Throughout three months deliberation, Navy members attempted to cause reduction in Army troop bases for 1943. Army members stood their ground on the premises of JCS and Presidential approval. A split report was averted by the Army members showing that adequate manpower was available for 1944 to meet both Army and Navy needs. . . . If the attitude of the Navy members on this subcommittee reflects the opinion of the Navy High Command, it is evident that inter-service controversy may result. . . . The Navy desires to reduce the Army in favor of augmenting the Navy, since it can be foreseen that a manpower ceiling will be reached in 1944.[75]

The memo accurately set forth the nub of the problem. Military leaders expected that the nation's manpower supply would run dry after 1944, leaving only enough men to replace losses. Because the navy had firm plans to continue adding ships during 1945 and beyond, navy planners had to go well beyond 1944 in determining the fleet's ultimate personnel requirements. To this end, navy representatives on the committee attempted to earmark as many men as possible for future growth and prevent the army from absorbing personnel that the navy would need two or three years into the future.

Reviewing JCS 154/2 the Joint Chiefs decided that military strength levels in the report were still too high. They therefore directed their deputy chiefs of staff to review the report, and in early June 1943 the latter group also concluded that the troop levels were excessive.[76] Thus, after more than six months of studies and debates, the joint staff system had failed to arrive at either a mutually satisfactory allocation of the nation's available military manpower or a clear vision of the number and type of units required for ultimate victory. To a nation trying to mobilize for total war in the most efficient manner, the delay constituted a significant setback.

Where did the fault for this failure lie? Navy leaders put the blame on overly ambitious schemes for army growth that totally ignored the realities of shipping and would waste manpower in units destined to languish in camps far from the fighting fronts. Although this criticism has some merit, the shipping issue was so complex that no one really knew what conditions would be like a year hence; in mid-1942 one army planner characterized estimates of 1944 shipping capabilities as "little more than guesses."[77]

Changes in ship construction, convoy scheduling, and especially loss rates would dramatically alter the army's ability to move its combat and support units to overseas theaters. Predicting future losses of cargo ships proved impossible, and army planners soon lost confidence in the wildly pessimistic figures that antisubmarine experts in Naval Intelligence provided.[78] In fact, the situation began to improve dramatically during 1943, and by that September army deployment targets for 1944 had risen by nearly a million men over what they had been a year earlier. Growing shipping possibilities would eventually threaten navy plans as army leaders began trying to reclaim the manpower they had been willing to forego when the situation appeared less favorable.

Army planners blamed the navy for obstructing force planning in an effort to undo joint manpower allocations agreed upon the previous autumn. During the first half of 1943 navy leaders had used the shipping issue to put considerable pressure on the army regarding its manpower requirements. Facing a military manpower freeze in 1944, navy leaders had no choice but to stockpile men, for the 1943 navy simply could not absorb everyone needed to man the great battle fleet being built for 1944, 1945, and 1946.

The navy eventually won this round of the mobilization debate by forcing Marshall to cut army expansion plans (chapter 6), but at a cost. Admiral King and his staff soon discovered that their tactic of intervening in army expansion planning could be turned against them, an almost inevitable consequence of politicizing the mobilization process. As a result of these debates, army and navy planners would increasingly eschew cooperative force structure planning for unilateral decisions about their own service's needs.

· 5 ·

THE RISE OF THE CRITICS
1943–1944

Throughout debates during late 1942 and early 1943 about resource priorities, all concerned parties generally accepted the navy expansion program as a given. Although possible delays to portions of the program in deference to other sectors of the war effort generated much debate, no one outside the navy was willing to question seriously the type of fleet taking shape in yards around the country. Inevitably, this state of affairs changed as the nation's leaders grappled with shortages of resources needed to fight the war. Most alarmingly, the pool of men required to create weapons and eventually use them had dropped to levels that threatened to disrupt the entire military effort. As the War Department and other agencies responsible for national war mobilization contemplated slowdowns or cuts in their programs, their leaders naturally began searching for others to share the burden.

In a sense, the navy thus became a victim of its own success. As one of the major resource users in the nation, it had come through the priorities struggle with its program largely intact. The fleet was slated to absorb an increasingly large portion of the military-age manpower still available for distribution, and the navy's industrial shipbuilding complex required millions of workers and masses of material. The navy program therefore became a prime target of those who, although claiming to act in the name of "efficiency" and "the good of the country," were often committed to diverting vital men and materials for reallocation to their own programs.

If the debates over steel, spare parts, and manpower in late 1942 and early 1943 prompted navy leaders to reassess their ideas regarding the size of the shipbuilding effort needed to win the war, their actions during the following six months gave no evidence of such second thoughts. Rather than attempting to integrate fleet growth with the rest of the war effort, they concentrated on seeing the existing program through and expanding it where possible. As a result, the first half of 1943 saw plans for navy expansion reach new levels of magnitude.

By early 1943 military and political developments had rendered completely obsolete the late prewar strategic concept of building a U.S. fleet to match the combined Axis fleets ton for ton and ship for ship. In January of that year, intelligence estimates indicated that Britain and the United States already enjoyed considerable superiority in combatant ships, possibly as great as a 2:1 ratio over their enemies. The United States alone had acquired a fleet that approximately matched in size the combined German, Italian, and Japanese fleets, while Great Britain had built its fleet up to a level second only to the Americans.[1]

By this point in the war, the Allied advantages in productive capacity were such that the sea power gap was almost certain to widen rather than shrink. U.S. Naval Intelligence believed it had a fairly accurate idea of Axis ship construction capabilities and enough confidence in its estimates to give them to naval officers testifying before Congress. The figures showed that the United States and Great Britain were building far more ships than their enemies in every class save submarines, where the Germans were concentrating the bulk of their effort.

In perhaps the most important category, aircraft carriers, the Allies were building more than fifty large units and a hundred escort carriers, as opposed to two or three large and six escort carriers in Axis shipyards. The intelligence summaries found similar ratios in the building of cruisers (82 Allied to 14 Axis) and destroyers (385 Allied to 54 Axis).[2] In short, assuming roughly equal losses (with dominance of the air and an increasing preponderance at sea balancing out the Allies' need to operate against enemy-held land areas), existing Allied building programs would eventually provide them with an overwhelming advantage in surface naval units.

THE UNSINKABLE FLEET

Much of the U.S. Navy's planned construction was due to enter service by the end of 1944, with aircraft carriers and light units taking the lead. Ten *Essex*-class fleet carriers were scheduled for completion during 1944, along with thirty-four escort carriers.[3] In contrast, battleships and heavy cruisers would trickle into service at a much lower rate, in part because of the time needed for construction and problems with armor supplies but also due to Admiral King's undoubtedly wise decision to give battleships a lower priority than other elements of the program.

Despite the Allies' increasing material advantages at sea and the troublesome resource and manpower shortages at home, navy leaders continued to press ahead in an effort to augment the current expansion program. As vice CNO, Admiral Horne had been entrusted by Admiral King to act as the CNO's chief deputy in the area of planning fleet growth. In May 1943, as interservice debates over manpower allocation intensified, Horne sent King a proposal regarding possible major additions to the building program. He noted that under existing authorization acts the navy had 921,000 tons of unallocated combatant tonnage authority.[4] This included the 200,000-ton surplus that had never been allocated from the 1.9 million tons authorized the previous summer plus 398,000 tons previously allocated to the five *Montana*-class super-battleships and four *Alaska*-class battle cruisers that had been suspended. Added to these were 193,000 tons to replace actual losses incurred during the war and 131,000 tons to "replace" overage ships, which would almost certainly remain in service.

Horne estimated that by the end of 1946 the nation's shipyards could complete approximately 2.3 million tons of combatants over and above those included in the current program. Thus, the 921,000 tons of existing building authority would use up only about 40 percent of the current excess construction capacity. Given these facts, Horne recommended seeking presidential approval for building the full tonnage possible under existing legislation and suggested that King consider seeking further legislative authority for even more tonnage. He presented the CNO with three possible mixes of ships that would use the navy's remaining tonnage authority, thus representing the maximum expansion possible without recourse to new legislation.

Admiral King approved Horne's recommendation, electing to build an additional battle cruiser, 4 aircraft carriers, 11 cruisers, 82 destroyers, 110 submarines, and 205 destroyer escorts, all of which could be completed by the end of 1946.⁵ Counting these ships, fleet strength by the beginning of 1947 would grow to 28 battleships and battle cruisers, 39 fleet and light carriers, approximately 100 escort carriers, 99 cruisers, 561 destroyers, 430 submarines, and 1,000 destroyer escorts, less any attrition suffered in the interim.

Within two weeks, the navy had secured presidential approval for this expansion totaling nearly a million tons of combatants. Without the need to consult Congress, the bureaus could immediately begin writing contracts and ordering materials.⁶ Before the war emergency began, prior approval from Congress had been necessary before the navy could begin work on ships built out of authorized tonnage. In order to streamline ship construction planning during the emergency, however, Congress had decided to allow the navy to proceed on particular ships pursuant to the general authorization acts without the need for specific legislative approval.⁷

Of course, money to pay for the ships could come only from Congress, and Admiral Horne was careful to explain the scope of the new program to members of the House Appropriations Committee responsible for spending on naval matters. The vice CNO described these additions as "replacements" for the five battleships, two battle cruisers, and one large carrier that previously had been suspended but were now definitely canceled and also for ships lost or becoming overage.⁸ The additions left the navy with only a thousand tons of unallocated building authority out of the several million tons authorized over the previous three years, approximately enough for one destroyer escort.

The inescapable conclusion from this episode is that navy expansion goals had become completely divorced from strategic planning and were influenced more by political possibilities than by any thorough reassessment of the fleet's long-term requirements for combatant ships. Despite serious resource shortages at home and strategic developments abroad during the preceding year, navy leaders increased their building program, apparently without even consulting their army counterparts. This augmentation of the fleet promised to increase the armed services' already serious competition for men.

With worrisome shortages afflicting many aspects of the war effort by the summer of 1943, potential critics of the fleet program awaited only the right opportunity to question the wisdom of navy expansion plans. The chance to create controversy arrived in early September 1943 with the surrender of Italy. In a few hectic days the bulk of the Italian fleet either surrendered to the Allies or was destroyed; the Germans captured only some light units, along with ships too damaged or mechanically deficient to leave port. Together with the scuttling of the French battle fleet at Toulon ten months earlier, Italy's surrender gave the Allies an overwhelming naval preponderance in the European theater. If fears of a major Axis naval resurgence still existed as late as August 1943, the arrival of the Italian fleet for internment in Malta harbor ended them for good.

Even before the Italian surrender, Admiral King and his staff had begun to feel the pressure of increased scrutiny by a powerful executive war agency and its director. In May 1943 the president had appointed former senator and Supreme Court justice James Byrnes to head the newly created Office of War Mobilization (OWM). Established by an executive order and in response to the perceived failure of Donald Nelson's War Production Board, the OWM was charged with the monumental task of coordinating all government agencies involved in war production. The president gave OWM sweeping authority "to unify the activities of Federal agencies and departments engaged in or concerned with production, procurement, distribution, or transportation of military or civilian supplies, materiel, and products, and to resolve and determine controversies between such agencies."[9]

As OWM director, Byrnes theoretically had authority to settle all priority disputes among various sectors of the war effort, including those involving the military services. A close political ally of the president, Byrnes made his headquarters in the White House just down the hall from the Oval Office. He refused to build OWM into a bureaucratic agency, relying on a few staff members to serve as his personal assistants; in effect, James Byrnes *was* the OWM. His friendship with and access to Roosevelt and to key senators, together with the powers inherent in his new position, combined to make him one of the most politically powerful men in the country; newspaper columnists dubbed him "assistant president."[10]

As Roosevelt's new mobilization czar, Byrnes believed that he had responsibility for ensuring that military procurement plans kept pace with developments in global strategy. To coordinate war production and assert his new authority, within a month of taking office Byrnes requested that all agencies involved in procurement, including the navy, make careful studies of their production requirements.[11] While the army and Maritime Commission readily complied with the OWM, navy leaders resisted, preferring to deal directly with the president. Not until Byrnes sought direct presidential intervention did the navy agree to establish a board of two retired officers and two civilians to review procurement. During July and August the procurement review board studied various aspects of the shipbuilding program, although its work was hampered by the navy's unwillingness to share information about future strategy with either the civilian board members or Byrnes's personal representative.

In late August 1943 the board submitted its report to the secretary of the navy and to OWM. Based on the board's findings, Byrnes decided that the navy program was out of balance with the rest of the war effort and with the changing strategic balance worldwide. A few days after he received the report, Byrnes wrote to the president to criticize the lack of realistic force planning within the Navy Department. He suggested that the nation's manpower problems demanded a critical review of the navy shipbuilding program, which, he believed, needed modification in light of the rapidly changing global military balance.[12]

Byrnes was primarily concerned about manpower problems in the shipbuilding industry, but he also discussed the overall scale of navy growth. He concluded that a combatant shipbuilding program designed to deal with the combined German, Italian, Japanese, and French navies had been "rendered partially obsolete by the tide of war," including the near-immobilization of the Italian fleet. In short, Byrnes argued that strategic developments since 1941, and the increasing difficulty of finding adequate numbers of shipyard workers, mandated a major review of navy expansion plans.

From anyone in so powerful a position, this recommendation constituted a major challenge to Admiral King's previously unquestioned authority to set targets for navy growth. Byrnes had not only power and the president's ear, but he also had experience and an intimate knowledge of the strategic rationale underlying the navy program. Before Roosevelt elevated him to the Supreme Court, Byrnes had served as chair of the Senate Appropriations Committee Navy Subcommittee, which oversaw the navy's budgets for fiscal years 1941 and 1942.[13]

Through congressional hearings and reports he would have received a fairly complete understanding of how the navy justified its building plans.

Byrnes's views quickly came to the attention of Secretary Knox and Admiral King, who took steps to limit the damage done to the navy's expansion plans and their own credibility. One of Byrnes's major complaints concerned the navy staff's failure to plan for possible cuts in combat ship construction in reaction to the decline in Axis naval strength. Perhaps anticipating Byrnes's criticisms, in late August 1943 Admiral King had the vice CNO institute a Navy Department survey of the ship construction program. The survey would cover all navy shipbuilding, with the goal of producing recommendations on possible reductions that seemed advisable in light of the progress of the war.[14] Armed with this information, Secretary Knox met with Byrnes and Roosevelt in early September and got Byrnes to retract his criticism of navy planning. Byrnes admitted that Admiral King and his staff were dealing with the situation adequately.[15]

Even before Italy's surrender Admiral King began taking some steps to adjust navy growth plans in light of certain strategic realities. The conquest of North Africa and Sicily opened the Mediterranean to Allied shipping, reducing the distance and danger of moving goods to India and the Mideast. At the same time, the war against Axis submarines had clearly turned in the Allies' favor; during a fierce summer campaign they had inflicted heavy losses on the U-boat fleet. These events, and the need to build larger numbers of landing craft, prompted the CNO to approve cancellation of 205 destroyer escorts and several dozen smaller patrol craft, with an understanding that the facilities and materials thereby released would be switched to landing craft construction.[16] Secretary Knox seconded this proposal, which received formal presidential approval in early September.[17]

The cancellation left 800 destroyer escorts in the program, and King soon proposed cancellation of 200 more in order to reduce production to 600 units.[18] The CNO's proposal drew a protest from the Bureau of Ships, which argued that such drastic cuts over such a short period would lead to waste and worker demoralization in the shipyards and in the plants producing ship parts. The bureau therefore recommended limiting the second program reduction to 100 units, leaving 700 as the planned building goal.[19] Admiral Horne seconded the bureau's views, noting that excess destroyer escorts could be converted into small transports (this was actually done), shore bombardment vessels, and specialized antiaircraft ships.[20]

Already concerned about criticism of possible overbuilding, King was in no mood to tolerate resistance from his staff. His reply to Horne's suggestion read in full: "It is necessary to reduce the DE program to a total of 600. Take steps accordingly."[21] The bureau's arguments caught the attention of Secretary Knox, however, who deferred cutting the destroyer escort production target below 700.

Not until the spring of 1944 did the navy manage to cut additional destroyer escorts from the program.[22] While King and his staff debated the number of antisubmarine escorts that the fleet needed, the core of the navy combatant shipbuilding program remained intact. Construction of traditional combatant types continued without let-up, with no signs that navy planners were reconsidering their original target strengths set the previous summer.

Outside intervention quickly threatened to change this comfortable status quo. Just a few days after the meeting of Roosevelt, Byrnes, and Knox that apparently settled OWM's critique of navy expansion, the Italian fleet sailed for Malta and internment. Whatever Byrnes may have promised Secretary Knox during that conference, Italy's surrender prompted him to again call for reductions in planned fleet strength.

In a second letter to Roosevelt, Byrnes cited the conclusions of the procurement review board to support his belief that the navy was absorbing a disproportionate share of the war production effort. Based on the board's findings and the elimination of Italian naval strength, Byrnes strongly recommended that the president order a review of the ship construction program for the purpose of cutting navy procurement.[23] The OWM director noted that the navy's long-range construction plans called for the fleet's combatant tonnage to triple by the end of 1946. The enormous building program established in 1941 and 1942 had been based on the prospect that the United States might face the combined Axis fleets without British assistance; Byrnes now argued that the surrender of Italy had "manifestly and permanently altered" the situation. He reasoned that "either this long range program was inadequate in January 1942, or else . . . it is over-size and beyond our needs in the summer of 1943."[24]

Byrnes correctly saw that the combat ship program placed a major burden on the war effort not just because of its monetary costs but by absorbing vast numbers of men and material that could be employed in other vital areas. He noted that the need to reduce the navy program was "dictated less by a lack of dollars than of the manpower to build these vessels . . . and to efficiently man them when they are completed." Byrnes also ruled out considering the negative effects that cancellations might have on shipyard employees or shipbuilding companies, stressing that the decision on "whether more ships are to be built should be reached wholly on the question of their essentiality in the present conflict."[25]

Taken alone, the letter from Byrnes, a powerful man, created a major threat to the established navy expansion program. Byrnes soon received support for his views from a most unexpected source. Six days after Byrnes set out his arguments, Under Secretary of the Navy Forrestal also wrote to the president to suggest that changed strategic conditions mandated a reexamination of the entire navy shipbuilding program. Despite Admiral King's earlier reorganization efforts, Forrestal still had primary responsibility for navy procurement, and his office remained the principal material coordinating agency of the Navy Department.[26] Forrestal argued that piecemeal cancellations like those in the destroyer escort program would ultimately prove wasteful and were the product of poor requirements planning. He now proposed that navy requirements be determined in a systematic fashion so that men and material would not be allocated for vessels that were no longer necessary.[27]

The president apparently agreed with Byrnes and Forrestal. Accordingly, he seemed inclined to order a review of the nation's entire ship construction program. In the meantime, he told Forrestal that he would refer Forrestal's letter to the Joint Chiefs.[28] Roosevelt believed that questions regarding navy shipbuilding primarily fell within the area of production priorities, and he wanted the problem handled by the newly created Joint Production Survey Committee (JPSC). Established just a few days earlier, the JPSC had been created through arrangements made at a meeting between the Joint Chiefs and Justice Byrnes. The review of the ship construction would therefore be the committee's first major project.

The JPSC had its origins in the requirements review studies Byrnes had ordered during the early summer. All the review boards' findings included recommendations that the services establish machinery that would continue to review military procurement; the JPSC was intended to be that machinery.[29] The JPSC consisted of two senior officers from the army and two from the navy and was responsible for advising the

The Rise of the Critics

Joint Chiefs on the means for balancing war production with military requirements in light of the strategic situation.[30] As a senior joint staff agency, it was authorized to obtain whatever studies or estimates it required from other joint agencies, as well as from the Navy and War Department staffs. Its charter mandated that it operate in a similar fashion to the Joint Strategic Survey Committee, studying all military production and passing on reports and recommendations directly to the Joint Chiefs.[31]

The assignment of the navy shipbuilding study to a joint planning group opened the door for the War Department to begin agitating for a say in controlling the process of navy expansion. By late summer 1943 army planners were fully aware that a substantial and growing share of the nation's male population was being devoted to creating and manning the fleet. From the War Department's perspective, bringing the shipbuilding program under joint supervision would be a first step toward balancing the navy's continuing influence over army troop basis planning.

Before Byrnes and Forrestal broached the subject to Roosevelt, navy representatives on joint manpower planning committees had been able to justify their requests simply by pointing out the number of ships expected to enter service in the coming years. At the same time, they persistently questioned the army's need to mobilize divisions that it could not ship, thereby challenging the very core of army force structure planning. If, as now appeared possible, the fleet construction program should become subject to joint control, both services would have to support their force structure requirements in conferences with representatives from the other service. Army planners would then have a way to regulate the flow of men into the navy and the shipbuilding industry by forcing cuts in fleet expansion plans. In sum, army staff officers had ample reason to support the idea of joint control over the navy program.

Interservice debates over bringing fleet expansion under joint control lasted from the autumn of 1943 through the spring and summer of 1944. Throughout these discussions, Admiral King's staff refused to acknowledge any army role in determining fleet strength and fought to prevent any joint supervision over combat ship construction. Despite the arguments that joint supervision was both fair and would promote greater efficiency in the war effort, the navy high command refused to give ground. Accustomed to complete freedom in setting fleet strength, King's staff was adamant in its refusal to accept army participation.

THE UNSINKABLE FLEET

The Joint Chiefs had intended that the JPSC would work closely with the Office of War Mobilization, but perhaps not as closely as the president now ordered. On 28 September 1943 he directed Byrnes to have the JPSC prepare a review of the entire national shipbuilding program, including ships for the army, Maritime Commission, and navy.[32] At the JPSC's first meeting, Byrnes said that Congress and the American public were demanding justification for the enormous war program and that Roosevelt was determined that his administration would lead the way on cutting excessive production. He added that the JPSC's report should include recommendations on reducing ship construction programs, taking into account national manpower shortages and the question of priorities among the army, navy, and Maritime Commission.[33]

Because combatant ship construction constituted a significant portion of U.S. war production, a review of the shipbuilding program was at least arguably within the JPSC's mandate. Navy leaders viewed the matter differently, however. Roosevelt apparently neglected to inform the Joint Chiefs that he had directed Byrnes to have the JPSC study the national ship construction situation. This may have been an oversight, but the president was notorious for his divide-and-conquer methods of dealing with subordinates. Based on the correspondence between Roosevelt and Forrestal, the Joint Chiefs believed that the decision on involving the JPSC was being left to them. Working under this misapprehension, they considered and rejected a proposal to forward both Forrestal's letter to the president and the latter's reply for study by the JPSC.[34]

The Joint Chiefs concluded that the navy program was not an appropriate subject for JPSC review and that questions regarding the size of the fleet should be resolved within the Navy Department. Admiral Leahy even drafted a letter for the president to send to Secretary Knox. Roosevelt was to ask the Navy Department to study ship construction goals because he agreed with the Joint Chiefs that an examination of the building program was not properly within the JPSC's cognizance.[35] The letter, if the president ever saw it, certainly did not represent his views; it was never sent.

One significant aspect of the mixup was General Marshall's apparent failure to deviate from his conviction that each service should set its own expansion goals. Byrnes and Forrestal had given Marshall a golden opportunity to assert some control over navy growth, but he apparently preferred to sacrifice the chance in order to promote harmony within the joint system. So long as the chief of staff steadfastly maintained this view, his subordinates could count on little support in the upcoming debates over joint participation in navy force planning.

The president's direct instructions to Justice Byrnes naturally superseded the Joint Chiefs' decision on the issue, and the JPSC study on shipbuilding went forward. Thus, on direct presidential orders, this subordinate joint agency would be conducting a major study on military requirements against the unanimous advice of the service chiefs. On 19 October 1943, Byrnes asked Secretary of the Navy Knox for the navy's help with the study, requesting that Knox submit recommendations to the committee regarding possible cuts in the navy program. Byrnes suggested that the elimination of the Italian and French fleets should permit the navy to accept reductions in combatant shipbuilding plans.[36]

Byrnes simultaneously attempted to influence the progress of ship construction directly. In a letter to Admiral Leahy, he noted that Forrestal had questioned the value of the final two *Iowa*-class battleships. He therefore asked Leahy to have the Joint Chiefs stop work on the two pending a full investigation of whether they were needed to further the war effort.[37]

The fact that the Joint Production Survey Committee study had presidential approval and paralleled a navy study did not placate Admiral King. He undoubtedly realized the crucial difference between an internal navy audit of the combat ship program and a review of that program by a joint agency; he could control one but not the other. Concerned about losing navy control over fleet force levels, Admiral King took the opportunity at a Joint Chiefs meeting to criticize the idea of the JPSC study openly, arguing that a review of the navy's combat ship program was not a proper task for that (or presumably any other joint) organization.[38] The CNO was supported in this view by his senior logistics officer, Admiral Horne. In meetings between Byrnes and Secretary Knox, the vice CNO repeatedly stressed that possible cutbacks in shipbuilding must be based on the strategic situation and operational plans and that only Admiral King was qualified to make recommendations in those areas.[39]

On the political front, King also had to deal with Byrnes's attempt to interfere with battleship construction. He quickly demonstrated that Byrnes did not have a monopoly on access to the president. King met personally with Roosevelt and then circulated a letter reporting that the president had approved completion of all four remaining *Iowa*-class battleships, thereby undercutting Byrnes's attempt to halt construction on the last two. King added that he and Roosevelt agreed that any investigation of navy shipbuilding should take into account the indefinite suspension of all five *Montana*-class battleships.[40]

Despite King's misgivings about the JPSC investigation, the matter had already been decided at the highest level. King wisely determined that the best course was to present the navy's case to the JPSC in the strongest possible fashion. On the same day he criticized the idea of the JPSC investigation, the CNO wrote Secretary Knox a letter in which he set forth the general strategic factors to keep in mind when considering reductions in the navy program.[41]

King argued that although the naval building program adopted in 1940 and 1942 had been premised on the assumption that the United States might be forced to fight alone against the combined Axis fleets, the initial rationale behind these early expansion plans was essentially defensive. He noted that the navy's mission since Pearl Harbor had expanded beyond the task of merely securing the Western Hemisphere against invasion. The planned offensive against Japanese forces in the western Pacific increased naval requirements; therefore, the virtual elimination of Axis naval strength in the European theater did not permit a corresponding reduction in the navy's combatant ship program.

The CNO also propounded a fleet requirement planning standard to which his subordinates would adhere in forthcoming debates over expansion plans. Admiral King declared that navy planners should not think in terms of minimum requirements for combat forces but instead should plan in terms of using all the combatant ships the fleet could get. Additional ships would permit more lines of advance, stronger assaults, lower losses, and a more rapid conclusion to the war. Unlike the army, the navy could readily employ all of the units (in this case ships rather than divisions) that could be provided in order to achieve an overwhelming advantage in strength and open new strategic possibilities. Any cuts in the approved building program would preclude certain lines of advance and reduce combat superiority, threatening heavier losses and a longer war.

Although the CNO made several valid points, his arguments suffered from some factual inaccuracies and failures of logic. First, the original navy program had never been purely defensive; the forces advocated

The Rise of the Critics

from 1939 through 1941 evolved from the premise that fleet units should be able to operate offensively in at least one ocean. In the Victory Program report of 1941, navy staff planners clearly stated that the proposed fleet would be sufficient for offensive operations in both oceans. The 1942 program was clearly intended to help the United States achieve naval supremacy at a time when the Axis powers seemed to be victorious everywhere.

Even if the original programs could be classified as defensive, King failed to explain why an offensive against the Japanese navy would require as many ships as would have been needed to face the combined fleets of all three Axis powers. Certainly there was heavy fighting ahead, and at great distances from major fleet bases, but by October 1943 the Japanese fleet was clearly on the decline. In a sense, King's claim that the navy should use all the ships it could get suggested that the CNO had given up on trying to link force levels with any particular foe, strategy, or set of planned operations. Navy ship construction would be limited by what the market would bear, taking into consideration industrial limitations, political costs, and the rival claims of other agencies also responsible for winning the war.

As to King's claims that a larger fleet would reduce the length and cost of the war, they failed to allow for the navy program's impact on the overall war effort. Although any commander would prefer to have the strategic options that overwhelming forces can provide, the nation simply lacked the means to provide that level of strength in every sector. If the power and flexibility King spoke of could be achieved only at the cost of weakening the other services, lives saved in the Pacific by enlarging the fleet might well be lost on the ground in France or in the air over Germany.

Armed with King's recommendations, Secretary Knox turned the issue of navy requirements over to the General Board for further study. The board basically echoed the CNO's arguments and added an economic dimension to help justify continued ship construction. It reported that the war was costing the United States some $200 million each day; if building more ships could appreciably shorten the war, the new construction would more than pay for itself.[42]

Based on the advice of the General Board and Admiral King, Knox informed Adm. Roland M. Brainard, the senior naval member of the JPSC, that the secretary could not recommend any further deletions from the navy's combatant ship program.[43] Knox fully embraced Admiral

King's argument that simple numerical comparisons of Allied and Axis combat tonnage had little meaning in connection with winning the war because each operation required a reasonable assurance of "decisive superiority" over the enemy. While Knox concluded that the war's end was not yet so definitely in view as to allow curtailment of the building program, he promised that cutbacks would come "when it becomes manifest that our superiority in any type is sufficient to warrant it." He pointed out that the navy had already canceled hundreds of destroyer escorts, indefinitely postponed five battleships and three battle cruisers, and placed two other battleships on a low priority for construction.

One important fact Knox failed to mention was that none of the canceled ships he listed could have been ready for service before 1946. Besides, by late 1943 even the most fervent battleship enthusiasts realized that carriers formed the primary striking force of the fleet. For these reasons, the tonnage originally allocated to the battleships Knox mentioned had already been reallocated to build other ships, making many of the "cancellations" in reality transfers of building tonnage from one type to another.

A few days after receiving the navy's recommendations from Secretary Knox, the Joint Production Survey Committee presented its report on the combatant ship program. Apparently Admiral Brainard and his navy colleague had completely dominated the discussions, for the report fully embraced Admiral King's views. The report noted that the JPSC had not examined the navy program with the idea of discovering the minimum requirements for victory.[44] The JPSC focused instead on "a *rapid* prosecution of the war with a view to reducing casualties and cost," goals that could not be achieved with the minimum forces necessary for victory. The report stated that setting minimum combatant ship requirements would be counterproductive because "an assured superiority of force will materially contribute in the long run toward an overall lessening of losses and expenses."

The approved building program would certainly assure naval superiority, with 7 capital ships, 28 carriers, 72 escort carriers, 73 cruisers, 251 destroyers, 541 destroyer escorts, and 257 submarines scheduled to come off the ways by late 1946. The new units would join the 713 combatants already in service, raising navy strength to more than 1,900 fighting ships. The JPSC concluded that national strategy was best served by building all of the ships called for in the navy's construction plans and therefore recommended that there be no reductions. Nothing in the report indicated that the JPSC had studied the effects that building and manning the fleet would have on the manpower problem or other military programs.

For all intents and purposes, the JPSC had simply accepted the arguments Admiral King used in his letter to the secretary of the navy. This should have surprised no one. Like the JSSC, the JPSC had no technical staff of its own and relied on other joint or single-service agencies for staff work.[45] Those JPSC members most qualified to judge navy combat ship requirements were navy officers, who presumably gave considerable deference to the work of King's staff and the General Board.

The net effect of the JPSC's first report was to reinforce the status quo, allowing navy leaders to proceed with their approved program of ship construction. On 18 November Admiral Horne duly notified Justice Byrnes that the Joint Chiefs had concluded that continued prosecution of the full navy building program was necessary to the war effort.[46] The JPSC's second report, covering transports and cargo ships, also endorsed the approved building program. In fact, the JPSC seemed so disinclined to disturb existing plans that Admiral Leahy feared the committee would lose credibility if it approved all scheduled production programs. Army Deputy Chief of Staff General McNarney worried whether the JPSC would be perceived as no more than a rubber stamp for the Joint Chiefs.[47]

The JPSC report assuaged navy leaders' concerns, but only briefly. Although Admiral King undoubtedly would have liked to see joint involvement with the navy program over and done with, the report included a rather ominous suggestion that combat ship construction should be kept under constant review as the strategic situation changed. The key question concerned which agency would perform this review. The JPSC would continue to work on production problems, with a representative of OWM present at all its meetings. When the JPSC subsequently attempted to initiate another study of navy combat ship requirements, it set off a second controversy over the role that joint planning agencies could or should play in reviewing fleet expansion goals.

By the end of 1943 the navy still had exclusive control over planning for fleet strength, answering only to Congress and the president on that issue. Although the navy had won the opening round, evidence continued to mount that some reduction in the combat ship program should occur. On the last day of 1943, the Munitions Assignments Board in Washington reported that the previous year had seen the global naval balance shift even more heavily in the Allies' favor. However, navy procurement would have a greater impact on the nation's material and manpower resources in 1944 than in 1943, despite the fact that the combined U.S. and British fleets already enjoyed a two-to-one or better advantage over the Axis in all ship classes save submarines.[48] The board noted that the navy was currently building 9 battleships and battle cruisers, 39 carriers, 101 escort carriers, 79 cruisers, 350 destroyers, and 297 submarines, many of which would not be completed until 1946 or later.

Figures like these were certain to attract attention; after a brief hiatus following its November report on navy shipbuilding the JPSC opened the door for more debates beginning in late January 1944. In a memorandum to the Joint Staff Planners the JPSC asked for a firm estimate of the U.S. combat ships that would be required for the war against Japan.[49] It noted that the defeat of Germany would release Allied (mostly British) naval forces for use against Japan. The United States could therefore expect the British fleet to provide a substantial number of naval units for a final campaign against the Japanese home islands. Based on expected British help in the Pacific, the JPSC reasoned that the "extensive" U.S. shipbuilding program would almost certainly be curtailed before the war's end. In order to plan those reductions in advance, the JPSC requested that the Joint Planners determine the number of combat ships required in the Pacific and estimate how many Allied ships could be expected to participate in that campaign.

By January 1944 the overwhelming bulk of U.S. Navy strength was committed to the Pacific. In essence, the JPSC was asking the Joint Planners to estimate the navy's ultimate combat ship requirements, with the expectation that the figure arrived at could be decreased in light of anticipated British assistance. The request touched off a debate between army and navy planners over whether any joint agency was competent to estimate combat ship requirements, especially if those estimates differed from the navy's own planned construction program. Such an estimate effectively would substitute the Joint Planners' views for those of the navy high command. This concept had presumably been rejected by the Joint Chiefs the previous autumn and would certainly meet resistance from the CNO and his staff.

The Rise of the Critics

The Joint Planners passed the JPSC request on to their subordinate planning agency, the Joint War Plans Committee (JWPC), which had replaced the Joint U.S. Strategic Committee in an organizational shakeup early in 1943. The planners directed the JWPC to estimate the number of combat ships needed to defeat Japan. In turn, the JWPC assigned the study to the joint planning team responsible for the Pacific theater.[50]

On 17 March 1944 the JWPC reported to the Joint Planners that no firm estimate of the number of U.S. warships needed to defeat Japan could be provided at that time.[51] It explained that because approved plans for operations in the Pacific extended only through the first three months of 1945, any calculation of requirements beyond that date would involve an unacceptable amount of speculation. In addition, the possible participation of British naval units was still in the planning stage. Given these uncertainties, any reliable estimate of navy requirements would have to wait until plans for the final defeat of Japan were completed.

At the next Joint Planners meeting, navy representatives seconded the JWPC's conclusions.[52] They argued that plans for the final defeat of Japan had not yet reached the stage where an estimate of the specific number of ships needed for victory was possible, a claim they buttressed with two related arguments. First, although attrition would affect ultimate requirements, the navy could not reasonably rely on past experience to figure future combat losses because sinkings might increase sharply as U.S. forces moved closer to Japan. Second, plans for future navy requirements could not safely be based on the state of the Japanese fleet because planned operations would for the first time bring U.S. ships within range of significant Japanese land-based air forces. In short, navy representatives insisted that the current building program reflected their best guess about ultimate combatant ship requirements and concluded that they lacked sufficient information to change their views.

Gen. Frank N. Roberts had replaced General Wedemeyer as the senior army representative on the Joint Planners, and he disputed the navy position. Pointing out that the army had repeatedly estimated the number of divisions it needed for planned operations, Roberts argued that the navy should be able to do the same with combatant ships. He insisted that a firm estimate was vital because the navy program had a direct effect on army plans through its impact on the nation's manpower.[53]

General Roberts suggested that an acceptable estimate could be based on known Japanese shipbuilding capabilities and worst-case scenarios for future operations. If the army could (unwillingly) subject its estimates of force requirements to joint scrutiny, Roberts was adamant that the navy should be required to do the same.

The tone for future confrontations was set, with each service determined not to alter its position. The meeting ended with a decision to return the initial report to the JWPC for a more definite estimate of ultimate combat ship requirements. As with other attempts to solve basic resource allocation disputes by having joint committees restudy issues, the decision produced only more conflicts.

A week passed before the JWPC issued its second report, which was little more than a rewrite of the first. This revised report also concluded that until the Joint Planners completed plans for the final defeat of Japan, the JWPC could not accurately assess the navy's ultimate needs. The JWPC therefore suggested that the Joint Production Survey Committee take its request to the Navy Department, which already had the building program under review.[54] Given the prior experience with the dynamics of the joint planning organizations, this deadlock should have surprised no one. Only the navy members of the committee were qualified to produce the requested estimate; if they declared the task was impossible, the army members could do little to oppose them.

In the Joint Planners meeting that followed the receipt of the second JWPC report, army and navy representatives again clashed over whether an estimate of combat ship requirements was necessary or even possible.[55] Both sides reiterated their old arguments, with the navy stressing the impossibility of estimating ultimate ship requirements because of many imponderables and the fluid state of strategic planning. General Roberts reminded the group that the army was constantly being called upon to estimate the number of divisions it needed and based those estimates on assessments of enemy capabilities. The AAF representative added that if his branch could determine the air groups needed for future operations, logic dictated that the same predictions could be made for combatant ships.

Senior navy member Adm. Bernard Bieri repeated Admiral King's argument that more combat ships meant more and stronger offensives and a shorter, less costly war. He added that the navy had never had enough ships in operation to meet all its requirements and therefore concluded that "the construction program is limited by our ability to construct the vessels required."[56] In other words, the navy intended to continue building ships as quickly as it could.

The debates demonstrated how far navy force planning had drifted from the requirements studies of 1938 through 1941. Navy planners faced no greater imponderables than their army or AAF counterparts, who had adjusted their programs to meet the realities imposed by resource limitations. The difference in approaches may be partially explained by the nature of anticipated losses. While army and AAF leaders could count on feeding replacements into existing formations as they took casualties, navy planners knew that in a single major action the fleet might lose key combatant units that would take years to replace.

The Joint Planners again reached no agreement on how to handle the JPSC's request, now more than two months old, and JPSC members were invited to attend the next Joint Planners meeting in an effort to resolve the impasse. At that meeting on 5 April 1944, Admiral Bieri repeated his earlier argument that the Pacific campaign had yet to reach the stage where the navy could delete ships from its current program. The admiral did concede that the navy might not have sufficient personnel to man all planned ships, and he suggested that some adjustment to the program might be possible if the Japanese fleet suffered a major defeat in upcoming operations.[57] The JPSC members left with the promise that the planners would have the JWPC prepare yet another report on the issue.

While these debates dragged on, navy leaders proceeded to obtain congressional approval and funding needed to proceed with the entire planned shipbuilding program. During March and April 1944 Admiral King and his subordinates testified on fleet expansion in hearings on the navy budget for fiscal year 1945. The CNO justified existing construction plans by testifying that enemy resistance was likely to grow rather than decrease as the Pacific campaign neared the Japanese home islands. Therefore, King concluded, the navy would require all the ships that could be provided.[58]

In response to questions from members of Congress about cutting combat shipbuilding, Admiral Horne noted that the construction program was already under constant review. He argued that U.S. preponderance in numbers was balanced by the need to operate several widely dispersed naval forces; in contrast, the Japanese navy kept its battle fleet concentrated and able to strike with its full power at a single spot.[59]

Navy leaders persisted with this argument even though, as Admiral Horne later admitted, by year's end the navy would outnumber the Japanese fleet by three or four to one.[60]

The third JWPC report on navy requirements, which appeared in early June 1944, raised an entirely new issue. Once again the JWPC professed its inability to make any estimate of navy combat ship needs. This time, however, it stated that the question was beyond its purview. The report noted, "While we may estimate the combat ship requirements for operations or campaigns, this is but one small factor influencing total naval requirements, which are also controlled by naval policies, developments in new weapons, expected attrition, needs for purely naval operations, and other factors which cannot readily be evaluated by this committee."[61] In light of this decision, the report recommended that the Joint Planners withdraw their directive for a JWPC estimate of navy requirements.

This abnegation of responsibility is somewhat puzzling in light of the JWPC's role in the joint planning system. As the working arm of the Joint Staff Planners, the JWPC's primary function was to prepare and submit war plans, studies, and estimates as directed by its parent agency.[62] The Joint Planners themselves had primary responsibility for "studies relating to the combined employment of military forces of the United Nations in the prosecution of the War."[63] Given this broad responsibility and the authority of the Joint Production Survey Committee to request studies necessary to perform its own duties, the JWPC's position on the combat ships issue was simply not supported by the facts. The most likely explanation for this is that the JWPC's action flowed from political rather than bureaucratic considerations, given the implications this issue had for army-navy relations.

Not surprisingly, navy representatives on the Joint Planners supported the JWPC's claim that it lacked authority to estimate navy combat ship needs. Adm. Donald B. Duncan, who had succeeded Admiral Bieri as senior navy planner, carried the JWPC's position to its logical conclusion. Citing the numerous factors involved in the question of navy combat ship requirements, he argued that the issue was outside the sphere of the Joint Chiefs of Staff or any of the supporting joint agencies.[64]

The JWPC's position on this issue probably represented the ideal solution from the navy perspective. While navy planners could put off the day of reckoning by claiming that an estimate of the navy's combat ship requirements would be premature, this tactic could only succeed in delaying the inevitable. Eventually, operations in the Pacific would reach a point where the argument lost credibility. The companion argument that the issue was too complex for solution also had its weaknesses. The army representatives could rightly reply that the issue was no more complex than that of army force requirements, which had repeatedly been subject to joint consideration. Also, how could the navy itself presume to find the correct solution if the issue were so complex as to be incomprehensible?

Because the Joint Chiefs had no precisely defined sphere of authority, army planners had no easy answer to the claim that navy expansion involved matters beyond joint responsibility. Precisely what those matters might be (political or postwar considerations, for example) seems not to have been stated with any certainty; this deliberate vagueness made the navy's position that much harder to refute.

Another factor that made this position attractive to the navy was that, unlike others that had been used in the past, it would endure the passage of time. The "beyond joint authority" rationale could be used as long as the war lasted, perhaps longer. By summer 1944, military and civilian leaders had begun seriously studying the topic of a unified department of defense. Admiral King opposed the idea but had to consider the distinct possibility that such an arrangement would be forced upon the navy after the war. His staff may well have been trying to set a precedent that would reserve to the navy any decisions on fleet strength should unification become a reality. The one major weakness of this argument was that it implicitly contradicted the president's decision that at least one joint agency, the JPSC, should have some responsibility for reviewing navy requirements.

Although General Roberts disagreed with the reasoning in the Joint War Plan Committee's report, he was willing to ask the JPSC to withdraw its request for an estimate of navy ship requirements.[65] The senior army planner's acquiescence must have surprised navy members, given Roberts's earlier statements about the JWPC being capable of producing the requested estimate. Perhaps Roberts had decided not to press the navy on this issue because of General Marshall's continuing desire to avoid any appearance of an open break within the joint staff system. Roberts also knew that the army was considering plans to ask for additional manpower to create new divisions. Pushing the issue of navy fleet strength at that particular time might result in controversy should the army attempt to increase its own forces.

If the Joint Production Survey Committee were willing to withdraw its request for an estimate of combatant ships needed to defeat Japan, the matter would presumably end there. However, if the JPSC persisted in its demand for an estimate, General Roberts wanted the Joint War Plans Committee to be prepared to submit an estimate of requirements based on information that various theater commanders submitted. When the JPSC declined the Joint Planners' invitation to withdraw their request, the planners once again directed the JWPC to prepare the necessary report.[66]

In late June 1944 the JWPC presented its fourth and final report on the navy's ultimate combatant ship requirements. Although once again the planners reiterated their claim that the matter was beyond their purview, the JWPC included in the report its best estimates of the numbers and types of combatant ships needed for approved operations through early 1945, some nine months into the future. However, it cautioned against fixing total combatant ship requirements by reference to an arithmetical summation of the requirements for specific tasks, suggesting that actual needs would exceed its estimate.[67] Echoing the navy argument that more ships equaled more flexibility, the JWPC concluded that projected operations through the end of 1945 would require all combat ships scheduled for completion by that date.

The War Department staff was unsatisfied with the fourth study. An internal Operations Division memorandum set forth the army staff's view that setting limits on navy combatant shipbuilding was definitely not beyond the purview of the Joint Planners. Army planners had seen no hard evidence supporting the JWPC's conclusion that all scheduled naval construction through 1945 was necessary to the war effort, and, they noted, they had no information on what the navy would do with ships coming off the ways in 1946.[68] Army staff officers were troubled by Admiral Bieri's statement that the building program was limited only by the navy's ability to construct vessels and frustrated by the navy planners' apparent determination not to deviate from this course.

Bieri's statement was seen as one of several major weaknesses in the navy's position. The navy had failed to demonstrate that all scheduled construction was actually needed to carry out strategic plans or that logistic facilities were sufficient to support the additional ships. Finally, and perhaps most important, chances seemed slim that the planned ships could be manned and supported without exceeding the navy's current troop basis. In this last assessment the Operations Division had hit upon the main obstacle to navy growth plans (chapter 6).

By the time the Joint Planners met in early August to consider the fourth JWPC report on navy requirements, the strategic picture on land and sea had changed dramatically. Allied forces had broken through German defenses in Normandy and were poised to begin a second landing on the Mediterranean coast. In the Pacific, American airplanes and submarines had shattered Japanese carrier forces in the Battle of the Philippine Sea, although many military leaders underestimated the extent of this important victory.

After reviewing the JWPC report, Admiral Duncan announced that the navy had established its own standing committee to study possible cutbacks in the combatant shipbuilding program. He recommended that planners refer the JPSC to this committee for any further information on navy ship construction plans.[69] General Roberts responded that the Joint Planners should provide a direct answer to the question the JPSC had presented them. Failing again to reach an agreement, the planners decided to defer any action on the JWPC report.

Several days after this meeting, the JWPC sent the Joint Planners a proposed memorandum that they could forward to the JPSC in order to justify their inability to produce an estimate of ship requirements.[70] The memo reiterated the claim that the building program involved factors (retirement of older ships, development of new designs) that required study by other agencies. The JWPC also recommended against any changes in the current program until future battles further reduced Japanese strength, and it predicted that British naval efforts in the Pacific would be too small to have any effect on American naval requirements.

In an effort to convince the JPSC to go elsewhere for information on navy requirements, the JWPC explained that the Joint Planners were able to make estimates of requirements only for planned operations. However, these same operational plans had been drawn up taking into account the anticipated availability of ships, perhaps explaining why the JWPC consistently reported that planned operations required all available ships. In a twist on Admiral King's theory that more ships allowed more operations, the JWPC concluded that any changes in the building program would change the operational plans that the Joint Planners

THE UNSINKABLE FLEET

relied upon to estimate ship requirements. In short, the JWPC claimed that the number of ships available controlled operational planning, not vice versa. This conclusion suggested that the naval planning staffs had taken to heart King's recommendation that they should base their calculations on using all the ships they could get.

The JWPC memo was practically the last word on joint oversight of navy shipbuilding. There is no indication that the JWPC ever produced the estimate of ultimate combatant ship requirements that it had set out to create in early 1944; instead, the matter was quietly and permanently dropped from the Joint Planners' agenda. As late as June 1945, the JPSC's request for the estimate of navy requirements remained outstanding.[71]

In the final analysis, navy planners had simply outlasted their army counterparts. Hewing to a consistent although at times illogical line, they had preserved all military decisions on fleet strength for the CNO and his staff. Without active help from their chief, Marshall's subordinates simply did not have the type of authority that might have compensated for their lack of expertise on this issue. They failed to gain anything for their efforts, and by midsummer the debate had already moved to a new arena within the Navy Department. Before decisions on ultimate navy strength became final, military leaders would have to clear up the still unsettled issue of manpower allocations to the fleet.

As secretary of the navy from 1940 until his death in April 1944, Frank Knox oversaw the fleet expansion program through its crucial years.

■ As the navy's principal field commander,
Adm. Chester Nimitz had a strong influence
on determining combatant ship requirements.

■ Vice Chief of Naval Operations Adm. Frederick Horne served as Admiral King's top deputy in overseeing the ship construction program.

■ Two fleet submarines take shape in the new building basin at Portsmouth Navy Yard, New Hampshire, April 1943, part of the facilities expansion at navy yards.

■ Facilities expansion at emergency shipyards: the Federal Shipbuilding and Drydock yard under construction, Port Newark, New Jersey, February 1942.

■ An emergency shipyard in action: Federal's Port Newark yard with destroyer escorts on the ways and others fitting out, April 1943.

■ A battleship rests in an advanced base sectional
dry dock, Manus Island, October 1944.

■ At a December 1942 lunch with key civilian war leaders, Admiral King is flanked on his right by Paul McNutt of the War Manpower Commission and on his left by Donald Nelson of the War Production Board. *U.S. Army Collection, National Archives*

■ Vice Adm. Roland Brainard was senior navy member of the Joint Production Survey Committee.

■ Rear Adm. Bernard Bieri was senior navy member of the Joint Staff Planners from late 1943 to May 1944 and King's point man on interservice debates over fleet expansion plans.

■ Vice Adm. Randall Jacobs, the wartime chief of the navy's Bureau of Personnel.

■ Capt. (later Admiral) Donald B. Duncan replaced Bieri on the Joint Staff Planners and served as senior navy member until July 1945.

■ Shift change at the Sea-Tac Shipyard, Tacoma, Washington, November 1943. Standardized designs and millions of laborers working round the clock helped the navy mass produce escort carriers on merchant hulls, quickly augmenting naval air power.

■ Admiral King stands somewhat uneasily
beside James Forrestal *(center)* as Forrestal
becomes secretary of the navy, May 1944.
Second from Forrestal's right stands Rep.
Carl Vinson, chair of the House Naval
Affairs Committee.

■ Rear Adm. Walter Delany, King's assistant chief of staff for readiness after March 1943 and senior member of the Special Navy Committee on Cutbacks (the "Cutback Committee").

■ Aircraft carriers outnumber battleships in this view of a navy task force steaming in the Pacific, February 1945. The new battle line was the result of changing technology and armor shortages.

■ The *Essex*-class aircraft carrier *Iwo Jima* at Newport News the day after navy leaders canceled construction in August 1945, a casualty of peace.

■ Adm. Ernest J. King and Army Chief of Staff Gen. George C. Marshall model their new five-star uniforms, January 1945.

■ James Byrnes, then-secretary of state, and President Harry S Truman meet with top military leaders en route to the Potsdam Conference, July 1945.

LAUNCHING U. S. S. CB 3

■ The battle cruiser USS *Hawaii* was launched in November 1945. The sheer momentum of the wartime program allowed the navy to continue building large numbers of ships months after hostilities ended.

· 6 ·

THE FLEET'S
PERSONNEL CRISIS
1943–1944

As intensive navy shipbuilding efforts began to bear fruit, unexpectedly severe personnel shortages led to very real fears that combat ship construction would outstrip the supply of men. Through late 1942 and early 1943, navy leaders had used political and bureaucratic pressure in an attempt to limit army expansion and maintain a military manpower reserve adequate to meet their service's future needs. Unfortunately, the navy failed to establish methods for accurately forecasting fleet personnel requirements, and planners had no idea whether manpower allocations would suffice to support the fleet they envisioned.

Throughout the war the navy based its manpower planning on the Force Operating Plan, an estimate of the numbers required to man and support the ships, airplanes, and base facilities that were expected to be in service at a given date. Projections in the Force Operating Plan usually proved inaccurate, leading to unexpected shortfalls that threatened to derail fleet expansion and upset the delicate agreement on manpower allocations that the navy planning staff had finally achieved with their army counterparts. Naval planners repeatedly failed to anticipate how unrelenting upward pressure of the combat ship program and the need to man advanced fleet bases would increase personnel requirements. As a result, they consistently underestimated personnel needs and were forced to ask for more men when shortages appeared after mobilization plans had been set. With the armed forces caught in a manpower squeeze, upward revisions in naval personnel requirements became the subject of inter- and intraservice controversy during the last two years of the war.

By late 1943 economic and political considerations had forced military leaders to place a definite cap on armed forces personnel. As the fleet continued to expand and its manpower requirements mushroomed during early 1944, Admiral King and his staff scrambled to procure enough men to meet demands that the rapid growth in combat strength created. Only the CNO's adroit manipulation of the joint planning system allowed the navy to avoid major cuts and kept planned fleet expansion on track.

The origins of the navy's wartime manpower crisis can be traced back to a significant bureaucratic victory, the 1943 War Department plan to reduce army mobilization goals unilaterally. By May 1943 General Marshall had decided that scheduled army growth for the remainder of the year was too high and ordered his staff to cut projected January 1944 troop strength from 8.2 million to 7.7 million, thereby saving more than half a million men.[1] The ensuing interservice problems resulted from the different expectations that this decision created. While Marshall envisioned the cutback as part of a joint military effort to conserve personnel, navy leaders saw it as an opportunity to obtain a larger share of the national manpower pool.

Several factors informed Marshall's decision, including a realization that movement of army units overseas lagged well behind mobilization rates and would probably remain behind for the foreseeable future. Shipping shortages prompted some of Marshall's subordinates to press for manpower savings through cutbacks in planned mobilization. Gen. I. H. Edwards, head of army personnel planning, told Marshall in February 1943 that studies of 1944 mobilization indicated the possibility and even desirability of deferring ten divisions in the 1943 program until the first half of 1944.[2] Because fewer than forty army divisions would be deployed overseas by the end of 1943, cutting ten divisions from the 100-division program would have no real effect on army combat capability in 1944. Edwards assured Marshall that the deferment would not disrupt the army's training establishment and would permit a significant reduction in the monthly induction rate for the second half of 1943.

In March and April other senior army planners echoed Edwards's reservations about continuing the planned buildup. They worried that the army could not publicly defend its use of men to fill out units that could not move overseas for lack of shipping. In April, Gen. Leslie McNair, commanding general of the army ground forces, suggested that induction rates be reduced in order to form new units on a one-for-one basis as others shipped out; he estimated that doing so would reduce army manpower requirements for 1943 by just over a hundred thousand men.[3]

The favorable progress of the war in early 1943 provided another rationale for a reduction in planned army strength; Allied successes on all fronts made such a move seem less risky than would have been the case three or four months earlier. When he explained the cutback to Congress in September, Marshall cited the conquest of North Africa, which permitted the army to reduce garrisons in the Western Hemisphere, as a major factor in his decision. He also noted the progress of the Russian army, which was steadily eroding the ground strength of the European Axis.[4]

Marshall undoubtedly hoped that his decision would deflect political pressure being applied by civilian leaders who had questioned the army's manpower demands in a series of congressional hearings during the first quarter of 1943. Although War Department representatives had apparently held their own during these hearings, a reduction in proposed troop strength for early 1944 would undercut any potential legislation aimed at closer civilian control over military growth. The chief of staff apparently worried about civilian intervention during this period, a concern he revealed to his colleagues in June 1943 when the Joint Chiefs became embroiled in arguments over the role of army and navy land-based aircraft. As General Arnold and Admiral King disputed the issue, Marshall told his fellow chiefs that he had become convinced that their procedure for settling interservice disputes was uneconomical. He warned that failure to solve such disagreements threatened military control of force planning and procurement issues and that "unless some definite action is taken as regards our own struggles, the matter will become public knowledge and something will be done for us."[5] Later Marshall confided to Secretary Stimson that he had his colleagues "scared to death" of the civilian intervention that would result unless the Army Air Forces and navy stopped fighting over which service would perform which mission.[6]

THE UNSINKABLE FLEET

The aggressive navy planning staff and its unrelenting criticism of army personnel planning played a major if unacknowledged role in influencing Marshall's decision to cut army growth. Attempts by the Joint Planners during the spring of 1943 to agree on military personnel strengths for 1944 and beyond had foundered on the navy's insistence that army expansion plans be scaled back. After months of often acrimonious debates the planners again appeared deadlocked by May 1943, yet the logic of efficient war production and resource allocation demanded that service strengths for 1944 and 1945 be settled quickly.

Given Marshall's aversion to open interservice wrangling, and the obdurate resistance of King's staff, the chief of staff probably saw the cut in army strength as a relatively painless way to preserve harmony on the Joint Chiefs and delay further disputes over manpower for six months or more. In late May he appointed a special army committee to study mobilization plans with an eye toward effecting the proposed reductions in force levels. The committee, led by Col. Ray T. Maddocks of the Operations Division, was directed to review the proposed army-navy troop bases and recommend changes consistent with current strategy.[7] On 1 June 1943 the committee reported that the army should cut its planned strength as of 31 December 1943 from 8.2 million to 7.65 million, deferring twelve divisions scheduled for activation during 1943 until further studies provided better information on ultimate ground force requirements.[8] Marshall and Secretary Stimson approved the committee's proposals in mid-June, and by 1 July the army had a new mobilization plan for 1943.

In a surprising move, Marshall gave the Maddocks Committee a secondary task: reviewing navy manpower requirements. Doing so marked a significant departure from his earlier statements about each service tending to its own expansion planning and leaving the others to do the same. Army interest in navy personnel strength continued to increase from this point on, as the services found themselves locked in a struggle over claims on a dwindling manpower reserve.

The Maddocks Committee report on navy personnel strength, a detailed, item-by-item accounting of the proposed troop basis pointing out "indications of excessive requests for manpower," was finished by early June.[9] Noting that the navy's planned 1944 personnel strength represented an increase of 1.2 million men over the approved 1943 ceiling, the committee identified several areas where members believed navy manpower requests to be unjustified. For example, the navy planned to have a hundred thousand officer candidates on its rolls in 1944, a number the committee felt was far too high for a service that would supposedly be nearing peak strength that year. The request for 215,000 men for construction battalions was also questioned. "There appears to be no sound reason for the navy to have such a large number of construction battalions, roughly twice the number of such units as are projected for the Army," the committee observed.

The committee also criticized other items in the navy troop basis, including 196,000 men allotted to unspecified "projects," 203,000 set aside to man new construction, and more than 350,000 recruits and students.[10] Without directly saying so, the Maddocks Committee implied that the navy was loading its 1944 personnel plan with extra manpower in order to provide for future growth, an assessment that was almost certainly accurate. The report concluded that the proposed troop basis was excessive and recommended postponing any agreement on cutting army induction rates until navy manpower demands were reduced.

General Marshall undoubtedly read the review of navy personnel demands along with the committee's primary report on reducing planned army strength for 1943. Overall, the chief of staff was pleased with the results, and he later commended the committee members for their work. However, their recommendation that the army force a personnel cap on the navy apparently ran afoul of Marshall's reluctance to interfere with naval requirements planning, and he failed to use possible cuts in planned army strength as a bargaining chip to negotiate reductions in navy manpower. Instead, he merely informed Admiral King of army cutbacks after the decision had been communicated to the president. In a memo to the CNO on 10 July, Marshall noted that cuts of five hundred thousand men and ten divisions would enable the War Department to effect "appreciable economies in 1943 without materially reducing the effectiveness of the Army for planned operations."[11] If Marshall hoped for a similar commitment from the navy, he was to be disappointed. Admiral King replied that he recognized the need to economize manpower but that the navy was already short of personnel needed to man new ship construction. The navy would therefore need all of the men called for in its approved 1943 troop basis.[12]

When King referred Marshall's letter to his staff for analysis, the Bureau of Naval Personnel concluded that the army's action would have little long-term significance. Even at the reduced induction rate the army would reach 93 percent of its 1944 manpower goal (7.7 of 8.25 million) by the end of 1943. By contrast, the navy would have on hand enough personnel to fill only 76 percent of its estimated 1944 manpower requirements by that time.[13] The bureau failed to identify the key effect of Marshall's decision, which placed half a million men who had previously been earmarked for the army back into the national manpower pool.

By informing Marshall that the navy already faced personnel shortages, King implicitly suggested that some of the men "saved" by the army cutbacks might now be claimed by the rapidly expanding navy. Within a few weeks, this is exactly what occurred. In September 1942 Admiral King had agreed that the navy (less the Marine Corps and Coast Guard) would need 2.15 million personnel for 1943, and that figure had been incorporated into the joint troop basis approved by the president and the Joint Chiefs of Staff.[14] As early as April 1943, however, navy planners concluded that they had seriously underestimated the number of men needed to meet navy and Marine Corps requirements. In appropriations hearings that month the chief of the Bureau of Personnel testified that navy personnel requirements for 30 June 1944 would exceed planned strength by more than a quarter million men.[15] Accordingly, navy leaders hoped to revise the 1943 troop basis upward as a head start in meeting their needs for mid-1944.

Coincidental or not, the navy's attempt to increase its 1943 personnel ceiling came directly on the heels of Marshall's decision to cut 1943 army strength. In late July Secretary of the Navy Frank Knox notified the Joint Chiefs and the president that by 31 December 1943 the navy would need an additional 221,000 men (plus 49,000 Marines) above and beyond those included in the 1943 troop basis.[16] Roosevelt approved the request and set navy personnel strength at just under 2.5 million men for 31 December 1943; Marine Corps strength was set at 411,000.[17] Thus, in a single stroke nearly half the army manpower that General Marshall had deferred until after 1943 effectively "transferred" to the navy and Marine Corps. Although the increase met no opposition, the president indicated that any requests for additional manpower should come through the Joint Chiefs of Staff rather than from the navy high command.

Army planners raised no objection to the navy request for more men in 1943, despite the obvious implications for further army growth in

1944 and beyond. The lack of controversy may have stemmed from the army staff's belief that the entire navy manpower question would be resolved by a special joint committee charged with setting personnel allotments for all services for 1944. War Department staff officers obviously envisioned an active role in determining the navy's 1944 manpower ceiling. As one senior officer in the army's Operations Division noted, "This increase in the navy is requested for the purpose of providing personnel necessary to man newly constructed naval vessels. This additional request is for 1943, and will be subject to later review when the 1944 troop bases are compiled, at which time the army will be prepared to investigate more thoroughly the over-all personnel requirements of the navy toward effecting the utmost economy in manpower."[18] By the autumn of 1943 at least some army planners were determined to abandon Marshall's live-and-let-live policy regarding navy manpower.

In late October 1943 the joint subcommittee that had been studying army and navy personnel strengths reached a tentative agreement on overall military manpower allocations through December 1944. The three members of the Maddocks Committee were assigned to the subcommittee, so most of their views on navy troop levels were probably communicated to the navy planners. Because the subcommittee members knew that they were allocating what was probably the nation's last reserve of military manpower, their investigations were unusually thorough. During the deliberations, each service had been required to present manpower requirements in detail and to justify each item in its proposed troop basis to the entire committee.[19]

The new joint manpower plan for 1944, known as JCS 154/7, set the stage for a final distribution of the national military manpower pool. Any increases over the agreed troop levels for one service would almost certainly come at the expense of the other service's expansion plans. Once the plan was approved, neither service could expect to obtain a significant increase in personnel strength without a fight, for such an increase might prevent the other service from carrying out its expansion plans.

It is worth noting that in early September 1943 Admiral King recommended to Secretary Knox that navy, Marine Corps, and Coast Guard strength be frozen at the levels approved for the end of 1943.[20] King believed that the navy, like the army, could achieve substantial manpower savings by reducing training bases and other shore establishments and also by cutting ship's complements. Just two weeks later he told the Senate Armed Services Committee that the navy was committed to manning all of the ships in the current construction program.[21] He apparently believed that savings from shore establishments and other sources would provide enough men to carry out this plan without increasing the navy's troop basis. Within a few months the CNO would be forced to acknowledge how misplaced his earlier optimism had been.

When the committee studying joint troop bases for 1944 completed JCS 154/7 in November 1943, the report proposed naval manpower allocations somewhat lower than navy planners had previously demanded. Combined 1944 personnel strength for the navy, Coast Guard, and Marine Corps shrank from approximately 3.8 million in the joint report of April 1943 (JCS 154/2) to 3.56 million in JCS 154/7, a decrease of almost 250,000.[22] More than half of the reduction came from the navy, primarily from men set aside for "unforeseen contingencies."

Although the figures in JCS 154/7 were smaller than earlier navy requests, they still represented an increase of more than half a million over the approved 1943 troop basis. The new report also noted that the navy would add approximately a hundred thousand men during the first six months of 1945, for a strength of about 3.06 million by 30 June 1945. The committee added that navy personnel strength would continue to increase after mid-1945 because of the ongoing ship construction program.

Nevertheless, at least one senior navy planner believed that the army staff was using the joint manpower report to pressure the navy into cutting its future manpower requests. Rear Adm. Charles Cooke complained that language in JCS 154/7 implied that the army had done its part to conserve manpower and that the navy now had the burden of justifying its personnel demands to the satisfaction of the War Department staff. Admiral Cooke worried that "the Navy is placed on the defensive and enjoined to undertake reductions when and if the situation permits. No such injunction upon the army seems to be included."[23]

He was undoubtedly referring to the passages in the early drafts of JCS 154/7 that stated that the army had no reserves and would be unable to take on additional commitments with the troop levels proposed. Although army planners probably hoped that their cutbacks would force the navy to follow suit, they were more concerned about preserving the possibility of future army growth. In either case, Admiral

The Fleet's Personnel Crisis

King successfully excised the objectionable language from the final draft that was sent to the president. Roosevelt approved the report and set strengths for 1944 at 2.9 million for the navy, 478,000 for the Marine Corps, and 174,000 for the Coast Guard.[24]

The final version of JCS 154/7 included another provision directly related to navy manpower limits. To compensate for the loss of the men slated for unforeseen contingencies, a special clause allowed the navy to accelerate its growth if necessary in order to reach its authorized 30 June 1945 strength by the end of 1944. Pursuant to this provision, navy leaders could raise the 1944 personnel limit by nearly a hundred thousand men.[25] Within three months after the president approved JCS 154/7, Admiral King sought to do just that. In a memorandum to the Joint Chiefs of Staff in late January 1944 he announced that the navy was seeking presidential approval to implement the plan to reach its authorized June 1945 strength by 31 December 1944.[26] Doing so would bring navy manpower (excluding the Coast Guard and Marine Corps) to just over three million. Forrestal, who was acting secretary because of Knox's health problems, had already contacted the president with the same proposal.[27]

In order to allay any doubts about the plan, both Admiral King and Acting Secretary Forrestal assured the president and the Joint Chiefs that accelerating navy growth would not result in a net increase in manpower requirements for 1945. They even appended copies of the latest navy personnel plan, which called for zero growth during the first six months of 1945. They thereby suggested that navy strength on 30 June 1945 would remain exactly as set forth in JCS 154/7; only the timing would change. This relatively small augmentation of just under a hundred thousand men, they promised, would fulfill the navy's manpower needs for some eighteen months, until the middle of 1945.

The navy's request for additional men in 1944 quickly ran into trouble. The president initially rejected the proposal, admonishing Forrestal to "make some improvements in the use of personnel, so as to keep within the figures I have already approved."[28] General Marshall and General Arnold were also cool to the idea. The navy's request came at a time when both the army and the navy were having difficulty procuring personnel; by early February 1944 the army was still more than three hundred thousand men short of its planned strength for 31 December 1943.[29]

In light of these problems the Joint Chiefs directed the Joint Logistics Committee (JLC) to study current personnel shortages as they related to the feasibility of Admiral King's proposal. The JLC reported in mid-February that neither the army nor the navy had yet reached its planned 1943 strength because of the Selective Service's inability to provide sufficient men. The shortages were caused by procurement and processing tie-ups, however, and the JLC concluded that the population of draft-eligible men contained enough bodies to fill out the planned 1944 troop bases for both services.

With the expectation that improved induction procedures would soon eliminate military manpower shortfalls, the JLC decided that accelerating navy mobilization would not hinder planned army expansion and therefore recommended approving the navy's request for a hundred thousand additional men in 1944.[30] Based on the JLC's findings, the Joint Chiefs gave the navy's latest personnel request their conditional approval, provided that it did not interfere with the army program.[31]

Joint approval of the plan rested on the premise that the hundred thousand additional men provided in 1944 would satisfy navy needs through the first half of 1945. Given the navy's personnel experiences in 1943 and the rapid pace of fleet expansion, King and Forrestal's promise of zero manpower growth during the first six months of 1945 hardly seems credible. In fact, even before Admiral King asked the JCS to increase the navy's 1944 manpower allotment, he had information indicating that navy planners had severely underestimated personnel requirements for 1944 and 1945.

In January 1944 a preliminary navy manpower study revealed that personnel requirements through mid-1945 would exceed the approved troop basis by four hundred thousand men, four times the number provided in the proposed augmentation plan.[32] Admiral King took steps to deal with the projected shortfall, but rapid fleet growth in the coming year promised to make a bad situation even worse. In late January 1944 the chief of naval personnel ordered field commanders to begin using reduced crew complements to conserve manpower, so that combatant ships were no longer being manned at their "optimum" crew strengths.[33] In mid-February King asked the Bureau of Personnel and Admiral Horne to investigate whether the navy was creating too many construction battalions, ship repair units, and similar specialized formations and to recommend personnel cuts in these areas.[34]

The CNO also tried to save manpower at navy bases in the United States. At Admiral King's request, Secretary Knox had created the Navy Manpower Survey Board in November 1943 to study shore installations and eliminate overstaffing.[35] Knox had hoped that the Survey Board would produce substantial manpower savings that could be transferred to the fleet. These hopes came to nothing; the board reported by February 1944 that in relation to the size of the forces being supported, navy shore installations were actually undermanned.[36]

Ominous signs of impending personnel shortages continued to accumulate. In early February Vice CNO Horne warned Admiral King that the navy faced increasing demands for personnel that had not been foreseen in the force operating plan for 1945. In order to stay within the June 1945 ceiling on manpower, Horne warned, the navy would have to make considerable cuts in planned operating forces.[37]

Incredibly, by this stage of the war the navy had yet to complete a comprehensive study of its manpower needs through June 1945. Only preliminary figures were available, and these indicated that the approved troop ceiling would be insufficient to meet all of the navy's commitments.[38] Navy planners had failed to appreciate fully the expansion of supporting activities that increases in ship and aircraft strength and the need to operate large forces at the end of a three-thousand-mile supply line required.

Faced with significant personnel shortfalls in the coming months, certain navy leaders began to backtrack on the promise of zero personnel growth for the first half of 1945. Testifying before the House Appropriations Committee in late February 1944, Navy Personnel Chief Adm. Randall Jacobs stated that the navy was considering increasing its June 1945 manpower goal by half a million men.[39] Jacobs blamed the shortfall on new strategic commitments that had forced revisions in the navy's operating force plan. Due to these revisions, Jacobs claimed, the navy could provide no firm estimates of its personnel requirements beyond the end of 1944.

The real cause of the navy's dilemma was its failure to establish a reliable method of estimating manpower requirements. Until 1944, navy mobilization plans had been based on equipment, not manpower. As the Bureau of Personnel's history admits, "Until mid-1944, the rest of the naval establishment was dominated by the idea of material and strategic planning, never recognizing that the wartime industrial power of the

United States was such that we would sooner reach shortages of men than of ships."[40] How such an attitude could have survived the army-navy manpower debates of early 1943 is a mystery that says little for King's planners.

As a result of this preoccupation with production and strategy, little or no consideration had been given to availability of personnel when determining navy expansion goals.[41] Although this approach had worked early in the war, worsening manpower shortages made it imperative that accelerating ship construction be coordinated with anticipated personnel levels. By early 1944 navy leaders faced a dilemma partly of their own making. They had accepted a cap on personnel without bothering to obtain reliable studies linking manpower levels to the forces they planned to keep in service.

With no reliable way to anticipate the personnel that the growing fleet would require, planners had become accustomed to submitting manpower estimates without any real hope of obtaining accuracy. The Bureau of Naval Personnel had routinely submitted the estimates with the knowledge that personnel planning throughout the navy would be "spotty" and that estimates of future manpower requirements were generally too low.[42] Based on this appraisal, which seems to have been valid, the bureau compensated by inserting a generous safety factor into its estimates of manpower needs. This safety factor accounted for the "unforeseen contingency" personnel in the navy troop basis that the Maddocks Committee found so objectionable and that had been reduced in the joint personnel agreement of late 1943.

This slipshod planning system was adequate so long as the navy could rely on increases in its manpower allotment like the ones it obtained in July 1943 and January and February 1944. Perhaps because navy leaders had successfully obtained such increases in the past, no real attempts to change the planning system were made until mid-1944.[43] Once an absolute troop ceiling was set, however, requests for additional men could no longer compensate for poor planning. Unanticipated shortfalls would have to be made up from men set aside for other purposes.

Having never developed an accurate estimate of the fleet's manpower needs, navy planners found in 1944 that they had left themselves without sufficient personnel to man and support the ships that would soon be coming off the ways. The personnel shortage threatened to grow over time, as more ships and planes entered service. By March 1944 unanticipated manpower requirements placed new demands on the troop basis at a rate of twenty thousand men every month. The latest projections suggested that by the end of 1944 manpower requirements would exceed the current personnel ceiling by more than 340,000 men, and by 1 July 1945 the deficit would reach nearly half a million.[44]

In late March, Admiral Horne told Admiral King that the current operating force plan would use up the navy's entire 1944 personnel allotment by August. Further increases in fleet strength would then be possible only by obtaining additional manpower.[45] The crux of the problem was that the navy planned to have in service by mid-1945 a fleet of unprecedented proportions in addition to a sizable land-based air force, all being supported in operations thousands of miles from major bases. The operating force plan for 30 June 1945 included more than 100 aircraft carriers of various types, more than 100 battleships and cruisers, more than 500 destroyers, and more than 300 submarines. Counting support ships, amphibious craft, and other smaller craft, more than 8,000 vessels would be in service by that date. Crews alone for these vessels would require an estimated 1.1 million men.

With no immediate prospect of personnel increases, the possibility of cuts in planned operating forces demanded consideration. Initially at least, Admiral King favored this solution over the alternative of presenting a new set of manpower demands to the president and the Joint Chiefs. Given his concern with maintaining the building program, King naturally thought in terms of decommissioning older ships rather than cutting production of new models. One study that Admiral Horne cited found that decommissioning 5 older battleships, 16 cruisers, and 128 destroyers would save nearly 200,000 men.[46] Even this fairly drastic plan, however, would reduce the expected July 1945 manpower deficit by less than half.

By late March 1944 Admiral King had apparently decided that he would cut fleet strength rather than ask for more men, and he formally announced his intentions at a meeting of the Joint Chiefs and the heads of civilian war agencies. The navy was doing its best to economize on manpower, King stated, and he promised that it would decommission older ships if that became necessary to stay within approved troop limits.[47]

Having guaranteed the army and civilian war agencies that his service would make do with current manpower allotments, King soon came under pressure from his staff to raise the navy manpower ceiling.

THE UNSINKABLE FLEET

One such proposal came in April 1944 from the Bureau of Navy Personnel, which noted that just over 109,000 of the navy's 3 million authorized personnel were women in the Naval Reserve. Because there was no national shortage of women, the bureau reasoned, these reservists should not be counted against the navy total. It recommended that the CNO ask the president to exclude these women from the navy's troop basis, thereby allowing an increase of 109,000 men without actually exceeding the personnel ceiling.[48] Admiral Horne seconded the bureau's plan, telling King that informal contacts in the War Department indicated that the army would not oppose it.[49] King rejected this rather disingenuous scheme outright, however, stating that the navy's current troop basis was sufficient to meet requirements until July of 1945. Based on that utterly unsupported determination, Admiral King reasserted his unwillingness to seek further increases in navy manpower.[50]

Once Admiral King definitely decided to stay within the manpower levels in JCS 154/7, navy force structure planning would have to change to accommodate the shortfall in personnel. For the first time, King's staff would have to create an operating force plan designed around a set number of men. In early April the CNO appointed a special committee to study navy force structure and report on changes needed in the operating force plan to keep within the authorized manpower ceiling.[51] The committee was also to report immediately any findings that indicated the desirability of reductions in ship or aircraft construction programs.

The committee's report, submitted in early May, provided a detailed look at the scale of cutbacks necessary to bring the navy's planned operating forces within the current troop basis.[52] The committee recommended cutting ships, aircraft, construction units, and support facilities to make up the anticipated shortage of 457,000 men by July 1945. It noted that it had revised the operating force plan to include only those units considered absolutely necessary to carry out currently approved strategy. The plan also called for significant cuts in the combatant fleet, including five old battleships, all old cruisers, more than forty destroyers, and twenty submarines. In addition, more than two dozen escort carriers would be reassigned to transport roles with reduced crews. The report also suggested the possibility of cuts in ship construction because the new operating force plan did not provide for manning ships to be completed after November 1944.[53]

The committee pointed out that because the Pacific theater absorbed most navy combat strength, requirements there should control navy force structure. It therefore recommended delaying any decision on cutbacks until the Pacific Fleet submitted an estimate of ships and aircraft required to defeat Japan. In an interesting twist, the special committee was chaired by the same Admiral Bieri who as a member of the Joint Staff Planners had spent the previous few months telling his army counterparts that the navy could not possibly give an accurate estimate of the number of ships needed to win the war. Apparently, Admiral Bieri had fewer qualms about suggesting such an estimate as part of an internal navy study.

The CNO forwarded the committee's report to Adm. Chester W. Nimitz, commander in chief of the Pacific Fleet, and asked for comments and recommendations on the overall requirements of Nimitz's command.[54] Although Nimitz and his staff concurred with many of the committee's suggestions, they balked at the prospect of laying up a large number of combatant ships.[55] Nimitz's counterproposal recommended that almost all of these ships be retained: the battleships for shore bombardment and the cruisers and destroyers for patrolling. Nimitz's chief of staff, Rear Adm. Forrest P. Sherman, subsequently told King's staff that Nimitz considered his counterproposal to be the lesser of two evils. More important, Sherman reported that Nimitz believed that even the compromise plan left him with insufficient forces to ensure success.[56]

The special committee's report had provided Admiral King with a glimpse of what the fleet might look like in the event that the navy failed to increase its current troop ceiling. Apparently, Admiral Nimitz's misgivings about the proposed reductions were shared by an influential portion of Admiral King's staff. As part of its report, the special committee recommended that the navy attempt to obtain another five hundred thousand men rather than cut operating forces.

In mid-June 1944 a "Personnel Committee" in King's headquarters proposed a less drastic plan for saving manpower, one that would require a substantial increase in the navy's personnel ceiling. The committee determined that through a rigorous review of obligations and the greatest practicable reductions in operating forces the navy could trim its July 1945 manpower deficit from 457,000 to 243,000.[57] The plan would still require significant cuts in fleet strength, but not as severe as those needed to stay within current troop limits. Under this less ambitious reduction plan the navy would decommission one battleship, eight cruisers, two escort carriers, twenty-four destroyers, and hundreds of smaller ships by 30 June 1945.

Included with the report was the draft of a memorandum that Admiral King could forward to the Joint Chiefs requesting an increase of 243,000 men in the 30 June 1945 authorized troop strength. The memorandum blamed the unforeseen increases on "changes in the building program since JCS 154/7 was approved" and noted that navy personnel requirements would exceed the current ceiling by October 1944.[58] Although the increased troop allowance would be sufficient to man all ships due to enter service through the end of 1945, the draft memo stated, an additional 94,000 men would be required to man ships entering service during 1946.

The report and the special committee's findings called into question the wisdom of continuing the navy's current construction program. Personnel savings from the proposed cuts in operating forces would go directly to man ships scheduled to enter service. Could the nation afford to spend the time and resources to build a new cruiser, for instance, if manning that vessel would be at the expense of decommissioning an older but still serviceable ship? Although a newer design would arguably be more effective, the material and labor devoted to providing the fleet with a possibly marginal increase in capabilities might prove prohibitive and would almost certainly cause controversy.

Apparently this consideration, together with Admiral Nimitz's misgivings about cuts in fleet strength, convinced Admiral King that the navy simply had to obtain more men. He was astute enough to realize the difficulty of pressing forward with the building program while simultaneously laying up large numbers of ships. Decommissioning combat ships also went against King's strategic concept of applying maximum force against the enemy. By the end of June 1944 the CNO had overcome his earlier reluctance to ask the Joint Chiefs for an increase in the navy's manpower allotment, and he was determined to find sufficient men to avoid cuts in fleet strength. The Personnel Committee's proposal for an additional 243,000 men was insufficient to achieve this end, and the CNO prepared to seek an even higher limit.

On 2 July 1944 Admiral King formally asked the Joint Chiefs of Staff to increase the June 1945 personnel ceiling by 390,000 men.[59] Doing so would raise navy strength (excluding the Marine Corps and the Coast

Guard) to just under 3.4 million. King explained that the increase would be used to man ships and installations entering service before 31 December 1945. Because more than 100 ships were scheduled for commissioning after that date (including 9 aircraft carriers, 3 capital ships, and 30 cruisers), King noted that the navy would require an additional 94,000 men during the second half of 1945.

Perhaps the most remarkable attribute of Admiral King's request was that it was presented in terms designed to overcome possible objections from the War Department. The CNO and his staff had obviously benefited from more than two years' experience in working out interservice disputes, for the proposal demonstrated a superior grasp of the bureaucratic and political considerations that underlay every joint decision on resource allocation.

Admiral King prefaced his proposal by explaining that the navy troop basis in JCS 154/7 actually represented a decrease from the figures in the Operating Force Plan that the secretary of the navy had approved in August 1943. The CNO thereby implied that the requested manpower increase would in part merely restore personnel who had been "cut" by the joint subcommittee the previous fall. This was a somewhat disingenuous approach; the operating force plan had never been subject to joint review.

In an astute bureaucratic ploy Admiral King then claimed that the bulk of the additional manpower was needed to provide crews and support personnel for the navy's expanded amphibious shipping program. The amphibious program, which had presidential approval, required developing the capability to transport twenty ground divisions simultaneously in assault shipping. King averred that 216,000 of the 390,000 additional men requested would be allocated to the amphibious shipping program. In contrast, his figures showed that only 16,000 of the additional personnel would be earmarked for combatant ships.[60] The amphibious shipping program had indeed increased since JCS 154/7 had set troop strengths for all services. In November 1943 the Joint Chiefs approved a program that would nearly triple the previous goals for assault transport and assault cargo ships.[61] In late November and early December, the landing craft construction program had been increased by an additional 35 percent over figures agreed to at the end of October.[62]

Manpower figures in navy planning papers cast doubt on Admiral King's claim that increases in the amphibious shipping program were

THE UNSINKABLE FLEET

the principal cause of the new manpower demands. The Navy Personnel Committee's report on 15 June had stated that the amphibious program would require an additional hundred thousand men; that this figure could have more than doubled in just two weeks seems improbable.

Whatever the source of King's figures, they would have been nearly impossible for army planners to challenge without access to internal navy studies. Such questions might well have been irrelevant; in essence the numbers represented not so much an accounting figure as an implicit threat. The unstated corollary to the CNO's statement about the cause of navy personnel shortages was that shortfalls in manpower would primarily affect amphibious shipping. The Marine Corps would field no more than six divisions, so the bulk of the twenty-division transport capability was destined for army use. By rejecting the navy's request for more men, the army would only be damaging the navy's ability to move army divisions to the scene of combat in the Pacific theater.

King's proposal put army leaders in a bind, for they were counting on an increase in amphibious shipping capabilities in order to carry out the two-pronged Pacific strategy that the Joint Chiefs had decided on in late 1943. The southern prong involved offensives through New Guinea toward the Philippines by Gen. Douglas MacArthur's forces, which were composed mainly of army units. At the same time, forces under Admiral Nimitz would advance through the islands of the central Pacific.[63]

In general, the navy's offensive in the central Pacific covered longer distances and required large assault transport and cargo ships, whereas MacArthur's command made do with smaller landing craft for their coastal amphibious operations.[64] By the summer of 1944 MacArthur's troops had nearly completed the conquest of New Guinea; the planned invasion of the Philippines and the invasion of Japan proper involved longer distances and would require more navy assistance. Shortages of assault shipping could therefore severely limit army participation in the final stages of the Pacific campaign. Given these considerations, some senior army planners were inclined to give the navy the benefit of the doubt rather than risk cutbacks in assault shipping. One OPD officer reflected this view when he pointed out that "amphibious lift is the basic army requirement from the navy."[65]

Admiral King's request for nearly four hundred thousand more men provoked a mixed reaction within the War Department, where officers were concerned about the army's own personnel situation. When King's memorandum arrived in July 1944, the army had already exceeded its personnel ceiling and was still growing steadily. By late August, the army was more than three hundred thousand men over its authorized strength of 7.7 million, chiefly due to the large number of men tied up in travel, hospitals, transit camps, and detached duty.[66] Under the circumstances, Deputy Chief of Staff McNarney thought the army was in a poor position to oppose the CNO. Also, he reasoned, if the navy were allowed to exceed its manpower ceiling, the army would no longer be the only service doing so. In that sense, granting the navy's request might even pave the way for official approval of the army's personnel overruns.[67]

Although the threat of diminished amphibious lift and the army's personnel problems dampened War Department resistance to the navy proposal, some planners opposed giving up a large reserve of men that the army might still need. These officers questioned whether the national manpower pool could stand the additional demands of the navy plan, and they wanted the matter handled by a joint agency. A study by the Army Service Forces concluded that the requirement to lift twenty divisions simultaneously had not been demonstrated and therefore the navy's request for personnel was not adequately supported.[68] Less dependent on the navy for transport, the Army Air Forces could afford to be more openly critical. Reflecting the growing AAF-navy rivalry, a senior AAF planner objected to King's plan on the grounds that the additional personnel would really be used to enlarge the navy's land-based air arm.[69]

At the suggestion of General Arnold, the Joint Chiefs sent King's proposal to the Joint Logistics Committee for review and recommendations. The JLC reported that the navy plan would negatively affect the national manpower situation by exacerbating the national labor shortage during 1945, perhaps to the extent that munitions production would be adversely affected.[70] The principal effect of the plan on the armed forces would be to increase the average age of men entering service. This was especially unwelcome news for the army, where the average age was twenty-five and increasing at what General Marshall considered an alarming rate.[71] Navy and Marine Corps personnel averaged less than twenty-four years of age, in part because the navy accepted seventeen-year-olds for voluntary enlistment. If the navy plan were implemented and the army later had to expand to meet some unforeseen contingency, it would have to induct men older than twenty-six, who were generally considered too old for combat service.

Despite these findings, and without any demonstrated need to simultaneously transport twenty divisions, the Joint Logistics Committee recommended provisionally approving all but 7,000 of the 390,000 men Admiral King requested. In order to settle the issue of whether an amphibious shipping program of the size contemplated was really necessary, the JLC proposed a study to determine the maximum amphibious lift required to defeat Japan. If that study revealed that some of the planned amphibious ships were unnecessary, the navy's personnel allotment could be retroactively reduced. Based on these findings, the Joint Chiefs of Staff approved the navy plan in mid-July.[72]

King's gambit had succeeded brilliantly, removing the last logistic obstacle to continued fleet expansion. Only the question of amphibious shipping requirements remained. Impeded by bureaucratic delays and misunderstandings, the Joint Logistics Committee did not complete the study on amphibious lift until November 1944. It concluded that under ideal conditions the planned amphibious shipping program would provide enough ships to transport twenty divisions simultaneously. Battle losses and ships under repair would reduce the actual lift capacity to about sixteen divisions.[73] That figure roughly corresponded to the simultaneous lift of fifteen divisions that the Joint Staff Planners believed would be necessary for the invasion of Japan. The JLC therefore recommended no cuts in either the assault shipping program or the navy's manpower allocation. The navy had weathered its greatest manpower crisis.

Of course, the navy's manpower estimates were still faulty, and new shortages soon occupied the planners. Even as the latest increase was under consideration, the CNO remained concerned about manpower. In a July 1944 conference with Admiral Nimitz, King explained that he had not formally requested the ninety thousand men needed to man ships that would enter service in 1946. Noting that the manpower situation was still serious, King again suggested decommissioning older ships. Nimitz wanted to keep these for shore bombardment, however, and, despite his reservations, King agreed.[74]

Even with the additional personnel King obtained, the navy's manpower needs again rapidly outstripped its resources. By April 1945 the operating force plan called for about 4.1 million personnel by 30 June 1945, approximately two hundred thousand more than the navy had allotted; a further quarter-million would be needed by mid-1946.[75] Fortunately, victory in Europe the following month prevented another manpower crisis by reducing navy commitments in that theater and easing the nation's overall manpower shortage.

In the final analysis, the navy's ability to expand despite increasing manpower shortages depended on Admiral King's firm commitment to the building program and his adept use of the joint planning system. By making the amphibious shipping program the centerpiece of his request for additional personnel, Admiral King ensured the approval, or at least the acquiescence, of the army planners. He and his staff demonstrated a clear grasp of bureaucratic imperatives when they used the army's requirement for assault shipping as a lever to prevent any significant opposition to their augmentation plan. By adroitly packaging their proposal to increase navy personnel, they achieved their objective while avoiding what might have been a debilitating clash with their War Department counterparts.

The navy would never have been in this position, however, were it not for failures in the area of personnel planning. In a letter written immediately after the war, the assistant chief of naval personnel summed up the problems with the navy's wartime manpower plans. He believed these stemmed from the planning staff's preoccupation with the number of ships in the fleet, to the exclusion of nearly all else: "Operations were geared to the number of ships we could reasonably expect to have, which in turn was geared to steel production and ship construction. The ships were believed, because of underestimating the country's productive capacity, to be the limiting factor, and therefore our plans and our planning methods were made on the assumption that we would always be able to get all of everything we needed except ships, and no system was developed to control the 'requirement' of any other item."[76] Personnel planning for advanced bases had been particularly bad, the letter continued, with estimates running at about 75 percent of what was actually needed. As a result, personnel constantly had to be diverted from other areas to fill urgent requirements that planners had not foreseen.

By going along with an unreliable and inaccurate system that relied on frequent upward adjustments, the navy staff threatened the viability of the building effort and perhaps even the integrity of the fleet. The personnel studies of 1944 showed how grievously planners had underestimated manpower requirements; had events overseas taken a turn for the worse, a crisis might have ensued. Although Admiral King and his staff managed to make good these shortfalls by procuring a large portion of the available manpower, such bureaucratic maneuvering was no substitute for sound planning.

·7·

THE INTERNAL DEBATE
1944

Through the early summer of 1944 navy representatives on the Joint Planners continued to dismiss the possibility of estimating U.S. combatant ship requirements for the benefit of the Joint Production Survey Committee. While these officers stridently maintained that any such estimate would be premature and overly speculative, Admiral King's staff was already engaged in its own attempt to gauge how closely the approved shipbuilding program matched the fleet's actual needs. Attempts by naval planners to estimate combatant ship requirements resulted from a growing awareness of the serious limitations imposed by manpower shortages and of the possibility that personnel might not be available to man all ships scheduled to enter the fleet. These studies and the accompanying shifts in procurement goals also stemmed from personnel changes at the very highest levels of the Navy Department, changes that brought two very different philosophies about expansion policy into direct conflict.

During the interminable Joint Planners debate over navy requirements, Admiral Duncan at one point suggested referring the Joint Production Survey Committee to a special navy committee that had recently been established to study the problem of fleet expansion. The navy created the Special Committee on Cutbacks, informally known as the

THE UNSINKABLE FLEET

Cutback Committee, in early June 1944 as a result of the growing disparity between the navy's planned construction program and the projected manpower available to the fleet. The establishment of the committee marked the navy's first serious attempt to determine exactly what forces it would need to prosecute the war successfully. Although the committee's efforts were colored at every juncture by internal navy politics, its work provides some insight into how U.S. naval leaders might have gone about setting parameters for fleet expansion.

The Cutback Committee was created on the orders of James Forrestal, who had replaced Frank Knox as secretary of the navy upon the latter's death in April 1944. Forrestal's initiative grew out of the navy's personnel shortage, which had reached crisis proportions by May 1944. Admiral King originally had decided that he would deal with the personnel crisis by deactivating a number of older combatant ships while simultaneously forging ahead with the scheduled production of new units.

King's views on this issue grew out of his belief that the navy had to prepare now for its role in the postwar world. By early 1944 the CNO and his staff were seriously contemplating the end of hostilities and considering the probable makeup of the postwar fleet. In late 1943 the navy had established a Special Planning Section to conduct studies and produce recommendations on the navy's postwar requirements.[1] Thus, by the spring of 1944 postwar planning had been under way for more than six months.

By the time the manpower shortage reached critical levels that threatened to affect planned fleet strength adversely, postwar planners had identified several major problems that the navy would face once hostilities ended. Not surprisingly, their principal concern was money. They worried that Congress, after years of nearly unlimited appropriations, would not adequately fund a fleet of the size that the country would need after the war. Most of the older naval officers recalled the slump in ship production that followed World War I and believed that history might well repeat itself after the present conflict.

A related issue was the danger of what navy planners called "block obsolescence." After the war, a large portion of the fleet's war-built combatant ships would be approximately the same age and so would become obsolete at about the same time. In order to avoid this problem and ensure some postwar construction, the navy would benefit by having a number of ships on the ways at the time hostilities ended.[2] Completing these ships would keep experienced shipyards and their trained work forces in business after the war and allow the navy to bring newer and updated units into the fleet.

Postwar considerations almost certainly played an important part in Admiral King's approach to manpower shortages as they affected the shipbuilding program and contributed to his preference for laying up older ships in order to continue construction of newer models. He was keenly interested in how wartime construction would affect the navy's postwar position, and in March 1944 he asked Forrestal to have the General Board review fleet building plans in order to keep the program in line with current strategy and establish goals for the postwar navy. The study was to concentrate not on the Japanese fleet but on the British Royal Navy, which King believed would be the world's second largest when the fighting ended.[3] Forrestal ordered the board to conduct such a study, although he probably hoped that the board would recommend reductions in overall procurement.[4]

Because this General Board study overlapped Admiral Horne's sphere of authority, the vice CNO quickly stepped in with his own suggestions on future ship construction. In a memo to Admiral King, Horne noted that prospective shortages of shipyard labor would slow work on combatants during the remainder of 1944 and into 1945, pushing back the completion dates of many ships to 1946 and, in the case of several cruisers, to 1947.[5] Nevertheless, Horne proposed adding new units to the program in order to use 400,000 tons of building authority that had become available through ship losses and cutbacks in planned destroyer escort construction. Although the navy already had on hand or was building forty-three aircraft carriers (not including escort carriers) and forty-one heavy and seventy-nine light cruisers, Horne recommended that the CNO expand the current program by choosing among three mixes of possible builds that stressed aircraft carriers and cruisers.

Just as he had done the previous May, Horne proposed filling the yards with the maximum combatant tonnage that the navy could produce without benefit of further congressional authorization. Evidently impressed by the vice CNO's arguments, King had Horne's memo forwarded to the General Board for use in the study he had requested. He told Forrestal that he favored increasing the current program by adding nine carriers, seven cruisers, and one battle cruiser, along with a number of destroyers and submarines.[6] When King then asked the vice CNO about the prospects for building an additional battle cruiser, however, Horne advised against such a plan.[7] He noted that three ships were already scheduled for delivery in 1944 and 1945 and that an additional unit of this type would take up to three years to complete.

On 17 May 1944 the board reported on navy ship requirements for the present conflict and for the postwar world. The report noted that existing ship construction efforts were probably sufficient to carry out current U.S. strategy, and therefore operational requirements did not demand any modifications to the program. Nevertheless, additional ships would be useful as insurance against unanticipated losses and negative changes in the overall strategic situation, as well as providing additional fighting power that could help shorten the war.[8]

To strengthen and modernize the postwar fleet, the board recommended that the navy maintain uninterrupted production of warships of all types. Unallocated construction authority could be used to place contracts now that would ensure continuous production of ships reflecting the latest advances in design and embodying the most recent innovations. To allow constant improvements in navy ship design and guard against unexpected losses, the board proposed adding a battleship, six carriers, nine cruisers, and a dozen smaller warships to the existing program. This construction would use 368,000 tons of the navy's remaining building authority, which by early May had reached 438,000 tons.[9]

The General Board's report came out at the same time that the Joint Planners were hotly debating possible cuts in the current shipbuilding program and in the midst of a manpower crunch that threatened to cripple fleet expansion. With pressure building to reduce ship production, the navy's senior officers were instead contemplating still further increases in fleet strength. These increases were intended primarily to enhance the navy's postwar position, yet naval leaders hoped to begin work on the proposed ships amid the severe manpower and material shortages that the war had created.

The apparent inconsistencies between future plans and current shortages disturbed senior members of Forrestal's office. The day after the board issued its findings, Assistant Secretary of the Navy Ralph A. Bard cautioned Forrestal about navy procurement planning. Bard had become assistant secretary under his old friend Frank Knox in 1941; since the latter's death he had acted in Forrestal's place as under secretary, a post he would soon fill in an official capacity.[10]

Bard was concerned about Admiral King's proposal to lay up a number of older ships due to manpower shortages, and he reminded the new secretary that there had been no careful examination of combat ship requirements since the Joint Production Survey Committee report the previous fall. He felt the navy would be in "quite a spot" politically if it continued to build new ships at a rapid pace while simultaneously meeting manpower shortfalls by decommissioning older units that were still serviceable.[11] Bard therefore recommended that Forrestal order a survey to determine whether all the ships in the building program were actually needed to prosecute the war.

Forrestal agreed and ordered Horne to provide him with monthly reports on possible cutbacks and deadwood in the building program.[12] He also inquired of Admiral King whether the existing programs for destroyers and submarines would produce an excessive number of these vessels. The sheer numbers alone might have given Forrestal pause. By late May 1944 the navy had 360 destroyers built and 181 more under construction; it also planned to add 211 submarines to the 195 already in service.[13]

King referred Forrestal's query on submarines and destroyers to his planning staff, who told the CNO that they could not establish ultimate requirements for these types until upcoming operations were completed. The staff also suggested that any reductions in planned strength come through elimination of older ships. King passed these findings on to Forrestal with the proviso that cuts in destroyer production would be unwise under any circumstances but that shrinking patrol areas and a diminishing number of targets might eventually allow a reduction in submarine building.[14]

Seeking to formalize his oversight of combatant shipbuilding, Forrestal in early June instructed Admiral King to begin regular periodic reviews of the navy construction program and submit monthly recommendations on what ships might safely be canceled.[15] In response, the CNO had Admiral Horne appoint a Special Committee on Cutbacks to report on possible deletions from planned construction. The nine-member Cutback Committee was headed by Adm. Walter S. Delany, chief of the readiness section of King's COMINCH staff.[16]

Unfortunately, by this time Forrestal and King had developed a strong mutual dislike that often degenerated into unconcealed animosity.[17] Forrestal's opposition had been partly responsible for foiling Admiral

King's repeated attempts to reorganize the Navy Department so that authority for procurement and material decisions would be taken out of civilian hands. Forrestal had earned King's disfavor by helping Secretary Knox block these changes and by maintaining the under secretary's authority over navy procurement.[18] Undoubtedly, Forrestal's role in involving the Joint Production Survey Committee in studies of combat ship requirements only deepened King's mistrust. After turning back attempts by Justice Byrnes and the army staff to interfere with fleet expansion planning, the CNO was determined that any future review of the navy's building program would be firmly under his control.

Admiral King's creation of the Cutback Committee allowed him to minimize civilian interference with expansion planning and ensure his continued control over the size and makeup of the fleet. The committee, filled with officers from King's own COMINCH planning staff, naturally supported the CNO's position and felt that the building program accurately reflected the navy's needs and that the postwar navy would benefit from further increases in existing construction. In practice, the term *Cutback Committee* was something of a misnomer. During the year or so between its creation and the end of the war, the committee consistently recommended that few or no ships be deleted from planned construction. Not surprisingly, Admiral King routinely approved these recommendations, passing the committee's reports on to Forrestal with his endorsement. The monthly reports gave King's arguments added legitimacy, being the product of deliberations by a professional planning staff rather than the views of a single individual.

Even with the Cutback Committee seconding his views, the CNO was realistic enough to acknowledge that changing strategic conditions and the manpower crisis might necessitate some reductions in the building program. In mid-June Vice CNO Horne had under preparation an overall navy logistic plan for the coming campaigns against Japan. In order to calculate fleet logistic requirements, Horne had to estimate the number of ships that would be available for operations during the closing phases of the war. He notified the CNO that his calculations were based on the assumption that the building program would be completed as planned.[19] King demurred, noting that completion dates on many vessels were likely to be pushed back and that he expected some cuts in construction of destroyers, destroyer escorts, and submarines.[20]

The Internal Debate

Destroyer escorts had already been cut in late 1943 after the U-boat crisis eased, and strategic developments now made reductions in submarine production seem advisable. Unlike surface ships, which often operated in large task forces, submarines operated independently in assigned patrol areas. By mid-1944 naval leaders realized that the number of available patrol areas in the dwindling Japanese sphere of influence would not permit the fleet to use all of the submarines scheduled to enter service.

In early June, Admiral King determined that this situation probably called for cuts in submarine production, and he directed Nimitz to estimate his command's submarine needs in light of the shrinking sea areas where Japanese ships were likely to be found.[21] The Pacific Fleet staff determined that Nimitz would need 157 submarines to patrol all assigned areas. Nimitz expected to reach this force level by August 1945, after which a steady monthly influx of seven new units would suffice to replace losses and allow retirement of older types.[22] King agreed to reduce submarine building, and on his recommendation Forrestal canceled 98 of the 204 remaining submarines in the planned program.[23] Production would drop to three units a month by May 1945, with building schedules arranged to keep two yards in operation in case requirements rose unexpectedly.[24]

King also proposed further cuts in the destroyer escort program, which competed for resources with landing craft and other amphibious shipping. Even after the massive cancellations of late 1943 and early 1944, navy expansion plans still included provision for 622 units. In late May, King noted that 57 of these ships had not been laid down, and he recommended immediate cancellation of 22, bringing the program to 600.[25] A week later the CNO canceled the remaining thirty-five units on which construction had not yet started. He questioned whether they could be manned if built and suggested to Forrestal that manpower considerations and the improving strategic situation called for cancellation of these marginally useful extra hulls.[26]

Although Admiral King acknowledged the desirability of some cuts in planned construction for submarines and patrol vessels, this view did not extend to major surface units. The Cutback Committee members therefore dutifully went about the process of supporting with studies the proposition that the established building program perfectly fit the navy's needs. Despite the committee's role as a political tool of the CNO,

the very creation of such a body marked a major step in navy requirements planning. For the first time since 1940–41, naval planners attempted to estimate the size and type of fleet needed to win the war—or at
least they tried to demonstrate how they believed the ships they were
building would actually contribute to ultimate victory.

By late summer of 1944 the successful landings in Normandy and
southern France limited U.S. naval requirements in the Atlantic to training and antisubmarine patrol. Most American naval units had been or
would soon be switched to the Pacific, where U.S. forces were still thousands of miles away from their ultimate objective. Given these facts,
planners in COMINCH headquarters, including the Cutback Committee, naturally had to accord considerable deference to any force estimates coming from Admiral Nimitz and the Pacific Fleet staff.

By the time the Cutback Committee began its work, planners in
Washington already had some ideas about what the Pacific Fleet thought
it needed in terms of ships. A few days before the committee was orga-
nized, Admiral Nimitz circulated a study detailing requirements for
naval aviation in the Pacific. With carrier task forces now forming the
centerpieces of the combatant fleet, aviation requirements probably
would have a decisive influence on the number of surface ships to be
built. Reviewing the aircraft carrier construction program, the navy's
top operational commander noted that current plans called for his fleet
to have forty-three fleet and light carriers, along with eighty-eight escort
carriers, by mid-1946.[27] Nimitz emphasized that he did not believe that
these figures should be cut but instead suggested that the carrier construction program be accelerated and augmented.

By mid-1944 Nimitz had become convinced of the carrier's dominant
role in the Pacific war. Soon after he reported on aviation requirements,
the Bureau of Ships proposed accelerating carrier production, thereby
moving up the completion dates of five carriers and two escort carriers
to 1945 instead of the originally scheduled dates in 1946. This could
only be accomplished by slowing work on other types, thereby delaying completion of several cruisers, two battleships, and a battle cruiser.[28]
Given these options, Nimitz quickly approved the bureau's plan, in
effect trading cruisers and capital ships for more flying-off decks and
settling the issue of aircraft carrier cutbacks.[29]

Carriers, however, were the class of combatants probably least threatened by Forrestal's economy drive. Battleships, battle cruisers, cruisers,

and destroyers would be pouring out of the yards from late 1944 through 1946, and navy planners had no clear-cut justification for a program of such magnitude. The Cutback Committee therefore concentrated on determining the proper mix of surface combatants in what had clearly become a carrier-dominated naval war.

The number of aircraft carriers that Nimitz wanted for Pacific operations provided some guidance on the need for other major combatants, but any definitive requirements estimate by the planners in Washington risked undermining Pacific Fleet staff. The Cutback Committee members therefore decided on a dual approach, awaiting the Pacific Fleet's estimate of overall ship requirements while trying to work out their own formula from the information available to them.[30]

The committee followed the lead of Nimitz's staff and began its calculations with an estimate of the fleet's requirements for shipborne aircraft. Two thousand aircraft flying from fast carrier task groups would be needed to form the primary strike force for major fleet engagements and raids on enemy bases. The fleet should also have approximately 1,000 additional airplanes based on slower escort carriers and dedicated to supporting amphibious landings that had become the centerpieces of the Pacific offensive.[31] Thus, committee members based their estimate of combatant ship requirements on a somewhat artificial target that the fleet would have no fewer than 3,000 carrier-based airplanes available at all times.

Applying this standard to fast carrier task groups, the committee based their calculations on standard fleet carriers, with eighty aircraft apiece and light carriers (converted from cruiser hulls) carrying thirty-five airplanes each. The fleet should have available twenty-one of the former and nine of the latter, carrying 1,995 airplanes. To allow for expected attrition of five fleet and two light units, plus repairs to three of the larger *Essex*-class ships, the committee decided on a requirement of twenty-nine fleet and eleven light carriers, almost exactly the numbers to be provided by the current building program.

The Cutback Committee carried out a similar exercise with escort carriers, which on the average (there were several types) carried twenty-four airplanes each. Forty-three of these ships in special task forces would provide the thousand airplanes necessary for support of amphibious landings. The planners estimated that attrition would claim three units and that five would be under repair at any one time. They also allowed for twenty-eight additional escort carriers employed as aircraft transports supplying front-line combatants with replacement airplanes and thirteen to fifteen more serving as convoy escorts.[32] Ninety-two to ninety-four escort carriers were required, again almost exactly the number built or under construction. The three 45,000-ton large carriers expected to enter service in 1945 and 1946 would allow for a margin of error by providing more aircraft for fast task forces, and incorporating war lessons into the fleet.

Having justified the carrier program by setting somewhat arbitrary figures for aircraft deployment, the committee then attempted to use carrier requirements to justify planned construction of other combatant types. In effect, it attempted to bootstrap the entire building program around the presumed need for 3,000 carrier-borne aircraft. Again planners divided the fleet into "fast" and "slow" carrier groups. The 30-odd carriers in fast task forces would require as escorts 10 fast battleships, 54 cruisers, and 180 destroyers. The slower escort carrier task forces would employ all 14 prewar battleships, 39 cruisers, and 240 destroyers. To the 93 cruisers needed for duty with the carriers the planners added 9 for detached service, 9 under repair, and 13 anticipated as future losses, a total of 124, again the total number in the program. In addition to the 420 destroyers in carrier task forces, the committee foresaw requirements for 36 on detached service—a total of 456. It estimated that 30 would be lost and 42 under repair, bringing destroyer requirements to 528, again nearly matching expected production.

The figures produced by the Cutback Committee's study supported the current building program, and Admiral Duncan, King's assistant chief of staff for plans, quickly adopted them. Duncan used the committee's figures to refute the claim that the navy should reduce the planned destroyer program of 528 units, a move that King's earlier statements indicated he was willing to consider.[33] Duncan noted that all 528 of the destroyers were needed to screen larger ships and escort convoys, and he warned that cuts to the program would eliminate new ships with improved features that the postwar navy desired.

Duncan also pointed out that an alternative method for figuring destroyer requirements produced roughly the same results. This method involved totaling the number of carriers, battleships, and cruisers that required destroyers as screening ships and multiplying that figure by the number of destroyers assigned to each ship (three for carriers and two for battleships, escort carriers, and cruisers). Duncan stressed, however, that both methods supported his opposition to reductions in planned destroyer strength.

In early August the Pacific Fleet planners finally provided King's staff with their estimate of the combatant ships needed for Pacific operations, an estimate that the CNO had requested at a July conference with Admiral Nimitz. Nimitz and his staff reported that for operations through September 1945 they would need 22 battleships, 33 aircraft carriers, 66 escort carriers, 68 cruisers, 396 destroyers, and 230 submarines.[34] In almost all categories the Pacific Fleet's estimates paralleled those at which the Cutback Committee had arrived in late June. The Pacific Fleet wanted a few more carriers and a few less old battleships than the Washington planners believed necessary, but overall the findings of Nimitz's staff supported the committee's work.

The similarity between the Pacific Fleet's estimates and those of the Cutback Committee undoubtedly reinforced the latter group's determination not to recommend any reduction in shipbuilding. Comparing the estimated operational requirements for September 1945 with expected ship production, the committee reported in November 1944 that the figures matched almost exactly. If the planners were correct, the existing expansion program would just barely produce the number of ships needed in the Pacific (and Atlantic if Germany remained undefeated) through September 1945.[35]

As an operational staff, the Pacific Fleet proved unable or unwilling to project its needs beyond the period that current operational plans covered, which extended through the first nine months of 1945. By late summer of 1944 strategic plans called for an invasion of southern Japan at the end of September 1945, presumably the ultimate naval enterprise of the campaign in terms of fleet requirements. A second invasion near Tokyo and a possible attack on the Chinese coast remained more distant possibilities, but only after the Allies had occupied a large portion of southern Japan.

The building program included a large number of ships scheduled for completion in the last quarter of 1945 and through 1946, including two battleships, thirteen aircraft carriers, thirteen escort carriers, thirty-nine cruisers, and fifty-seven destroyers.[36] None would enter service in time to participate in the invasion of southern Japan, and they did not appear in any existing operational plans. The Cutback Committee, therefore, had no outside support for its continuing insistence that all ships in the existing program were necessary to prosecute the war successfully. The problem of justifying the large number of ships scheduled to enter service after the invasion of Japan would continue to plague navy planners until the end of the war.

Although Admiral King seconded the committee's recommendations, he also had his subordinates prepare for the possibility of additional cuts. He directed the Bureau of Ships to prepare a list of vessels in the construction program, showing the last possible date that each unit could be canceled without unduly disrupting overall production. In order to save any appreciable amount of money and material, the bureau replied, ships would have to be canceled no later than one month before launch; the earlier a ship was canceled, the more resources would be saved.[37] The bureau noted, however, that other factors mitigated against canceling vessels on which work had hardly begun. The ships farthest along in construction were generally of earlier designs, and the navy therefore might benefit from canceling these in favor of completing improved types that had been laid down afterward.

Even as he investigated the distribution of possible shipbuilding cutbacks, however, the CNO remained interested in further expansion of the existing program. On 23 June, King informed Forrestal that he favored additional ship construction along the lines that the General Board report had suggested the previous month.[38] In late July 1944 King decided to approve, for planning purposes only, adding one battleship, nine cruisers, six carriers, and several smaller ships to the existing program, as recommended by the General Board.[39]

All of this bureaucratic maneuvering resulted in very little action on shipbuilding, which may well have been the CNO's primary goal. Throughout the late summer and fall of 1944, King consistently approved the Cutback Committee's reports, recommending no major changes in the combatant building program. The one significant exception to this pattern occurred in early September. The Bureau of Ships notified Admiral King in late August that the acceleration of aircraft carrier construction, combined with the growing labor shortages in navy shipyards, would delay the completion of four planned light cruisers until late 1947. The units were of an earlier design and would actually enter service after several units of improved wartime designs originally intended to replace them.[40] King told Forrestal that he favored cutting these four ships from the current program, noting that they would be obsolete by the time they entered service.[41]

Except for this cancellation, the CNO continued to support going forward with the approved program or possibly even augmenting it. In notes to the secretary seconding the recommendations of the Cutback Committee, Admiral King emphasized three major factors militating against cuts in planned construction. First, a large number of ships had already been cut. The list of cancellations included antisubmarine vessels, especially 440 destroyer escorts, and 98 submarines, along with the 5 *Montana*-class battleships, 3 battle cruisers, and 4 light cruisers.[42] King failed to mention, however, that none of the larger ships could have been completed for several years and that much of the tonnage authority freed by these cancellations had already been reallocated to other types.

Second, the CNO also claimed that the ships in the current program were necessary to allow for periodic overhauls of operating units and combat testing of the latest advances in ship design. King argued that the ultimate size of the fleet

> is not the sole factor to be considered in the study of the necessity for continuing the building program. Many naval vessels of all types have actually been engaged in the war in the Pacific since its beginning, almost three years ago. They have had little or no opportunity for overhaul except that incident to battle damage. We must, therefore, give consideration to building new ships either to replace these ones that are wearing out, or to provide sufficient of the types to permit requisite upkeep time and at the same time keep an adequate combatant force available to win the war. The continuing program permits us to build war lessons into the ships.[43]

Finally, the CNO assured Forrestal in late September 1944 that all planned ships were necessary to the war effort because both losses and operational requirements were likely to rise as the Pacific campaign neared the Japanese home islands.[44] Echoing the arguments of his planners, Admiral King noted that losses might increase markedly once the navy began operations within range of the substantial enemy air forces based in Japan proper. He also predicted that Japanese submarines would soon be diverted from their supply missions and begin taking a heavier toll of U.S. ships. At the same time losses would be rising, planned large-scale amphibious operations around Japan would tax the navy's ability to provide sufficient cruisers and destroyers to escort troop transports.

The need to compensate for future losses was a constant refrain in King's statements, and it figured prominently in the Cutback Committee's calculations as well. Any long-range construction plan naturally would have to allow for substantial attrition in predicting actual fleet strength at a given date. Unfortunately, such predictions required considerable speculation, adding another layer of uncertainty to the already problematic estimates of fleet requirements.

Navy planners based their estimates of future combat losses on past experience. Almost certainly King's staff continued to be influenced by the heavy ship losses of 1942, when U.S. and Japanese naval and air strengths were roughly equal. As a result of that experience, navy studies consistently overestimated losses for 1943 and beyond, especially regarding the larger classes of ships.

At times, loss estimates nearly equaled construction rates in some categories of ships, so projected fleet strength rose only slightly despite the massive building program. For example, in July 1943 the navy estimated that during the next twelve months the fleet would be augmented by 2 battleships, 14 carriers, 51 escort carriers, 11 cruisers, and 130 destroyers. Estimated losses during the same period were three battleships, five carriers, fourteen escort carriers, eleven cruisers, and forty-six destroyers, about half of the combatant tonnage scheduled to enter service.[45] If these predictions were realized, carrier strength would grow significantly, whereas battleship and cruiser forces would actually decline, threatening to unbalance the fleet.

When in January 1944 navy planners calculated expected gains and losses for the coming calendar year, they reached similar conclusions. The fleet would commission 4 battleships and lose 3, add 9 carriers and lose 5, add 13 cruisers while losing 8, and add nearly 100 destroyers and lose 47.[46] Only in mass-produced escort carriers would the fleet's net gains far outdistance expected attrition.

Fortunately for the navy and the United States, actual events turned out quite differently. Exploiting its growing numerical and technological superiority, after 1942 the navy lost only one light carrier, six escort carriers, and three cruisers.[47] No battleships or fleet carriers and just one heavy cruiser were lost from 1943 on, although several of these types

TABLE 2. Actual versus Estimated U.S. Navy Ship Losses, 1943–45

	Battleships	Aircraft Carriers	Escort Carriers	Cruisers	Destroyers	Destroyer Escorts	Submarines
Estimated losses 9/30/43 to 12/31/44	3	5	8	13	63	93	27
Actual losses 9/30/43 to 12/31/44	0	0	4	0	26	9	25
Estimated losses 5/1/44 to 9/30/45	4	9	12	14	43	97	29
Actual losses 5/1/44 to 9/30/45	0	1	5	1	27	11	22

were badly damaged. Destroyers fared more poorly, in part because they were easier to sink than large ships and because they often operated on hazardous detached duty where enemy units could overwhelm their defenses. However, without minimizing the heavy price paid by navy men and ships during the last two and a half years of the war, overall losses never once approached the cataclysmic levels reflected in planning documents. Estimated losses for 1944 and 1945 far exceeded the actual number of ships sunk (table 2).

In part because the planners' estimates of losses were too high, during 1943 and 1944 the fleet grew faster than navy leaders had anticipated. Ironically, the navy suffered lower-than-anticipated losses in late 1943 and early 1944, which exacerbated the manpower crisis of mid-1944. One obvious solution would have been to cut ship production, but Admiral King and his senior commanders had already rejected that option.

Lower losses created no insurmountable obstacles and were undoubtedly welcome despite the manpower problems they created. The real trouble lay in the planners' use of unrealistically inflated loss projections to justify additional ship construction. For instance, when Admiral Horne suggested in March 1944 that Admiral King take steps to expand the building program, he based his recommendation on heavy navy losses in the Pacific in 1943. Horne noted that losses during 1943 were 50 percent for carriers, nearly that rate for heavy cruisers, and more than 16 percent for light cruisers and destroyers, based on the number of ships available at the beginning of that year.[48] Because the navy lost only one escort carrier, one heavy cruiser, and one light cruiser during all of 1943, Horne's figures reflected more the Pacific Fleet's weakness in January 1943 than any substantial successes by the Japanese. The numbers were really intended to imply that heavy loss rates might be expected in 1944 and beyond, thereby providing a rationale for Horne's proposal to further increase the existing shipbuilding program.

Although plans for Pacific operations extended through the first nine months of 1945, anticipated ship losses provided a separate rationale for building ships that would be completed in late 1945, 1946, and 1947. When in mid-1944 naval planners looked ahead to September 1945, they foresaw losses so severe that the fleet would not have all the ships they believed necessary to carry out planned operations against Japan.[49] If Germany remained undefeated through September 1945, the planners calculated that between 1 May 1944 and that date the navy would lose four battleships, fourteen cruisers, nine carriers, twelve escort carriers, and forty-three destroyers. If these estimates proved correct, the fleet would need the ships coming off the ways in the last quarter of 1945 and beyond just to reach a strength commensurate with operational requirements.

Fortunately, the dire predictions of 1943 and early 1944 proved overly pessimistic, yet through the end of 1944 and beyond the Cutback Committee continued to claim that fleet requirements equaled the number of ships in the building program.[50] As the program surged on unimpeded and the second half of 1944 brought unexpectedly light losses, by the end of the year navy planners could anticipate the day when fleet combatants would nearly equal the totals suggested in the doomsday studies of 1939 and 1940. Projecting just a year and a half ahead to mid-1946, the flow charts showed a fleet of 27 battleships, 39 carriers, 84 cruisers, 462 destroyers, and 289 submarines.[51] Compared to the 1940 program, the 1946 fleet would be short about five capital ships and three cruisers but replete with aircraft carriers, destroyers, and submarines. These would be augmented by more than a hundred escort carriers unsuitable for operations with fast task forces but perfectly capable of supporting landings and providing air cover for slower surface units. In addition, hundreds of destroyer escorts not anticipated in the prewar plans would be available to fill in for destroyers against the remaining Japanese submarine assets.

Almost all of these ships would be engaged in the final offensive against Japan, but not without associated costs. That offensive might have to be delayed because a shortage of transport and cargo shipping would limit troop redeployment capabilities after Germany's defeat, a situation not helped by a continuing shortage of service units in the Pacific.[52] Still, in terms of meeting long-range production targets, the program planners had achieved miracles.

Perhaps the most astounding feature of the navy's situation was the fact that the enemy fleets that this huge force was designed to defeat had all but disappeared by late 1944. The navy's intelligence service confirmed that the great Axis naval threat no longer existed; Hitler's navy, when it dared to leave port in the face of overwhelming Allied air power, had barely enough ships to protect Germany's Baltic Coast. Only the Japanese fleet remained a viable force through most of 1944. However, the crushing defeat in Leyte Gulf gutted the Imperial Japanese Navy; by January 1945 Nimitz's units outnumbered it by five to one or more in almost every category.[53]

During this same period, America's principal naval ally had not only survived but also flourished, a development not necessarily to the CNO's liking. By the end of 1944 the Royal Navy had reached a strength roughly equivalent to the prewar U.S. fleet, partly by manning lend-lease ships built in American yards. Unfortunately, Admiral King's antipathy for the British spilled over into plans for their participation in the Pacific war. When Churchill suggested after Italy's surrender that British units might operate with Nimitz, King successfully opposed the idea. The CNO argued that U.S. forces represented the maximum that logistic facilities could support, and he claimed that nothing could be gained by sending Royal Navy ships to the Pacific.[54] What King really felt about the British was perhaps best expressed in a letter to Admiral Stark about this time. In it he complained that "what they wish in their hearts is that we would haul down the Stars and Stripes and hoist the White Ensign in all of our ships."[55]

In September 1944, with the European naval campaign all but over, the British tried again. They offered ten aircraft carriers and supporting units for participation in Pacific Fleet operations. Once again the CNO objected, suggesting that the British occupy themselves by tying down Japanese forces in the Indian Ocean. This time Roosevelt and Admiral Leahy overruled King in the interests of inter-Allied harmony, and by late 1944 plans had been worked out to provide Nimitz with a substantial all-British task force (TF 57) for the 1945 Pacific campaigns.[56] Despite these developments, Cutback Committee planners in Washington continued to act as if the Royal Navy did not exist, except perhaps as a yardstick by which to measure postwar U.S. naval requirements.

As 1944 drew to a close, the CNO and his staff could look back on the year's bureaucratic struggles with a sense of accomplishment. Having turned back the army's push for joint oversight of navy expansion and at least temporarily solved the fleet's manpower problem, by late 1944 Admiral King had gained the freedom he needed to continue the current shipbuilding program. Although Forrestal obviously distrusted King on this issue, he had no independent source of information to dispute the conclusions of King's planning staff. The navy's internal debate over fleet expansion had ended, and King clearly had won.

The key question that remained involved the CNO's ability to augment the existing program in order to ensure a modernized postwar fleet. Admiral King had approved—for planning purposes only—the General Board's recommendation to add several ships to the program. Given Forrestal's doubts, he could probably do no more. Actually adding these ships, however, would require presidential approval and at least acquiescence from Forrestal, both of which seemed unlikely. Yet for a brief period in early 1945 a combination of political circumstances seemed to put this goal tantalizingly within King's reach.

· 8 ·

FORRESTAL'S CONVERSION
AND THE ENDGAME
1945

By December 1944 the existing navy expansion program appeared secure from both external and internal interference. Although Admiral King flirted with the idea of further increases, there seemed little chance that he could overcome Forrestal's resistance to any additional combatant construction. To go on the offensive in this field the CNO would need a strong ally who could override the secretary's misgivings about further ship procurement.

Admiral King found such an ally in Rep. Carl Vinson, who still possessed great influence over military policy as chair of the House Naval Affairs Committee. Always a strong supporter of the navy, Vinson seems to have developed a close relationship to the CNO. King described Vinson as an enthusiastic supporter of the navy who communicated with him frequently and offered to back him in any potential struggle with the new secretary.[1]

In late December 1944 Vinson questioned the secretary's staff about the combatant building program. The Naval Affairs Committee chair wanted to know how much unallocated building authority remained, as well as how much combatant tonnage the navy actually could build if Congress passed legislation for additional construction authority. Vinson

Forrestal's Conversion and the Endgame

also demanded an explanation for the navy's failure to proceed with construction on its authorized tonnage of combatant ships.[2]

Forrestal's staff replied that because of cancellations, losses, and ships becoming overage, the navy still had 750,000 tons of congressional authorization for combatant ship construction. Estimates showed that if Congress approved additional ships, the nation's building yards could turn out approximately one and a quarter million tons by the end of 1947. However, the reply to Vinson emphasized that the CNO saw no strategic need for new ships and that increases in the building program would require the navy to induct and train more men.

These findings failed to dissuade Vinson, who had direct access to Admiral King and presumably to the CNO's views on the desirability of enlarging the shipbuilding program. In early January, Forrestal notified the president that Vinson had asked the navy to obtain funding and begin contracting for the unused 750,000 tons of building authority.[3] Vinson's direct interference in navy procurement planning amounted to gross overstepping of his responsibilities and probably would not have occurred without King's approval. Whether King or his staff had a hand in Vinson's move remains uncertain, but Vinson's proposal for more ships certainly echoed the CNO's comments on the subject. The navy might suffer drastic losses as the Pacific fighting moved closer to Japan, Vinson argued, a claim that navy planners often made.

Forrestal remained somewhat ambivalent about the proposal in light of the navy's existing preponderance of strength but gave the idea at least lukewarm support. "Both Admiral King and I have misgivings on this in view of the very large fleet we have now," he explained to Roosevelt, "and the substantial building program as yet unfinished, and also in view of the availability of elements of the British Navy in the Pacific. On the other hand, . . . getting the appropriations and starting the building program would give us insurance which would not be very expensive."[4]

Given the tone of earlier directives from Forrestal that had forced Admiral King to justify the existing program on a monthly basis, his grudging approval of Vinson's proposal marked a significant shift in attitude. After less than a year on the job, Forrestal may have been unwilling to alienate such a powerful legislative leader, or he may have believed that the combination of King and Vinson would simply override his objections by taking their case directly to the president. His

THE UNSINKABLE FLEET

subsequent actions suggest, however, that he may have had a true change of heart on the issue.

By late 1944 the Anglo-U.S.-Soviet grand alliance had begun to develop serious cracks. Although American leaders differed in their assessments of Russian intentions, problems over postwar control of Eastern Europe defied easy solution. Some top leaders, including Forrestal, had already concluded that Stalin's impressive war machine was likely to become the principal postwar threat to U.S. interests around the world. Forrestal thus became one of the first and most influential cold warriors. As secretary of the navy, he determined that the United States must maintain military forces adequate to curb postwar Soviet ambitions.[5] Thus, his fears of Russian imperialism may well have influenced his views on the necessity of further navy expansion; by late December 1944 he had certainly grown more receptive to plans for additional shipbuilding, as his comments and actions over the following few weeks demonstrated.

In November 1944 Forrestal had decided to hold weekly meetings of a navy Top Policy Group consisting of the secretary, the CNO, and their principal assistants. The group was supposed to operate as a sort of navy board of directors, discussing important policy matters involving the Navy Department.[6] At one meeting in early January the discussion turned to submarine production. Admiral Cooke noted that U.S. submarines were currently operating in about one million square miles of ocean and suggested that as the operating area decreased, the public might question why the navy needed more units of this type. Forrestal replied, "I can answer why you are building more. I won't be able to answer why you didn't build more." When a participant then asked what the word *requirements* really meant in relation to combatants, Forrestal shot back, "It means whatever you want it to mean at a particular moment and in a particular instance. . . . What you are really saying is, this is what we propose to build."[7] Such comments suggest that by early 1945 the secretary held a broader view of navy requirements than had previously been the case and that he would not hesitate to justify additional construction before Congress and the public.

On 6 January 1945 Forrestal, Vinson, King, and their key subordinates met in Forrestal's office to plan for new additions to the navy building program. The timing was hardly auspicious. During the first week of January both services were considering further expansion but for very different reasons. During the preceding two weeks Allied armies in Western Europe had struggled through some of the most bitter fighting of the war. The German Ardennes offensive so alarmed Secretary of War Henry Stimson that he strongly urged General Marshall to obtain more manpower to form additional fighting divisions.[8] Eventually, only Marshall's threat to resign thwarted this scheme, which would have placed an additional burden on the already difficult manpower situation.

Admiral King ran the meeting in Forrestal's office, which took place with no army representatives in attendance. He began by explaining that through the end of 1947 existing shipyard facilities would have room to build only eighteen large (more than 7,000 tons) combatants above and beyond those included in the current program.[9] This limitation would not affect escort carrier construction because those large combatants were built in merchant shipyards. The current program already included two battleships and one battle cruiser scheduled for completion in 1946 or 1947, so King preferred not to add additional units of these types. He did recommend adding two 45,000-ton aircraft carriers and six *Essex*-class carriers, bringing planned strength to five of the former and thirty-five of the latter. The navy was building twenty-seven heavy cruisers, including eight of an advanced type with rapid-fire guns. King wished to add four of these to the program, along with six light antiaircraft cruisers that would tail on to the twenty-five light cruisers already on order. The eighteen cruisers and carriers that King proposed, along with eight additional escort carriers, would use up the bulk of the navy's available tonnage authorization.

Although the navy had 372 destroyers in service, and 128 more scheduled for delivery in 1945 and 1946, King asked for 36 units of a newer, larger design with higher speed. The CNO noted that he did not want any more of the standard fleet submarines currently under construction, but he did request twelve of a new advanced type under development. In the meantime, the navy could build six additional units of the old design in order to keep the yards in operation while designers perfected the new model. In sum, King wanted the program expanded by eight carriers, twelve escort carriers, ten cruisers, thirty-six destroyers, and eighteen submarines. All except the twelve yet-to-be-designed new submarines could be laid down within a few months.

Vinson said that he was extremely pleased with the new program. He noted that the additional ships would keep the navy abreast of the latest design improvements and "at the same time keep the yards and the unlimited resources of the country being utilized in the war effort."[10] The navy would need approximately 55,000 more men to man the proposed ships, the CNO said, but he promised to junk or give away older ships if manpower became a problem. This solution suited Vinson, who remarked that he had suggested additions to the program in order to keep the navy in modern ships. With these increases, planned navy strength for 1 January 1948 would rise to 25 battleships, 3 battle cruisers, 50 fleet and light aircraft carriers, 94 escort carriers, 122 cruisers, 540 destroyers, 386 destroyer escorts, and 320 submarines.

Apparently Forrestal had no immediate objection to the proposal. At the meeting he seconded King's views and later informed his subordinates of the decision to expand the current construction program.[11] On 8 January Admiral King sent Forrestal his plan for using the remaining tonnage in the navy's authorization.[12] The CNO formally requested approval for 664,000 tons of additional construction, or eighty-four combatant ships. King noted that the new units would incorporate the lessons learned during the war with Japan but would include no radical departures from current designs.

At the next meeting of Forrestal's Top Policy Group the secretary explained that the new building program would tail on to the existing one, with the additional ships being laid down as units now under construction were completed. Admiral King explained that the navy was "looking at the postwar situation and trying to get the most modern types all the way along the line."[13]

After this meeting Forrestal duly sent the proposal to Roosevelt, requesting final approval for the additional construction.[14] The president, however, was busy preparing for his trip to Western Europe and ultimately to the Yalta summit and did not have time to give the expansion plan much attention.[15] He did indicate that he favored granting the navy's request and sent the proposal on to the Bureau of the Budget for further analysis.[16]

There the navy plan ran into trouble. Harold Smith, a New Dealer and presidential confidant, headed the Bureau of Budget. Before James Byrnes took charge of mobilization at OWM, Budget had expanded its influence in pursuit of Smith's vision of using his organization as the president's chief policy coordinating arm. Although Byrnes saw the bureau as a tool serving OWM, a view Smith disputed, it remained active as an ad hoc technical staff reporting directly to the president.[17]

After reviewing the new shipbuilding plan, the budget director sent Roosevelt a memorandum questioning the advisability of any further increases in the navy program. Smith noted that both manpower and material were in critical supply and that he feared that any further construction would only exacerbate existing shortages. He pointed out that the current construction program already involved hundreds of ships, including nearly 30 fleet carriers and more than 100 cruisers.

Smith doubted that the navy's proposed use of scarce labor and material would contribute to the war effort and reminded Roosevelt that production of additional equipment should be undertaken only if it were essential to winning the war. He refused to accept the navy's official explanation of the ships being needed to ensure against possible losses in the final stages of the Pacific campaign. If the Japanese were already badly outnumbered, he reasoned, then equal losses on both sides would only increase the relative advantage of the United States. Smith strongly opposed Admiral King's policy of attempting to assure a cheap and speedy victory by building up an overwhelming superiority in strength: "No matter how many vessels we build, we cannot completely eliminate the element of risk when we finally meet the Japanese main fleet in decisive battle. . . . I sometimes ask myself—what kind of insurance does the navy want? Must it have several times the fleet of the enemy to establish self confidence? I cannot believe it. It may be time to call a halt."[18]

Forrestal took the lead in responding to Smith's challenge. At the next Top Policy Group meeting, the secretary noted that he had spoken directly with Roosevelt, who had given the expansion program the green light. Nevertheless, the Bureau of the Budget had interposed an objection: "The obvious causes of that question are: Why do we need all this? If we have administered these spankings to the Japanese navy, why do we need more ships? What is the British Fleet doing? What is it going to do?"[19]

Forrestal explained that he saw the extra ships as insurance against unforeseen contingencies. He believed that beginning work under the program would not be very costly and that construction could be canceled without too much loss if the navy decided the ships were not needed. When informed that the ships would have to be contracted for immediately in order to avoid any gaps in construction and keep the yard work forces together, Forrestal replied, "That is exactly what I want."

In order to remove the roadblock Smith had placed before the new program, Forrestal turned to Admiral King for help. The secretary's staff had prepared a response to Smith's objections that could be sent to the president. At this meeting Forrestal gave the proposed reply to King, asking the CNO to see whether it fit his views.

Admiral King apparently was determined to push his program through, and he backed Forrestal's plan to override Smith by sending Roosevelt a direct reply to the budget director's memorandum.[20] Forrestal sent the reply to Roosevelt but indicated that it had originated with the CNO. Perhaps Forrestal feared that the document went too far, or he may have believed that King's word would carry more weight, but in any case he seemed anxious to distance himself from its contents.

The memorandum argued that the additional ships in the new program would be needed should the navy suffer heavy losses in the final approach to Japan. The CNO pointed out that because mines and land-based aircraft caused most sinkings, even the elimination of the Japanese fleet would not reduce the hazards to be faced. Therefore, a simple comparison of U.S. and enemy strength was "not a sound criterion by which to challenge the proposed program of the Navy Department for the additional 664,000 tons of combatant vessels."[21]

By late January 1945 such claims were wholly inconsistent with the realities of strategy and production. Certainly, Japan's growing use of suicide aircraft threatened to increase navy losses, but the existing building program already provided a significant margin of safety. Construction of the additional ships would just be starting as the fighting intensified in the area around Japan. None of the larger ships would be completed until late 1947; even the smaller vessels would not be finished until late 1946.[22] The odds of any seeing action in the conflict were exceedingly low, and both Forrestal and King knew it. Admiral King had stated repeatedly that his primary purpose in contracting for the ships was to modernize the postwar fleet, and Forrestal had argued for months that military requirements would allow cutbacks in shipbuilding. Nevertheless, the CNO and the secretary were willing to use specious claims of military necessity to keep the program alive.

Vice Adm. Wilson Brown, the president's naval aide, transmitted the memorandum from Forrestal and Admiral King to Roosevelt on the last day of January and recommended that the president approve the program.[23] Apparently the president was convinced; he endorsed the proposed reply to Budget Director Smith that same day. Faced with what amounted to a direct presidential order, Smith had no choice but to capitulate. On 7 February he notified Forrestal that the proposed addition of 664,000 tons of combatants had been approved.[24] Within a week Admiral King ordered navy bureau chiefs to begin contracting for construction of all eighty-four ships in the new augmentation plan.[25]

The navy bureaucracy immediately began planning material allocations and placing construction contracts. Because of the large number of ships already building, the first units from the new program would not be finished until mid-1946 in the case of escort carriers and mid-to-late 1947 in the case of cruisers.[26] Before construction could even begin, however, the enlarged program had to be worked into the navy appropriations request for fiscal year 1946, which would soon go before Congress. The navy's Office of Budget and Reports estimated that the additional ships would cost $1.8 billion.[27] However, only about one-sixth of that amount—Forrestal's "insurance premium"—would be spent during the 1945–46 fiscal year.[28]

When hearings on the 1946 navy appropriations bill began in mid-March, Forrestal and King's proposal to increase ship construction immediately met resistance. At least some members of the House Appropriations Committee believed that the navy should grow only if such growth could help win the war. King testified that all of the new ships would be completed by the end of 1947, although many would not enter service until 1948. This, he claimed, showed that the current conflict was the primary motivating factor in the navy's decision to build the units.[29]

Despite the CNO's assurances, members of Congress questioned the necessity of the ships, the Japanese fleet's decline, and the expected assistance from British units. One committee member predicted difficulty in justifying the increase to the full House and the public and demanded details on Japanese naval strength. King demurred, refusing to put "numbers against numbers," but Forrestal rose to the challenge. He pointed out that U.S. naval forces were operating in seven different areas of the Pacific and that the navy was "committed to having sufficient strength in each area to meet the maximum power the Jap[anese] can bring into any one of them."[30] This new strategic force "requirement" appears to have come directly from the secretary's fertile mind, perhaps on the spur of the moment. Such statements indicate how flexible navy leaders could be in justifying expansion plans and the difficulties civilian leaders had in criticizing those plans authoritatively during wartime.

By the time congressional budget hearings were under way, the new expansion program had run into more trouble on the executive front. For a second time James Byrnes intervened in navy production plans, this time decisively. Byrnes had accompanied Roosevelt to the Yalta Conference, a trip that ultimately earned him the position of secretary of state in the early Truman administration. Upon his return, Byrnes learned of the proposal to increase the fleet and immediately urged the president to cancel the new program on the grounds that it was a waste of resources.[31] Although Roosevelt was weakened by his travels and nearer death than anyone knew, his experience as a former assistant secretary of the navy probably had taught him enough to realize the fallacy of King's arguments. By his own account, Byrnes needed only a day to convince Roosevelt that the proposed additions would not contribute to the war effort.

At a cabinet meeting in mid-March, Roosevelt questioned the wisdom of further navy expansion and expressed concern that the new program would aggravate existing manpower and material shortages. Although Roosevelt recalled giving oral approval, he could not remember whether he had signed anything authorizing further construction. At the same meeting, which neither King nor Forrestal attended, Byrnes told the group that Admiral King had admitted to him that the proposed ships were not really needed to help win the war.[32]

In early March, Byrnes had asked Forrestal to defer construction of these new ships until the matter could be studied further. Byrnes noted that he had discussed the navy program with Roosevelt and concluded that "if the ships available to the navy, now under construction, suffice for the war against Japan, we should avoid further authorization at this time."[33] In late March Roosevelt formally ordered Forrestal to cancel all proposed ships save for a dozen escort carriers that Admiral King had stated were actually required for planned operations.[34]

The attempt to increase the combatant building program thus ended in ignominious defeat; the major question now concerned the political price that naval leaders would have to pay. Roosevelt died shortly after the affair ended, and Byrnes soon resigned from his post at OWM. Thus, overall damage on the executive side was probably minimal. The serious repercussions of the aborted attempt to increase the fleet seem to have occurred in Congress, where the affair undoubtedly undermined lawmakers' faith in the navy's ability to police itself. This constituted an important defeat, for Congress would control postwar purse strings and play a decisive role in the ongoing debate over military unification.

Shortly after the ships were canceled, legislators stripped the navy of a large measure of its autonomy in ship procurement. In April the House Appropriations Committee reported on the navy appropriation bill for 1946, which no longer included funding for the new building program. This report noted that the navy was expected to undertake no additional construction of combatant vessels unless Congress first specifically approved funding for those ships.[35] Such language reversed nearly three years of congressional policy that allowed the navy to contract freely for ships within the limits of the construction authority Congress granted. King asked that the language be changed so that the navy need only seek approval from the naval subcommittee before contracting for more ships.[36]

King's request was refused by Representative Shepard, chairman of the Appropriation Committee's naval subcommittee. Shepard explained to Admiral Horne that members were concerned that the navy was building vessels not needed for the war. If the CNO actually believed that more ships were necessary, he could bring his case before the committee. If the needs were real, Shepard was confident that Congress could pass a joint resolution in just a few days authorizing additional construction.[37] The navy had therefore lost not only a major battle to use the full measure of combatant building authority but also its ability to present Congress with a fait accompli by making unilateral commitments on the remaining unallocated tonnage.

Although Roosevelt's decision on the eighty-four-ship program thwarted the navy plan to augment current construction, it did nothing to disturb the massive building program already in place. Even without the Vinson-King expansion proposals, by late March 1945 the navy was building or planning to build 2 battleships, 16 carriers, 31 escort carriers, 48 cruisers, 111 destroyers, and 50 submarines. Many would not be finished until 1946, and some of the cruisers were scheduled for completion in 1947 (tables 3 and 4).[38]

TABLE 3. Wartime Navy Fleet Expansion Targets, 1942–45

	Battleships	Aircraft Carriers	Escort Carriers	Cruisers	Destroyers	Destroyer Escorts	Submarines
Approved program, as of November 1942	30 (work on 5 suspended)	35 (plus 4 pending authorization)	114	114 (4 battle cruisers suspended)	500	750	314
Approved program through 1946, as of June 1943	25	39	approx. 100	102	561	1,000	430
Proposed Vinson-King program of January 1945	25	50	94	125	540	386	320
Projected fleet strength for mid-1947, as of March 1945 (no attrition)	23	42	96	109	485	359	255

TABLE 4. U.S. Navy Fleet Strength and Building Programs, 1941 and 1945

	Battleships	Aircraft Carriers	Cruisers	Destroyers	Destroyer Escorts	Submarines
On hand, July 1941	15	6	37	224	0	100
Building or authorized, July 1941	17	12	54	180	0	85
On hand, January 1945	23	25 (plus 65 escort carriers)	62	367	376	235
Under construction, January 1945	2	17 (plus 13 escort carriers)	41	110	10	62

THE UNSINKABLE FLEET

With the Axis powers in retreat everywhere, army leaders again began challenging their naval counterparts to justify the fleet building program's enormous cost in labor and material. By late March 1945 the Third Reich clearly was on the verge of collapse, and the United States would soon be able to concentrate all its military resources in the Pacific. The impending shift from a two-front to a one-front war had major implications for navy expansion, some positive and some negative. On the one hand, victory in Europe would free some Allied ships occupied there for redeployment to the Pacific. Navy personnel serving as armed guards on merchantmen and in various shore establishments could soon be reassigned to man new construction. More important, Germany's final defeat would drastically cut overall military manpower requirements, making available additional personnel to meet the navy's needs.

On the other hand, the large army forces employed in Europe, especially air units, soon would start moving to the Pacific. These AAF squadrons promised to strain theater logistic capacity while competing with naval aviation for important force-justifying missions. With sufficient strategically located bases and adequate logistic support, the availability of additional Army Air Force airplanes and a British carrier task force threatened to undermine the navy's rationale for the expansion program as it existed in spring of 1945.

As the Joint Chiefs and their subordinate agencies finalized plans for the decisive campaign against Japan, top army leaders began to question the need for continued fleet expansion beyond the scheduled invasion dates for the Japanese home islands. In late March 1945 the Joint Planners produced a single-front deployment study that postulated final victory in Europe by the end of June. The document revealed that the navy planned to continue adding combatant ships to the fleet well after March 1946, and by then planners believed that the United States and its allies would have mounted the final invasion of the main Japanese island of Honshu.[39]

The planned assault on Honshu was to be preceded by the invasion of Kyushu (Operation Olympic) in late 1945. One of the primary military aims of Olympic was to secure air bases so that land-based airplanes could establish air supremacy over the entire Japanese homeland. After the deployment study of March 1945 army planners had serious questions about future navy growth, especially the construction of additional aircraft carriers.

Forrestal's Conversion and the Endgame

One army member of the Joint Production Survey Committee suggested to General Marshall that the navy's policy of building ships to the limit of productive capacity had skewed planned U.S. deployments against Japan. Faced with a request from the Office of War Mobilization and Reconversion (the successor to OWM) questioning the proposed single-front aircraft production program, Gen. R. C. Moore criticized the plans for continued growth in navy carrier strength. Moore argued that because army ground forces and their supporting air units would be limited by availability of shipping and air bases, the fleet would enjoy a far greater preponderance of force over its enemies than army ground or air forces.[40] He suggested that cuts should come from the navy if the national economy required a reduction in military forces, but he noted, "From my past experience on this committee, I do not believe the Navy members of the Joint Chiefs of Staff will accept any such conclusion."

At this late date General Marshall finally began to reconsider his hands-off approach to the issue of navy force structure. He told the Joint Chiefs that he disagreed with elements of the proposed single-front deployment, especially as it called for armed forces of eleven million some eighteen months after Germany's surrender. Marshall criticized the proposed expansion of air forces after V-E Day and questioned the usefulness of further navy growth beyond the final invasion of the Japanese home islands. The chief of staff concluded that the Joint Chiefs should obtain better justification of the proposed deployments before approving this use of scarce resources.[41]

One can only speculate about the effects on American force structure had Marshall taken this stand a year or a year and a half earlier. By the time he had his change of heart, the war in Europe was nearly over and the great armies he had helped to create would soon begin to disband. From this point forward army ground forces would diminish while naval and air power assumed dominant roles in the war effort.

Not surprisingly, the end of fighting in Europe changed the dynamics of army-navy rivalry. With the Pacific now the only active front, the ground army could not hope to sustain its dominant role in War Department force planning. The remaining theater of operations simply could not support, and did not demand, even half of the army's existing combat divisions. On the other hand, the Pacific offered the army's air arm a new arena in which to demonstrate its usefulness, subjecting Japanese territory to the same level of aerial punishment that had been inflicted on Germany and occupied Europe. Unlike Europe, how-ever, the theater contained a rival American air arm also looking for new targets as the Japanese fleet rapidly disappeared. Due to these fac-tors, in the final few months of the war the Army Air Forces replaced the ground army as the principal military opponent of navy expansion plans.

As early as autumn 1944 AAF leaders were devoting considerable attention to what would happen after the war. AAF lobbying had all but guaranteed an independent postwar Air Force, but the relative stature of that organization had yet to be determined. In order to obtain congressional and public support for a strong and independent air force once the fighting ended, AAF leaders were determined to obtain maxi-mum favorable publicity for their wartime achievements.[42] Once plan-ning began for the final campaigns against Japan, AAF leaders tried to ensure a maximum role for their service so the future air force would not be overshadowed by navy aviators. In Europe, the AAF's role had been clear-cut, but in the Pacific theater the navy's own air arm threat-ened to steal the spotlight.

In this atmosphere, planners began openly to discuss the political repercussions of particular strategic options and deployment decisions. For example, in late September 1944 the Joint Planners estimated the tactical air units needed to defeat Japan; the more than 16,000 combat planes would participate in the final Pacific offensive; just under half of these would be navy or Marine aircraft.[43]

General Arnold approved these figures because they would allow the AAF to retain a large fighting force to the end of the war. Some army planners had their doubts about this approach, however, believing that the navy would dominate air action in the decisive theater and thereby reap the rewards of favorable publicity. One Operations Division paper noted of the report, "The AAF desires the largest possible air force in being at the end of the war to ensure that the AAF continues to be the dominant U.S. air arm after the war. . . . The Army goal, however, to obtain post-war dominance in the United States, should be to insure its position in the opinion of the public and of Congress. This requires AAF dominance in the final kill on Honshu, with minimum dispersion to minor areas."[44] "Minor," of course, meant less important in terms of publicity on the home front and therefore less useful in terms of postwar political maneuverings.

Navy leaders refused to remain on the defensive and were entirely capable of criticizing proposed AAF deployments for the assault on Japan. In his review of the Joint Planners' single-front deployment study, Admiral King found the aircraft deployment figures for the Pacific "unrealistic and unnecessary."[45] As he had no plans to limit aircraft carrier production and deployment, King's comment was almost certainly directed at the land-based air deployments that the AAF proposed.

By the spring of 1945 Secretary Forrestal believed that only an all-out effort to promote the navy and its accomplishments would guarantee the service's status with the public after Japan surrendered. He feared that large numbers of Americans did not understand how important a role the navy had played during the war and that the average citizen would not strongly support maintenance of a large postwar fleet. While Forrestal worked on getting the navy's message to the public, AAF officers maneuvered to limit naval aviation in the postwar world.

Quite naturally, AAF planners' criticism was primarily directed against the navy's air arm rather than its ship program, but where aircraft carriers were involved, the two issues overlapped. Because carrier strength provided the clearest rationale for the remainder of the shipbuilding program, an AAF attack on carrier production threatened the navy's entire force structure plan. The key target of AAF criticism was the navy's desire to continue expanding the number of carrier air groups by adding new carriers throughout 1946.

By late spring 1945, long-range strategic plans anticipated that the final invasion of Honshu would take place by March 1946, and army planners began to question whether the United States had any reason to continue increasing navy air power beyond that date. During the year following the scheduled invasion date, the navy planned to add six aircraft carriers and sixteen escort carriers, along with a battleship, twenty cruisers, and numerous smaller combatants.[46] The number of tactical combat aircraft in navy hands was scheduled to increase from 6,000 in April 1945 to 9,500 two years later, primarily due to the number of new aircraft carriers set to enter service.[47]

These deployment plans appeared excessive to army and AAF planners on the Joint War Plans Committee. Writing just after V-E Day, one OPD officer reflected the ambivalence of army planners over the apparently excessive navy expansion program for carrier aircraft: "As to what

THE UNSINKABLE FLEET

excuse the Navy can present to an inquiring Congress or Executive for the projected aircraft increases during calendar 1946, I am at a loss to say. . . . Further, it is beyond me to explain how authorization for such a program has apparently gotten by the Bureau of the Budget. . . . My guess is that a day of reckoning is near, but I'm afraid we can't get our oar in on a sister service's business."[48]

If this hands-off attitude reflected the views of most planners, it quickly changed. By June, army and AAF representatives were demanding that the JWPC produce military deployment estimates "capable of being defended before the American people."[49] Army and navy planners on the JWPC failed to agree on the crucial issue of whether navy carrier aviation should continue to expand beyond the March 1946 date set for the invasion of Honshu. Just as in previous years, the planners issued a split report on an issue that had impact on service strengths, in this case the desirable military deployment for defeating Japan. Navy representatives saw no problem with their service's plans to bring more than twenty carriers into service after March 1946. They argued that the new ships were needed due to uncertainty over future losses. In any case, the building program had already been approved at the "highest levels" and therefore needed no further justification.[50]

Army and AAF planners refused to accept that additional airplanes would be needed after the Honshu invasion (Operation Coronet) landed major ground forces on the Tokyo plain. Surely the presence of substantial numbers of AAF units operating from captured airfields on Kyushu was intended to obviate the need for even more carrier task forces. As one army paper asked, if "Jap[anese] air forces will have been almost completely annihilated after Coronet, why do we anticipate a need for larger carrier forces for this period?"[51]

Whatever arguments the army planners might make, the combat ship construction program was still firmly under navy control. Only the new president had the power to alter the status quo, and Harry S. Truman was still too occupied with pressing political and strategic issues to question the seasoned military and civilian leaders he had inherited from Roosevelt. Under Admiral King's supervision, the navy's own Cutback Committee showed no inclination to curb fleet expansion. Under the bootstrapping rationale the committee had employed since 1944, the "requirement" for more carriers created a further requirement for all manner of other combatants to escort and support them. Even after

Germany's surrender in May 1945, the committee refused to recommend any reductions in the construction schedule.

In its first report after V-E Day, the Cutback Committee cited its usual arguments on the possibility of heavy losses and the large number of ships expected to be out of action due to battle damage. However, it also argued that victory over Germany had actually exacerbated navy repair problems by creating a complacent attitude among shipyard workers, who were leaving the yards by the thousands. Thus, the committee argued, longer repair layovers caused in part by Germany's defeat actually increased the number of ships the fleet would require in service in order to keep operational task forces up to strength.[52] The committee concluded that the navy would have to build more ships because euphoria after V-E Day would prevent it from adequately repairing the ones it already had.

By this very late stage of the war, plans for the postwar navy significantly affected how all concerned viewed the existing building program. Without going into a detailed examination of this issue, a few facts are worth noting. The postwar navy would undoubtedly be smaller than the wartime fleet, even if the enormous number of inactive mothballed ships (6 battleships, 47 cruisers, 23 aircraft carriers, and 200 destroyers, among others) were counted.[53] The postwar plan presented by Admiral King to Forrestal in late April 1945 anticipated that 243 combatants would be scrapped after the war, including 7 battleships, 19 cruisers, 4 carriers, and 111 destroyers. In terms of pure numbers, cancellation of the remaining ships on order in the spring of 1945 would have little or no effect on plans for the active postwar fleet.

In the five years since the building program took shape, the navy's methods for gauging its overall force requirements had undergone very few changes. When Forrestal testified before Congress in June 1945, he noted that the postwar U.S. Navy should be large enough to have superiority over any possible combination of foes in the western Atlantic or the Pacific.[54] Navy leaders still employed the same formula for fleet strength in 1945 that planners had used in 1938 and 1939, but they had no specific future opponent against which to plan. For this reason, any requirements estimates were necessarily tentative and short-term in nature.[55]

Although naval leaders' advocacy of this yardstick for measuring fleet requirements showed a due appreciation for American industrial capacity, such a course may have been politically unwise in the face of an inevitable postwar stand-down. With Britain as the only other nation with a fleet of any consequence, members of Congress might well have wondered why the navy sought to base its postwar strength on the need to outnumber our closest ally. Of course, most American military leaders did not anticipate a war with Britain, but they had found that a preponderance of force within a coalition gave the dominant military power greater weight in any interallied debates, a consideration that received explicit acknowledgment in planning postwar fleet strength.[56] Nevertheless, the lack of potential naval enemies undermined navy leaders' reliance on the old prewar strategic formulas for setting fleet strength.

Naval leaders also faced the problem of postwar modernization. Because almost all of the units on order in 1945 were follow-ons to standardized types already in service, technological improvements would probably consist of useful but not groundbreaking wartime adjustments. Thus, most ships still on the ways could be described as newer but not necessarily more modern than their predecessors. To continue the current program in the name of postwar preparedness might not provide returns commensurate with the financial and political costs of doing so. At least one officer in King's postwar planning branch adopted this view. He argued that the inevitable return to peacetime methods would slow ship construction after the war, pushing back completion dates even further into the future. He therefore recommended cutting the present program for battleships and cruisers and directing efforts into designing and then building ships of more modern design.[57]

By late spring, navy leaders were already proposing postwar construction programs specifically intended to provide the fleet with modern designs. Foiled in the attempt to increase the war program, Secretary Forrestal sought to improve the fleet by contracting for new designs in the name of postwar preparedness. In late March, just days after Byrnes had forced the cancellation of the eighty-four-ship program that Vinson and King proposed, Admiral Horne urged the CNO to adopt a much smaller program featuring ships of the most advanced design.[58] Forrestal favored this approach and soon after V-E Day ordered the bureaus to develop plans for new classes of aircraft carriers, antiaircraft cruisers, destroyers, and submarines. These were to be the best designs possible; the only restriction was that each type be suitable for mass production.

Forrestal noted that he hoped to get immediate approval for twelve new ships in order to keep alive the art of combatant design and construction, adding that his proposal was "not a war program."[59]

The secretary sought to gain approval for the program on the basis of preserving the navy's technological and industrial base. Explaining the need for additional construction to the new president, Forrestal stated that the requirements of wartime mass production had frozen the designs of many ship types, the major exceptions being heavy and light cruisers. He therefore asked Truman to approve construction of a handful of new antiaircraft cruisers, destroyers, and submarines in order to help maintain the design bureaus and shipyards capable of producing advanced combatants.[60] Similar letters went out to the chairs of the House and Senate Naval Affairs Committees.[61] In all cases, Forrestal stressed that the ships were intended for postwar service only.

In late June 1945 Forrestal directed the General Board to work this expansion proposal into a more comprehensive plan for postwar building that he could present to congressional leaders anxious for information on navy intentions.[62] Although little came of these proposals during the war, the overt change to postwar construction planning constituted a tacit admission that the navy had on hand or was building all the ships it would need to prosecute the Pacific campaign. On the issue of wartime requirements, only the question of further cutbacks remained.

In light of progress at the front and the impending invasion of Japan, eventually even Admiral King's closest staff raised doubts about the wisdom of continuing the building program as established. In October 1944 King had created the new position of deputy COMINCH/deputy CNO to assist him in handling military policy. This important post went to Adm. Richard Edwards, who had been King's chief of staff in the COMINCH organization. In this new capacity Edwards took over responsibility for postwar planning and policing the construction program, allowing Admiral Horne to concentrate on logistics.[63]

Edwards proved to be less enthusiastic than Horne about going forward with all approved combatants come what may. In early June he wrote to King of his concerns about the program being oversized. Long experience with the CNO prevented him from actually questioning his chief's judgment, however. "I am beginning to think that the cruiser program is possibly too large," Edwards wrote. "At the present time there are 46 under construction or authorized. However, in view of the uncertainties of the future, it does not seem desirable to make any cutback as yet."[64]

While the CNO's staff edged toward a debate on whether to continue shipbuilding without letup, Forrestal made up his mind. During prolonged congressional testimony and debates over unification, the secretary had grown acutely sensitive to the possibility that overbuilding would damage the navy's public image and thereby limit its postwar prospects. Forrestal also had to consider the wishes of his new commander in chief, who had made his reputation heading investigations of military overspending. Truman asked Forrestal in early July to tell his subordinates that the president demanded "the most exacting review of expenditures" where there was even the slightest possibility of misuse of government funds.[65]

Faced with possible presidential intervention, Forrestal decided to act. On 24 July 1945, just three weeks before the war ended, the secretary urged Admiral King to terminate construction on a portion of the current program in order to save money. Forrestal warned that this step was necessary to protect "the Navy's future position with the country and particularly with the taxpayers."[66] Navy leaders discussed the issue at the next Top Policy Group meeting, where they learned that the navy was building 213 combatants, including 14 carriers, 26 escort carriers, and 42 cruisers.[67] When someone pointed out that the navy could save more than $2 billion by cutting these ships, King reminded the group that the ships currently under construction would form the backbone of the postwar fleet.

By this point even the CNO could no longer deny that the Japanese were on the brink. On the last day of July the Cutback Committee reported that certain ships could be cut from the program on the assumption that any vessel completed after April 1946 would not be vital to winning the war—the same argument army and AAF planners had used for the previous three or four months. Based on this assumption, the committee believed that the navy could safely cut two carriers, twelve escort carriers, thirteen cruisers, seven destroyers, and nineteen auxiliary ships from the program, with the provision that construction would start again if losses proved heavier than expected.[68]

In his formal reply to Forrestal's plea for cutbacks, Admiral King recommended cutting the ships that the committee specified. He noted that

these cuts would save the navy $419 million and added that such can-
cellations were possible only because U.S. losses had been lighter than
expected, whereas Japanese losses had been extremely heavy. The CNO
pointed out that the expendable ships had been included in the program
as insurance against heavy losses (the same claim he made regarding the
eighty-four-ship program defeated by Byrnes), which now appeared
unlikely. However, he noted that the navy would continue work on
some ships not due for completion by April 1946, notably the newly
designed rapid-fire light and heavy cruisers and the two remaining unfinished battleships.[69]

King's proposal failed to satisfy Forrestal, who ordered even deeper
cuts. In early August he directed the CNO to terminate contracts for
one battleship, two carriers, sixteen escort carriers, twenty cruisers,
eleven destroyers, and six submarines.[70] Less than a week later the news
broke that Japan had accepted Allied surrender terms. Both the war and
the wartime building program had finally come to an end.

The war's end failed to settle the issue of cutbacks in navy shipbuilding. In late August the Cutback Committee recommended that it
be disbanded but not before urging the CNO to restore plans for building five cruisers of advanced design that Forrestal had canceled.[71] By
early September the navy had reduced the building program for combatants from 202 to 146 ships; including auxiliaries, the vessels cut
totaled almost 1 million tons.[72]

These cuts were only the beginning. Over the next several months
navy planners fought a rear-guard action against pressure for ever-
deeper reductions in planned construction. By year's end Forrestal was
willing to reduce the combatant building program to just under eighty
ships on the condition that work on new types could start after further
research (including atomic bomb tests) provided more information on
the best postwar designs.[73] Because work on many ships had advanced
beyond the point where cancellation would produce any savings, however, new units continued to join the fleet. From the war's end through
1947, the navy succeeded in adding twelve carriers, ten escort carriers,
twenty cruisers, seventy-seven destroyers, and thirty-two submarines
from the war program.[74] Thus, the successful defense of wartime building plans helped the navy maintain the fleet and the shipbuilding industry through the early years of the cold war.

CONCLUSION

During World War II the United States conceived and carried out a program to build a fleet capable of taking on any possible combination of enemies. The navy that resulted reflected the fears of 1940, tempered by the harsh experiences of 1941 and 1942. By 1943 and 1944 the early fears had been replaced by a burning determination to bring the war home to America's enemies, especially to Imperial Japan. Throughout the war the navy staff retained its determination to continue naval expansion. This continuity of purpose linked speculative prewar estimates with planned deployments for the final advance against Japan and with schemes designed to maintain postwar naval dominance.

All attempts to limit warship construction foundered on resistance by Admiral King and his subordinates, who were determined to justify and protect the fleet growing in American shipyards. Employing bureaucratic and political skills of a high order, the CNO used his position to shield navy combatant ship construction against all outside interference. He deftly turned aside all attempts to interfere seriously with navy expansion policy, giving in where necessary and holding firm or counterattacking whenever possible. The actions of King and his staff exerted a profound influence on the makeup of America's armed forces and ensured that the nation would end the war with the greatest fleet in history.

Several important factors combined to make the navy's defense of its fleet expansion program so successful. The tightly knit nature of the navy staff when compared with similar army planning organizations clearly contributed to the final result. Admiral King imposed a strict discipline on his two staffs, as he did in every command he held. The CNO's subordinates followed his lead without deviation, presenting navy critics with a united front at all levels of the joint staff system. The uniformly aggressive navy approach to joint planning consistently placed army representatives on the defensive, while army and civilian attempts to bring naval force planning under the joint umbrella met with a solid wall of resistance.

In contrast, the War Department staff lacked this top-to-bottom unanimity. Marshall remained ambivalent about his role in controlling navy growth and clung to his prewar belief that the entire system would work better if each service refrained from meddling in the other's growth plans. Navy leaders accepted, and indeed insisted on, this approach when dealing with navy policy but were quick to criticize army demands for men and equipment once the conflicts between the two service programs became apparent. Marshall's subordinates showed more willingness to question fleet expansion goals actively and demand a say in resource distribution, but they were undercut by their chief's reluctance to create interservice controversy. Significantly, most of the army documents that openly criticize navy intransigence are internal; only the most assertive War Department officers actually tried to force the fleet issue out into the open for debate and resolution.

Without the chief of staff's active support, army planners found themselves at a distinct disadvantage in the joint planning groups that attempted to study and rationalize American force structure and procurement. The makeup of the joint staff system itself aided the navy's efforts, for in each joint planning agency, only the navy members were considered qualified to evaluate the fleet's needs. Their army and AAF counterparts could criticize navy expansion plans but lacked the expertise to support their claims adequately.

In practice this lack of acknowledged expertise, together with interservice competition and unclear lines of joint authority, resulted in the multiservice agencies operating more like bargaining sessions rather than cooperative planning organs. Without support from Marshall, army planners found they could not force concessions on their navy counterparts, who were following the party line passed down from above. The drawn-out debates and criticism ultimately had no effect on navy planning, while in contrast the army quickly found that the shipping issue made its mobilization schedule vulnerable to public attack from navy and civilian leaders.

The navy staff's bureaucratic skill and zealous dedication to a long-range plan combined with America's reliance on its industrial might and its penchant for machine-oriented fighting forces to give Admiral King real advantages at the highest levels of procurement planning. America excelled at industrial production, and most U.S. leaders were determined to use this advantage to out-build the nation's enemies in a massive war of attrition. As the most machine-intensive branch of the armed services, the navy benefited from this national desire to achieve victory through increased industrial output.

During World War II American leaders adopted an "ethos of production" that greatly affected how the country fought the war. Most Americans believed that the nation's ability to out-build the Axis was the key to victory, and most military planners worked under the unstated corollary that if a weapon could be built, it should be built. The navy and to a lesser extent the AAF were machine-driven services; their force levels depended on the number of machines that could be built and manned. By trying to force cuts in ship construction, the navy's critics were fighting the unspoken assumption that the country would be doing less than it should if it failed to produce to its utmost. To argue against maximum war production, especially of fighting machines, was to go against the grain of the entire U.S. war effort.

The other side of the production ethos was a national abhorrence of a "mass" infantry army. Both leaders and the public associated the idea of a large ground army with the slaughter and frustration of World War I, even though actual experience showed that American manpower had brought that conflict to an end rather quickly and cheaply. A national fascination with industrial accomplishments made the idea of building a new ship more attractive than that of organizing more foot soldiers, if only because Americans seemed to believe that reliance on more and better machines would somehow make the war less costly in human terms.

The long-term nature of the navy's expansion plan contributed to this effect. Once facilities and work forces had been assembled and trained at great expense, once materials had been allocated and work begun, the building process represented an investment that most leaders were reluctant to sacrifice. After building was well under way, partially completed ships on the ways created their own nearly unassailable argument for the expenditure of more resources, including labor, materials, and crewmen.

The time required to build ships added another element that worked in favor of fleet expansion. It took a bold leader to declare in 1943 or even 1944 that ships in the construction pipeline would not be needed in 1945 and 1946, given the ever-present possibility of catastrophic losses that would take years to replace. The urge to provide insurance for whatever might occur two years in the future was nearly overwhelming and seemed to sway a number of leaders, even in 1945. Capital investment and long building times thus combined to give the entire process a momentum at least partially independent from strategic and operational considerations.

The reverse side of this coin was the inability or unwillingness of navy planners to agree on operational requirements. While prewar plans set building goals based on enemy fleet strength, during the war navy leaders correctly argued that the number of U.S. ships available, not enemy strength, controlled the tempo of offensive operations. Instead of asking about relative U.S.-Axis naval strength, critics of the navy program after the fall of 1943 should have framed their inquiry in terms of what scale and pace of attacks Allied strategy demanded and what risk of delay the Allies could accept should ship losses prove higher than expected.

Admiral King and his staff faced an entirely different problem when dealing with civilian leaders inside the Navy Department. Forrestal's objections to continued expansion stemmed from his desire to avoid political embarrassment that would damage the navy's postwar political influence. Here the contest involved officers who wanted the hardware in hand when the fighting stopped and civilians who believed that good will would provide more benefits in the long run. Given the longevity of the ships involved and America's notoriously short political memory, proponents of more building may well have been right. The fortuitous (for military budgets) appearance of the Soviet-U.S. rift and the search for new missions in the atomic age made the debate somewhat academic. The fleet would remain in a kind of stasis until leaders worked out the implications of new technologies and political alignments.

Conclusion

Finally, Admiral King's unique personality played a significant role in pushing through the navy program despite all resistance. Although King could compromise on peripheral issues, the CNO remained doctrinaire in his determination that he alone would decide what ships the fleet would procure. King's approach to this issue was somewhat parochial and rigid, but he did succeed in preventing encroachment on his domain.

Pursuing his vision of undisputed naval supremacy, King was willing to break promises on navy manpower limits and to alienate powerful civilian leaders. In the process he established his own undisputed control over fleet expansion policy, but only as long as the war lasted. While the country as a whole may have been better served by leaders who would rationalize national mobilization rather than exploit a flawed planning system, King demonstrated that he was a formidable bureaucratic infighter who would serve the navy's interests as he saw them.

NOTES

Abbreviations Used in the Notes

ABC	American-British Conversations
CCS	Combined Chiefs of Staff
CINCPAC	Commander in Chief, Pacific Fleet
COMINCH	Commander in Chief, U.S. Fleet
FDRL	Franklin D. Roosevelt Library
JCS	Joint Chiefs of Staff
NA	National Archives
NHC	Naval Historical Center, Washington, D.C.
OPD	War Department Operations Division
RG	Record Group
SecNav/CNO	Secretary of the Navy/Chief of Naval Operations
WPD	Army War Plans Division
00 Files	Double-Zero Office Files of Admiral King

Chapter 1. A Two-Ocean Fleet

1. Bureau of Ships, *An Administrative History of the Bureau of Ships during World War II*, 1:4.
2. Davis, *A Navy Second to None*, 359.
3. Reynolds, Jr., "America and a Two-Ocean Navy," 16.
4. Ibid., 29.
5. Ibid., 34.

6. Davis, *A Navy Second to None*, 390.
7. Reynolds, Jr., "America and a Two-Ocean Navy," 99–104.
8. Enders, "The Vinson Navy," 100–101.
9. Davis, *A Navy Second to None*, 374–78.
10. Chairman General Board to Secretary of the Navy, 7/25/38, Subject: "Ten-Year Shipbuilding Program," General Board 420.2, 1937–1938, RG 80, NA.
11. Memorandum by Captain Cooke, 11/6/39: Navy Strategic Plans Division series 5, box 89, NHC.
12. Richardson, *On the Treadmill to Pearl Harbor*, 56.
13. Statement of the Assistant Secretary of the Navy, 10/7/39, Records of the Navy Office of Budgets and Reports, Budget Preparations and Estimates, 1941–1948, RG 80, NA.
14. "Annual Estimate of the Situation of the Chief of Naval Operations for the Fiscal Year 1942," 4/15/40, SecNav/CNO Secret File 1940–41, L-1-1, RG 80, NA.
15. Furer, *Administration of the Navy Department in World War II*, 107–8.
16. Ibid., 123.
17. Miller, *War Plan Orange*, 224.
18. Ibid., 313.
19. Hayes, *The History of the Joint Chiefs of Staff in World War II*, 7.
20. Secretary, Joint Board to Joint Planning Committee, 11/12/38, Subject: "Study of Joint Action in Event of Violation of Monroe Doctrine by Fascist Powers," Joint Board 325, Serial 634, RG 225, NA.
21. Chart dated 12/15/38, Title: "Requirements of United States for Operations in Both Oceans Against Japanese, German, and Italian Strength, Built and Building," General Board 420.2, 1937–38, RG 80, NA.
22. Joint Planning Committee Exploratory Studies, 4/21/39, Joint Board 325, Serial 634, RG 225, NA.
23. General Board to Chief of Naval Operations, 5/2/39, Subject: "Two Ocean Navy," General Board 420.2, 1939, RG 80, NA.
24. Ibid.
25. Miller, *War Plan Orange*, 252–53.
26. Op-12 to Chief of Naval Operations, 9/26/39, Subject: "Two Ocean Navy—Numbers and Types," General Board 420.2, 1939, RG 80, NA.
27. Captain R. S. Crenshaw to Chief of Naval Operations, 10/24/39, Subject: "Increase of Navy-Special Program Twenty-Five Percent Increase of Authorization," Navy Strategic Plans Division series 5, box 89, NHC.
28. Memo on CNO Conference, 11/3/39, Subject: "Increase of the Navy-Special 25 Percent Increase of Authorization," General Board 420.2, 1939, RG 80, NA.
29. Chief of Naval Operations to Representative Vinson, 11/4/39, Harold R. Stark Papers, "Senate Naval Affairs Committee," NHC.
30. Albion, *Makers of Naval Policy, 1798–1947*, 513.
31. Congress, House, Committee on Naval Affairs, *Bill to Establish the Composition of the United States Navy*, 8 January 1940, 1719–21.

32. Statement of Admiral Harold R. Stark, Chief of Naval Operations, before the Naval Affairs Committee, 1/11/40, General Board 420.2 1940, RG 80, NA.
33. Congress, House, Debate on HR 8026, 2731–34.
34. Simpson III, "Harold Raynsford Stark," 121–22.
35. Congress, Senate, Committee on Naval Affairs, *Construction of Certain Naval Vessels,* 15 April 1940, 3.
36. Congress, Senate, Committee on Naval Affairs, *Hearing before the Committee on Naval Affairs on HR 8026,* 7 May 1940, 344–46.
37. Lowenthal, *Leadership and Indecision,* 241–42.
38. Leutze, *Bargaining for Supremacy,* 75, 85.
39. Joint Planning Committee, "Joint Army and Navy Basic War Plan Rainbow No. 4," 5/31/40, Joint Board 325, Serial 642–4, RG 225, NA.
40. Memorandum, General Board to Admiral Stark, 6/17/40, SecNav/CNO Secret File 1941, A1–3, RG 80, NA.
41. Congress, House, Committee on Naval Affairs, *Hearing on HR 10100,* 18 June 1940, 3578.
42. Walter, "Congressman Carl Vinson and Franklin D. Roosevelt," 303.
43. Congress, House, Debate on HR 10100, 9064–67.
44. Weinberg, *A World at Arms,* 175–76.
45. Congress, Senate, Debate on HR 10100, 9418–20.
46. Enders, "The Vinson Navy," 128–29.
47. Bureau of Ships, *An Administrative History of the Bureau of Ships during World War II,* 2:318.
48. Congress, House, Committee on Appropriations, *Navy Department Appropriation Bill for 1942,* 18 February 1941, 238–39.
49. Lobdell, "Frank Knox," 677.
50. Memorandum, Director Navy War Plans Division to Assistant CNO, 7/25/41, Subject: "Building Program, Combat Ships Fiscal Year 1943," SecNav/CNO Confidential File 1941, A1–3, RG 80, NA.
51. Chairman, General Board to Secretary of the Navy, 7/18/41, Subject: "Building Program, Combatant Ships-Fiscal Year 1943," SecNav/CNO Confidential File 1941, A1–3, RG 80, NA.
52. Testimony of Rear Admiral R. K. Turner, 6/27/41, General Board Hearings, 1941, RG 80, NA.
53. Director, War Plans Division to Assistant CNO, 7/25/41, Subject: "Building Program-Combatant Ships, Fiscal Year 1943," Navy Strategic Plans Division series 5, box 89, NHC.
54. Buell, *Master of Sea Power,* 123–27.
55. Admiral King to General Board, 7/30/41, Subject: "Priorities in Two-Ocean Navy Building Program," General Board 420.2 1941–1942, RG 80, NA.
56. Chief of Naval Operations to General Board, 9/9/41, Subject: "Extension of Current Building Program," General Board 420.2 1941–1942, RG 80, NA.
57. Matloff and Snell, *Strategic Planning for Coalition Warfare, 1941–1942,* 32–48.

58. Under Secretary of War to Secretary of War, 4/18/41, Subject: "Ultimate Munitions Production Essential to Safety of America," WPD 4494, RG 165, NA.

59. Watson, *Chief of Staff: Prewar Plans and Preparations,* 335–36.

60. Wedemeyer, *Wedemeyer Reports!* 16.

61. Acting Assistant Chief of Staff, War Plans Division, to Chief of Staff, 8/29/41, Subject: "Ultimate Production Requirements," WPD 4494–1, RG 165, NA.

62. Acting Assistant Chief of Staff, War Plans Division, to Admiral Turner, 9/3/41, Subject: "Ultimate Production Requirements," WPD 4494–6, RG 165, NA.

63. Chief of Staff to Secretary of War, 9/10/41, WPD 4494–9, RG 165, NA.

64. Report, "Army-Navy Estimate of U.S. Overall Production Requirements," appendix 2, part 2, section 2, 9/11/41, Joint Board 355, serial 707, RG 225, NA (hereafter, Ultimate Requirements Study).

65. Wedemeyer, *Wedemeyer Reports!* 74–75.

66. Kirkpatrick, *An Unknown Future and a Doubtful Present,* 84–91.

67. Ultimate Requirements Study, appendix 2, part 2, section 1.

68. Futrell, *Ideas, Concepts, Doctrine,* 44–46.

69. Ultimate Requirements Study, appendix 2, part 3.

70. Ultimate Requirements Study, appendix 1.

71. Ibid.

72. Acting Assistant Chief of Staff, War Plans Division, to Chief of Staff, 9/10/41, Subject: "U.S. Over-all Production Requirements," WPD 4494–10, RG 165, NA.

73. Acting Assistant Chief of Staff, War Plans Division, to Chief of Staff, 9/12/41, Subject: "Ultimate Tonnage Requirements," WPD 2789–12, RG 165, NA.

74. Chief of Staff to Admiral Stark, no date but sent 9/10/41, Subject: "U.S. Over-all Production Requirements," WPD 4494–10, RG 165, NA.

CHAPTER 2. The Impact of Pearl Harbor, 1942

1. Bureau of Ships, "U.S. Navy Shipbuilding Program: Statistical Summary of Progress," 1/1/42, Bureau of Ships World War II Command File, NHC.

2. Admiral Stark to the President, 12/11/41, General Board 420.2, 1941–1942, RG 80, NA.

3. Chairman, General Board, to Secretary of the Navy, 1/12/42, Subject: "Naval Requirements of Ships for Maximum War Efforts," General Board 420.2, 1941–42, RG 80, NA.

4. C. A. Jones to Senator David Walsh, 1/26/42, Bureau of Ships General Correspondence 1940–1945, A1–3, RG 19, NA.

5. Report by the Office of the Chief of Naval Operations, "Combatant Ship-building, 1-1-42 to 7-1-46," 133–34.

6. King and Whitehall, *Fleet Admiral King,* 356.
7. Captain Duncan to Admiral King, 3/5/42, Subject: "Aircraft Carriers—Future Provision For," King Manuscript Files, March 1942, NHC.
8. Minutes of Conversations between COMINCH and Commander-in-Chief, Pacific Fleet, 4/27/42, King Manuscript Files, April 1942, NHC.
9. General Board to Secretary of the Navy, 4/24/42, Subject: "1943–1944 Combatant Shipbuilding Program," General Board 420.2, 1941–1942, RG 80, NA.
10. Chief of Naval Operations to Secretary of the Navy, 5/8/42, Subject: "1943–1944 Combatant Ships Building Program," 00 Files 1942–1947, box 1, folder 1, NHC.
11. King and Whitehall, *Fleet Admiral King,* 298.
12. President to Secretary of the Navy, 5/22/42, 00 Files 1942–1947, box 1, folder 12, NHC.
13. Admiral King to the President, 5/29/42, Subject: "Building Program, 1943–1944," King Manuscript Files, May 1942, NHC.
14. President to Secretary of the Navy, 8/12/42 and President to Admiral Leahy, 9/16/42, both in SecNav/CNO Secret File 1942, A3–1, RG 80, NA.
15. General Board to Secretary of the Navy, 10/6/42, Subject: "Composition of Carrier Task Groups-Cruisers versus 2100-Ton Destroyers," SecNav/CNO Secret File 1942, A3–1, RG 80, NA
16. Secretary of the Navy to the President, 10/23/42, Subject: "Composition of Carrier Task Groups," Map Room Files, box 162, folder A2–A3, FDRL.
17. President to the Secretary of the Navy, 8/12/42, Map Room Files, box 162, folder A1–3, FDRL.
18. President to Secretary of the Navy, 9/14/42, Map Room Files, box 162, folder A1–3, FDRL.
19. Report by the Office of the Chief of Naval Operations, "Combatant Ship-building, 1-1-42 to 7-1-46," 147.
20. Congress, House, Representative Vinson Speaking for HR 7184, 5374–75.
21. Enders, "The Vinson Navy," 137.
22. Congress, House, Committee on Naval Affairs, *To Establish the Composition of the U.S. Navy,* 17 June 1942, 4–6.
23. Acting Director, Bureau of Budget, to President, 7/6/42, Subject: "Proposed Authorizations for Naval Vessels, HR 7159 and HR 7184," SecNav/CNO Confidential File 1942, A18–3, RG 80, NA.
24. Bureau of Ships, *An Administrative History of the Bureau of Ships during World War II,* 2:319–20.
25. Secretary of the Navy to the President, 7/18/42, SecNav/CNO Confidential File 1942, A1–3, RG 80, NA.
26. "General Board Summary of Building Program, 1943–44," 11/24/42, General Board 420.2 1941–42, RG 80, NA.
27. Hewes, Jr., *From Root to McNamara,* 82–84.
28. Historical Section, Commander in Chief, U.S. Fleet, first draft narrative, *Commander in Chief,* 55.

29. Ibid., 63–64.
30. Davis, *The History of the Joint Chiefs of Staff,* 2:264.
31. Cline, *Washington Command Post: The Operations Division,* 103.
32. Davis, *The History of the Joint Chiefs of Staff,* 2:278–79.
33. Ibid., 358.
34. Interview of Lt. Gen. Marshall S. Carter (Ret.).
35. Interview of Adm. Donald B. Duncan.
36. Acting Chief of Staff to Secretariat, Joint Chiefs of Staff, 1/16/43, Title: JCS 202, Subject: "War Planning Agencies," ABC 381 (12-19-42) section 1, RG 165, NA.
37. Minutes, Joint Chiefs of Staff 50th Meeting, 1/19/43, CCS 334 JCS Meetings (11-10-42), RG 218, NA.
38. Directive from Joint Chiefs of Staff to Committee members, 1/20/43, Title: JCS 202/1/D, Subject: "War Planning Agencies," CCS 300 (1-8-43) section 1, RG 218, NA.
39. Army Members of Subcommittee to Joint Staff Planners, 2/2/43, Title: JPS 123, Subject: "War Planning Agencies," ABC 381 (12-19-42) section 1, RG 165, NA.
40. Committee on JCS War Planning Agencies to Joint Chiefs of Staff, 3/25/43, Title: JCS 202/2, Subject: "War Planning Agencies," ABC 381 (12-19-42) section 1, RG 165, NA.
41. Minutes, Joint Chiefs of Staff 93d Meeting, 6/20/43, CCS 334 JCS Meetings (5-21-43), RG 218, NA.
42. Charter of Joint War Plans Committee, Title: JCS 202/14/D, ABC 381 UN (1-23-42) section 3–B, RG 165, NA.
43. Admiral King to Secretary of the Navy, 2/20/42, Subject: "Priorities of Production of Material," King Manuscript Files, February 1942, NHC.
44. Chief of Naval Operations to the President via the Secretary of the Navy, 3/26/42, Subject: "Priorities for Naval Shipbuilding Program," King Manuscript Files, March 1942, NHC.
45. President to Donald Nelson, 5/1/42, 00 Files 1941–1946, box 35, folder 130, NHC.
46. Report by the Office of the Chief of Naval Operations, "Combatant Shipbuilding, 1-1-42 to 7-1-46," 66.
47. Matloff and Snell, *Strategic Planning for Coalition Warfare, 1941–1942,* 266–68.
48. Ibid., 283–84.
49. Army Chief of Staff to the President, 8/10/42, Subject: "Augmentation of the Army in 1943," Chief of Staff Top Secret File 1941–1943, 320.2, RG 165, NA.
50. Chief of Staff to Joint Chiefs of Staff, 8/24/42, ABC 370.01 (7-25-42) section 1, RG 165, NA.
51. Assistant Chief of Staff G-3 to Chief of Staff, 7/3/42, Subject: "Troop Basis for Calendar Year 1943," Chief of Staff Correspondence File 1942–43, 320.2 section 6, RG 165, NA.

52. Acting Director, Bureau of the Budget, to the President, 8/22/42, Chief of Staff Correspondence File 1942–43, 320.2 section 5, RG 165, NA.
53. President to Admiral King, 8/24/42, ABC 370.01 (7-25-42) section 1, RG 165, NA.
54. Chief of Staff to Chief of Naval Operations, 8/26/42, Chief of Staff Correspondence File 1942–43, 320.2 section 5, RG 165, NA.
55. Chief of Naval Operations to Chief of Staff, 8/27/42, Subject: "Strength of Army for Calendar Year 1943," OPD 320.2 case 374, RG 165, NA.
56. Ibid.
57. Chief of Staff to President, 8/42, Chief of Staff Top Secret Correspondence File 1941–1943, 320.2, RG 165, NA.
58. Army Member, Joint U.S. Strategic Committee, to Chief, Strategic Plans and Policy Group, Operations Division, 7/21/42, Subject: "Estimate of Air and Ground Forces (Troop Basis as of 4/1/44)," ABC 381 (9-25-41) section 2, RG 165, NA.
59. Senior Army Member, Joint U.S. Strategic Committee, to Chief, Strategic Plans and Policy Group, Operations Division, 7/21/42, Subject: "Estimate of Air and Ground Forces (Shipping Implications as of 4/1/44)," ABC 381 (9-25-41) section 2, RG 165, NA.
60. Commanding General, Services of Supply to Assistant Chief of Staff, Operations Division, 7/28/42, Subject: "Estimate of Air and Ground Forces (Shipping Implications as of April 1, 1944)," OPD 320.2 case 268, RG 165, NA.
61. Joint U.S. Strategic Committee to Joint Staff Planners, 9/2/42, Title: JPS 53, Subject: "Personnel Strength for U.S. Armed Forces," ABC 370.01 (7-25-42) section 1, RG 165, NA.
62. Ibid.
63. Ibid.
64. Assistant Chief of Staff, G-3 to Wedemeyer, 9/7/42, ABC 370.01 (7-25-42) section 1, RG 165, NA.
65. Minutes of Joint Staff Planners 32d Meeting, 8/31/42, CCS 334 JPS Meetings (4-7-42), RG 218, NA.
66. Unsigned memo to JPS, 9/2/42, Subject: "Distribution of Manpower to the Armed Forces," ABC 370.01 (7-25-42) section 1, RG 165, NA.
67. Notes on JPS 34th Meeting, 9/9/42, ABC 370.01 (7-25-42) section 1, RG 165, NA.
68. Directive to Joint Staff Planners, 9/7/42, Title: JPS 57/D, Subject: "Troop Bases for All Services, Calendar Year 1943," CCS 320.2 (7-25-42) section 1, RG 218, NA.
69. Joint Chiefs of Staff to Director, Selective Service System, 9/1/42, Subject: "Manpower Available for the Armed Forces," CCS 320.2 (7-25-42) section 1, RG 218, NA.
70. Director, Selective Service System, to Secretary, Joint Chiefs of Staff, 9/10/42, Subject: "Requested Data," CCS 320.2 (7-25-42) section 1, RG 218, NA.
71. Flynn, *The Mess in Washington,* 16.

72. Bureau of the Budget, *The United States at War,* 184–89.
73. Joint Chiefs of Staff to Chairman, War Manpower Commission, 9/12/42, ABC 370.01 (7-25-42) section 1, RG 165, NA.
74. Chairman, War Manpower Commission, to Secretary, Joint Chiefs of Staff, 9/16/42, ABC 370.01 (7-25-42) section 1, RG 165, NA.
75. Minutes, Joint Staff Planners 34th Meeting, 9/9/42, CCS 334 JPS Meetings (4-7-42), RG 218, NA.
76. Joint Staff Planners Subcommittee to Joint Staff Planners, 9/21/42, Title: JPS 57/3, Subject: "Troop Bases for All Services, Calendar Year 1943," ABC 370.01 (7-25-42) section 1, RG 165, NA.
77. Joint Staff Planners to Joint Chiefs of Staff, 9/27/42, Title: JCS 115, Subject: "Troop Bases for All Services, Calendar Year 1943," ABC 370.01 (7-25-42) section 1, RG 165, NA.
78. Chief, Strategy and Policy Group, Operations Division, to Colonel Young, 10/15/42, Chief of Staff Top Secret Correspondence File 1941–1943, 320.2, RG 165, NA.
79. Notes on JCS 35th Meeting, 9/29/42, ABC 370.01 (7-25-42) section 1, RG 165, NA.

Chapter 3. The Apparatus of Growth

1. Bureau of Ships, *An Administrative History of the Bureau of Ships during World War II,* 1:5.
2. Ibid., 1:14.
3. Reynolds, "America and a Two-Ocean Navy," 39.
4. Congress, Senate, *Investigation of the National Defense Program,* 9 July 1941, 1435.
5. Congress, Senate, *Debate on HR 10100,* 10 July 1940, 9412.
6. Congress, Senate, Committee on Naval Affairs, *Authorizing Major Alterations to Certain Naval Vessels,* 27 January 1941, 9
7. Congress, Senate, Committee on Naval Affairs, *Additional Shipbuilding, Ship Repair,* 15 July 1941, 5.
8. Bureau of Yards and Docks, *Building the Navy's Bases in World War II,* 1:169.
9. Hooks, *Forging the Military-Industrial Complex,* 158.
10. Bureau of Yards and Docks, *Building the Navy's Bases in World War II,* 1:174–75.
11. Winslow III, *Portsmouth Built,* 86.
12. McVoy, Rinehart, and Palmer, "The Roosevelt Resurgence," 179.
13. Ibid., 183.
14. Barksdale, Jr., "History of the Norfolk Navy Yard in World War II," 53.
15. Annual Report of the Secretary of the Navy to the President, Fiscal Year 1945, A–99.
16. Lane, *Ships for Victory,* 153.

17. Smith and Brown, "Shipyard Statistics," 1:165–67.
18. Congress, Senate, Committee on Appropriations, *Second Supplemental Defense Appropriation Bill for 1941,* 13 August 1940, 169.
19. Congress, House, Committee on Appropriations, *Navy Department Appropriation Bill for 1942,* 18 February 1941, 667–68.
20. Ibid., 239.
21. Bureau of Ships, *An Administrative History of the Bureau of Ships during World War II,* 2:164–65.
22. Ibid., 175.
23. Farr and Bostwick, *Shipbuilding at Cramp & Sons,* 14, 56.
24. Smith, *The Army and Economic Mobilization,* 459–60.
25. Bureau of Ships, *An Administrative History of the Bureau of Ships during World War II,* 2:186–88.
26. Connery, *The Navy and the Industrial Mobilization,* 349.
27. White, *Billions for Defense,* 74.
28. *Fifty Years,* 55.
29. Snow, *Bath Iron Works,* 327–29.
30. Weir, *Forged in War,* 22–23.
31. Friedman, *U.S. Destroyers,* 152.
32. Bureau of Ships, *An Administrative History of the Bureau of Ships during World War II,* Appendix 9, 9.
33. Silverstone, *U.S. Warships of World War II,* 164–66.
34. Heiner, *Henry J. Kaiser,* 145–46.
35. Lane, *Ships for Victory,* 608.
36. Congress, House, Committee on Appropriations, *Navy Department Appropriation Bill for 1945,* 18 March 1944, 952.
37. Assistant Secretary of the Navy to Chairman, General Board, 5/23/40, Subject: "Readiness of the Naval Establishment to Meet a Serious Emergency," SecNav/CNO Secret File 1940–1941, A16–1, RG 80, NA.
38. Chief, Bureau of Ordnance to Director of Budget and Reports, 6/16/41, Subject: "Who Is Behind and Why," SecNav/CNO Confidential File 1940–1941, A16–1, RG 80, NA.
39. Bureau of Ships to General Board, 6/26/41, General Board 420.2, 1941–1942, RG 80, NA.
40. Congress, House, Committee on Appropriations, *Navy Department Appropriation Bill for 1942,* 17 February 1941, 319.
41. Congress, House, Committee on Appropriations, *Supplemental Navy Department Appropriation Bill for 1943,* 18 February 1943, 335.
42. Congress, House, Committee on Appropriations, *Navy Department Appropriation Bill for 1941,* 27 May 1940, 2.
43. Congress, House, Committee on Appropriations, *Navy Department Appropriation Bill for 1942,* 2 February 1941, 9.
44. King, *U.S. Navy at War, 1941–1945,* 149.
45. Mansfield, *Historical Review,* 89.
46. Lott, *A Long Line of Ships,* 221.

47. Lane, *Ships for Victory,* 250.
48. Congress, House, Committee on Appropriations, *Navy Department Appropriation Bill for 1945,* 18 March 1944, 944.
49. Congress, House, Committee on Naval Affairs, *Investigation of the Progress of the War Effort,* 80.
50. Bureau of Ships Memorandum, 2/14/44, Subject: "Progress of Naval Shipbuilding Program in 1943," Navy Library Microfiche F-157, NHC.
51. Snow, *Bath Iron Works,* 332.
52. Gemery and Hogendorn, "The Microeconomic Bases of Short-Run Learning Curves," 161–63.
53. Congress, House, Committee on Appropriations, *Navy Department Appropriation Bill for 1945,* 18 March 1944, 948.
54. Bureau of Ships Memorandum, 2/14/44, "Progress of Naval Shipbuilding Program in 1943."
55. Gene Duffield to Secretary of the Navy, 10/30/44, Records of Secretary of the Navy James Forrestal, 1944–1947, 42-1-25, RG 80, NA.
56. Congress, House, Committee on Appropriations, *Navy Department Appropriation Bill for 1946,* 30 March 1945, 521–22.
57. Ibid., 530.
58. Secretary of the Navy to Chairman, War Production Board, 1/29/45, SecNav/CNO Secret File 1945, A1–3, RG 80, NA.
59. Bureau of Yards and Docks, *Building the Navy's Bases in World War II,* 1:210–13.
60. Congress, House, Committee on Appropriations, *Navy Department Appropriation Bill for 1942,* 25 February 1941, 805–7.
61. Furer, *Administration of the Navy Department,* 904.
62. Bureau of Ships, *An Administrative History of the Bureau of Ships during World War II,* 1:42–44.
63. Albion, *Makers of Naval Policy, 1798–1947,* 530.
64. Hoopes and Brinkley, *Driven Patriot,* 137–39.
65. Furer, *Administration of the Navy Department,* 840.
66. Connery, *The Navy and Industrial Mobilization in World War II,* 72–73.
67. Hoopes and Brinkley, *Driven Patriot,* 162–63.
68. Connery, *The Navy and Industrial Mobilization in World War II,* 147.
69. Ibid., 392–93.
70. Hoopes and Brinkley, *Driven Patriot,* 164.
71. Congress, House, *Navy Department Appropriation Bill for 1943, Hearings before the Committee on Appropriations,* 12 January 1942, 9.
72. Quoted in Buell, *Master of Sea Power,* 528–29.
73. Chief of Naval Operations to listed officers, 3/17/42, Subject: "Military Organization of the Navy Department," King Manuscript Files, March 1942, NHC.
74. Vice Admiral Robinson to Chief of Naval Operations, 5/23/42, Subject: "Reorganization of the Navy Department," King Manuscript Files, May 1942, NHC.

75. Albion, *Makers of Naval Policy, 1798–1947*, 534.
76. Admiral Sexton to Chief of Naval Operations, 5/29/42, Subject: "Navy Department Organization," King Manuscript Files, May 1942, NHC.
77. Buell, *Master of Sea Power*, 236.
78. Albion, *Makers of Naval Policy, 1798–1947*, 537.
79. Rogow, *James Forrestal*, 102.
80. Lobdell, "Frank Knox," in *American Secretaries of the Navy*, ed. Coletta, 713–14.
81. Ibid., 715.
82. Buell, *Master of Sea Power*, 237.
83. Albion, *Makers of Naval Policy, 1798–1947*, 539.
84. Hoopes and Brinkley, *Driven Patriot*, 179.

CHAPTER 4. Holding the Line on Resource Allocations, 1942–1943

1. Chairman, War Production Board, to Joint Chiefs of Staff, 10/19/42, ABC 400 (2-17-42) section 3, RG 165, NA.
2. Bureau of the Budget, *The United States at War*, 105, 380.
3. Minutes, Joint Chiefs of Staff 38th Meeting, 10/20/42, ABC 400 (2-17-42) section 3, RG 165, NA.
4. President to Chairman, War Production Board, 10/29/42, ABC 400 (2-17-42) section 3, RG 165, NA.
5. "Victory Program" Study by Air War Plans Division, 1/6/42, WPD 4494 (misc.), RG 165, NA.
6. Major Magruder to Col. Wedemeyer, 12/4/41, Subject: "Notes Concerning Victory Program," WPD 4494 (misc.), RG 165, NA.
7. Chief of Naval Operations to Joint Board, 11/26/41, Subject: "Review of Priorities for the Four-engine Bomber Program," WPD 3807–103, RG 165, NA.
8. Joint U.S. Strategic Committee to Joint Staff Planners, 10/20/42, Title: JPS 151/1, Subject: "Priorities in Production of Munitions Based on Strategic Considerations," ABC 400 (2-17-42) section 3, RG 165, NA.
9. Memorandum by Navy Members of Joint Staff Planners, 10/30/42, Subject: "Priorities in Production of Munitions Based on Strategic Considerations," ABC 400 (2-17-42) section 3, RG 165, NA.
10. Minutes, Joint Staff Planners 44th Meeting, 11/4/42, ABC 400 (2-17-42) section 3, RG 165, NA.
11. Chief, Office of Procurement and Material, to Commander in Chief, U.S. Fleet, 11/3/42, Subject: "Aircraft Program—Effect of Machine Tool Priority on Naval Program," ABC 413.1 (11-5-42) RG 165, NA.
12. Minutes, Joint Chiefs of Staff 41st Meeting, 11/10/42, ABC 400 (2-17-42) section 3, RG 165, NA.
13. Joint Staff Planners to Joint Chiefs of Staff, 11/17/42, Title: JCS 146/1, Subject: "Priorities in Production of Munitions Based on Strategic Considerations," ABC 400 (2-17-42) section 3, RG 165, NA.

14. General B. E. Meyers to Joint Staff Planners, 11/14/42, Subject: "Priorities in Production of Munitions Based on Strategic Considerations," ABC 400 (2-17-42) section 3, RG 165, NA.

15. Chairman, War Production Board, to Admiral Leahy, 12/3/42, ABC 400 (2-17-42) section 4, RG 165, NA.

16. Notes on Joint Chiefs of Staff 45th Meeting, 12/8/42, ABC 400 (2-17-42) section 4, RG 165, NA.

17. R. S. Edwards to Admiral King, 12/8/42, 00 Files 1941–1946, box 35, folder 130, NHC.

18. Joint U.S. Strategic Committee to Joint Staff Planners, 11/21/42, Title: JPS 74/10, Subject: "U.S. War Production Objectives, 1943," ABC 400 (2-17-42) section 4, RG 165, NA.

19. Matloff and Snell, *Strategic Planning for Coalition Warfare, 1941–1942,* 353–55.

20. General Somervell and Admiral Horne to Joint Chiefs of Staff, 1/4/43, Title: JCS 186, Subject: "Production Priorities," ABC 400 (2-17-42) section 4, RG 165, NA.

21. Notes on Joint Chiefs of Staff 49th Meeting, 1/5/43, ABC 400 (2-17-42) section 4, RG 165, NA.

22. Joint Staff Planners to Joint Chiefs of Staff, 3/7/43, Title: JCS 146/11, Subject: "Priorities in Production of Munitions Based on Strategic Considerations," 00 Files 1941–1946, box 35, folder 130, NHC.

23. Chief of Naval Operations to Vice CNO and Assistant Chief of Staff (Plans), 3/10/43, Subject: "Priorities in Production of Munitions Based on Strategic Considerations," 00 Files 1941–1946, box 41, file 31 (VCNO), NHC.

24. Joint Staff Planners to Joint Chiefs of Staff, 3/15/43, Title: JCS 146/12, Subject: "Priorities in Production of Munitions Based on Strategic Considerations," 00 Files 1941–1946, box 35, folder 130, NHC.

25. Donald Nelson to Admiral Leahy, 4/14/43, Title: JCS 146/14, 00 Files 1941–1946, box 35, folder 130, NHC.

26. Goldberg, "Production Planning and Organization," in *The Army Air Forces in World War II,* ed. Craven and Cate, 6:285–86.

27. General Arnold to All Concerned, 1/5/43, Subject: "Saturation Point of the Air Power of the United States," H. H. Arnold Manuscript Collection, Official File 1932–1946, folder 74, LC.

28. Lane, *Ships for Victory,* 340.

29. War Shipping Administration to President, 10/16/42, ABC 411.5 (10-4-42) section 1, RG 165, NA.

30. Joint Military Transport Committee to Joint Chiefs of Staff, 11/13/42, Title: JCS 151, Subject: "Modification of the 1943 Shipbuilding Program of the Maritime Commission," ABC 411.5 (10-4-42) section 1, RG 165, NA.

31. Director, Services of Supply Requirements Division, to Joint Staff Planners, 10/24/42, Subject: "Additional Merchant Shipbuilding Program," CCS 561.4 (5-14-42) section 1, RG 218, NA.

32. Chaikin and Coleman, *Shipbuilding Policies,* 15.

33. Admiral Land to Admiral Leahy, 11/27/42, Title: JCS 151/2, 00 Files 1941–1946, box 35, folder 130, NHC.

34. Chief of Procurement and Material to Vice Chief of Naval Operations, 12/2/42, Title: JCS 151/3, Subject: "U.S. Maritime Commission—Additional Building Tonnage during 1943," ABC 411.5 (10-4-42) section 1, RG 165, NA.

35. Admiral Leahy to Donald Nelson, 12/16/42, Title: JCS 151/5, Subject: "Modification of the 1943 Shipbuilding Program of the Maritime Commission," 00 Files 1941–1946, folder 130, NHC.

36. Minutes, Joint Chiefs of Staff 48th Meeting, 12/29/42, CCS 334 JCS Meetings (11-10-42), RG 218, NA.

37. Lane, *Ships for Victory,* 342.

38. Congress, Senate, *Investigation of Manpower,* 9 February 1943, 31–32.

39. Joint Chiefs of Staff to Chairman, War Production Board, 1/6/43, ABC 411.5 (10-4-42) section 1, RG 165, NA.

40. Admiral Leahy to Admiral Land (Draft), 3/2/43, Title: JCS 151/16, Subject: "Modification of the 1943 Shipbuilding Program of the Maritime Commission," 00 Files 1941–1946, box 35, folder 130, NHC.

41. Chaikin and Coleman, *Shipbuilding Policies,* 100.

42. Joint Staff Planners to Joint Chiefs of Staff, 12/11/42, Title: JCS 157/3, Subject: "Coordination of Synthetic Rubber, 100 Octane Gas, and Escort Vessel Programs," 00 Files 1941–1946, box 35, folder 131, NHC.

43. Admiral King to Joint Chiefs of Staff, 12/15/42, Title: JCS 157/6, Subject: "Coordination of Synthetic Rubber, 100 Octane Gas, and Escort Vessel Programs," 00 Files 1941–1946, box 35, folder 131, NHC.

44. Chief of Strategy and Policy Group, Operations Division, to Secretary of Joint Staff Planners, 10/1/42, Subject: "Troop Bases for All Services for 1944 and Beyond," ABC 370.01 (7-25-42) section 2, RG 165, NA.

45. G-3 to Chief of Staff, 9/15/42, Subject: "Mobilization Plans," OPD 320.2 case 441, RG 165, NA.

46. Assistant Chief of Staff, Operations Division, to Assistant Chief of Staff, G-3, 10/20/42, Subject: "Mobilization Plans," OPD 320.2 case 441, RG 165, NA.

47. Report by Joint Staff Planners Sub-committee, 10/22/42, Title: JPS 57/6, Subject: "Troop Bases for All Services for 1944 and Beyond," ABC 370.01 (7-25-42) section 2, RG 165, NA.

48. Ibid.

49. Congress, Senate, Committee on Military Affairs, *Lowering the Draft Age to Eighteen Years,* 14 October 1942, 12.

50. Congress, House, Committee on Military Affairs, *Lowering the Draft Age to Eighteen Years,* 14 October 1942, 5.

51. Notes on Joint Staff Planners 43d Meeting, 10/28/42, ABC 370.01 (7-25-42) section 2, RG 165, NA.

52. Joint Chiefs of Staff Memorandum for Information, 11/5/42, "Meeting on Manpower Held Nov. 3," ABC 370.01 (7-25-42) section 2, RG 165, NA.

53. Minutes, General Council Meeting, 11/9/42, OPD 334.8 General Council, case 28, RG 165, NA.

54. Ibid.

55. Minutes, Joint Staff Planners 44th Meeting, 11/4/42, ABC 370.01 (7-25-42) section 2, RG 165, NA.

56. Draft Report, Joint Staff Planners to Joint Chiefs of Staff, 11/21/42, Subject: "Troop Bases for All Services for 1944 and Beyond (JCS 154)," CCS 320.2 (7-25-42) section 2, RG 218, NA.

57. Minutes, General Council Meeting, 11/23/42, OPD 334.8 General Council, case 30, RG 165, NA.

58. Joint Staff Planners to Joint Chiefs of Staff, 11/24/42, Title: JCS 154, Subject: "Troop Bases for All Services for 1944 and Beyond," ABC 370.01 (7-25-42) section 2, RG 165, NA.

59. Minutes, Joint Chiefs of Staff 44th Meeting, 12/1/42, CCS 334.8 JCS Meetings (11-10-42), RG 218, NA.

60. Minutes, Joint Chiefs of Staff 40th Meeting, 11/3/42, CCS 334 JCS Meetings (6-23-42), RG 218, NA.

61. Minutes, Joint Chiefs of Staff 44th Meeting, 12/1/42, CCS 334.8 JCS Meetings (11-10-42), RG 218, NA.

62. Joint Strategic Survey Committee to Joint Chiefs of Staff, 12/24/42, Title: JCS 154/1, Subject: "Troop Bases for All Services for 1944 and Beyond," ABC 370.01 (7-25-42) section 2, RG 165, NA.

63. Notes on Joint Chiefs of Staff 48th Meeting, 12/29/42, ABC 370.01 (7-25-42) section 2, RG 165, NA.

64. Joint Staff Planners to Subcommittee Members, 1/3/43, Subject: "Troop Bases for All Services for 1944 and Beyond," ABC 370.01 (7-25-42) section 2, RG 165, NA.

65. Chief of Staff to Secretary of War, 2/5/43, Subject: "Manpower," Chief of Staff Top Secret Correspondence File 1941–1943, 320.2, RG 165, NA.

66. Secretary of the Navy to Secretary of War, 2/8/43, Secretary of War "Safe" Correspondence File, "Navy Department," RG 107, NA.

67. Secretary of War to Secretary of the Navy, 2/12/43, Chief of Staff Top Secret Correspondence File 1941–1943, 320.2, RG 165, NA.

68. Congress, Senate, *Investigation of Manpower,* 17 February 1943, 275–79.

69. Ibid., 193.

70. Matloff, "The 90-Division Gamble," in *Command Decisions,* ed. Greenfield, 370.

71. Joint Staff Planners to Joint Chiefs of Staff, 5/7/43, Title: JCS 154/2 (original version JPS 57/8), Subject: "Troop Bases for All Services for 1944 and Beyond," ABC 370.01 (7-25-42) section 2, RG 165, NA.

72. Assistant Chief of Staff G-3 to Chief of Staff, 11/30/42, Subject: "Mobilization Plan, 1944," Chief of Staff Secret Correspondence File 1942–43, 320.2 section 4, RG 165, NA.

73. JCS 154/2, "Troop Bases for All Services for 1944 and Beyond."

74. Ibid.

75. Notes on Joint Staff Planners 72d Meeting, 5/5/43, ABC 370.01 (7-25-42) section 2, RG 165, NA.

76. Joint Deputy Chiefs of Staff to Joint Chiefs of Staff, 6/9/43, Subject: "Troop Bases for All Services for 1944 and Beyond," CCS 320.2 (7-25-42) section 3, RG 218, NA.

77. Paper by E. W. Chamberlain, Organization and Training Division, War Dept. General Staff, 7/24/42, G-3 320.2, RG 165, NA.

78. "C. L. J." to General Roberts, 11/3/44, ABC 560 (2-4-43), section 2, RG 165, NA.

CHAPTER 5. The Rise of the Critics, 1943–1944

1. Chart, "Total Aircraft and Total Tonnage of Combatant and Merchant Vessels—United Nations and Axis," 1/14/43, Navy Strategic Plans Division series 12, box 184, NHC.

2. Director of Naval Intelligence to Director of Central Division, 3/21/43, Subject: "Statement of the Vice CNO to be made before the Naval Subcommittee, House Appropriations Committee, on 1943 Estimates," SecNav/CNO Confidential File 1943, A18–4, RG 80, NA.

3. Chart, "Summary of Building Program," 1/1/43: General Board 420.2 1943–1945, RG 80, NA.

4. Vice Chief of Naval Operations to Admiral King, 5/7/43, Subject: "Recommendations Relative to New Construction," General Board 420.2 1943–1945, RG 80, NA.

5. Chief of Naval Operations to Admiral Horne, 5/19/43, Subject: "Recommendations Relative to New Construction," Navy Strategic Plans Division series 12, box 175, NHC.

6. Vice Chief of Naval Operations to Navy Bureaus, 5/28/43, Subject: "New Construction—Authorization Of," General Board 420.2 1943–1945, RG 80, NA.

7. Vice Chief of Naval Operations to Representative Harry Shepard, 5/22/43, SecNav/CNO Confidential File 1943, A18–1, RG 80, NA.

8. Vice Chief of Naval Operations to Representative Shepard, 6/1/43, SecNav/CNO Confidential File 1943, A18–1, RG 80, NA.

9. Somers, *Presidential Agency,* 47.

10. Robertson, *Sly and Able,* 326–28.

11. Somers, *Presidential Agency,* 117–18.

12. Director of Office of War Mobilization to President, no date, King Manuscript Files, September 1943, NHC.

13. Office of Budget and Reports to Senator James F. Byrnes, Chairman of Subcommittee on Naval Appropriation Bill, 2/12/40 and 3/13/41, Office of Budget and Reports, Budget Preparations and Estimates, Fiscal Years 1941–1942, RG 80, NA.

14. Vice CNO to Assistant CNO for Logistic Plans, 8/20/43, Subject: "Survey

of Ship Construction Program," Navy Strategic Plans Division series 14, part 3, box 204, NHC.

15. Secretary of the Navy to Admiral King, 9/3/43, King Manuscript Files, September 1943, NHC.

16. Chief of Naval Operations to Vice CNO, 9/6/43, Subject: "Revision of Ship-building Program," Navy Strategic Plans Division series 12, box 175, NHC.

17. Secretary of the Navy to the President, 9/9/43, SecNav/CNO Top Secret File 1945, A1–3, RG 80, NA.

18. Secretary of the Navy to the President, 9/21/43, SecNav/CNO Top Secret File 1945, A1–3, RG 80, NA.

19. Chief, Bureau of Ships, to Vice CNO, 9/27/43, Subject: "Destroyer Escort Program—Curtailment of Program," SecNav/CNO Top Secret File 1945 A1–3, RG 80, NA.

20. Vice CNO to Chief of Naval Operations, 9/29/43, Subject: "Destroyer Escort Program—Curtailment of," SecNav/CNO Top Secret File 1945 A1–3, RG 80, NA.

21. Chief of Naval Operations to Vice CNO, 10/7/43, Subject: "Destroyer Escort Program—Curtailment of," SecNav/CNO Top Secret File 1945 A1–3, RG 80, NA.

22. Chief, Bureau of Ships, to Chief of Naval Operations, 2/20/44, Subject: "Destroyer Escort Program—Further Cancellation of," SecNav/CNO Top Secret File 1945 A1–3, RG 80, NA.

23. Director of Office of War Mobilization to the President, 9/15/43, JCS Chairman's File 1942–48, Admiral Leahy, folder 127, RG 218, NA.

24. Ibid.

25. Ibid.

26. Rogow, *James Forrestal,* 92–93.

27. Under Secretary of Navy to President, 9/21/43, OPD 561 case 17, RG 165, NA.

28. President to Under Secretary of the Navy, 9/28/43, Subject: "Shipbuilding Program," ABC 561 (11-7-43), RG 165, NA.

29. Statement by President (for release), 9/24/43, CCS 334 JPSC (9-18-43), RG 218, NA.

30. Charter of Joint Production Survey Committee, 9/21/43, Title: JCS 202/26/D, ABC 334.8 JPSC (9-20-43), RG 165, NA.

31. Army Chief of Staff to General McNarney, 9/18/43, Subject: "Production Survey Committee," OPD Executive File 9, book 12, no. 36, RG 165, NA.

32. President to Director of Office of War Mobilization, 9/28/43, SecNav/CNO Secret File 1943, A1–3, RG 80, NA.

33. Minutes, Joint Production Survey Committee 1st Meeting, 10/2/43, CCS 334 JPSC (10-2-43), RG 218, NA.

34. Secretary, Joint Chiefs of Staff for Record, 10/15/43, Subject: "Navy Building Program," CCS 561.4 (9-21-43) section 1, RG 218, NA.

35. Draft letter, President to Secretary of the Navy, 10/15/43, JCS Chairman's File 1942–1948, Admiral Leahy, folder 127, RG 218, NA.

36. Director, Office of War Mobilization, to Secretary of the Navy, 10/19/43, SecNav/CNO Secret File 1943 A1–3, RG 80, NA.
37. Director, Office of War Mobilization, to Admiral Leahy, 10/21/43, CCS 561.4 (9-21-43) section 1, RG 218, NA.
38. Minutes, Joint Chiefs of Staff 120th Meeting, 10/26/43, CCS 334 JCS (9-14-43), RG 218, NA.
39. Vice CNO to Admiral King, 10/23/43, 00 Files 1941–1946, box 41, folder 31, NHC.
40. Chief of Naval Operations to Secretary of the Navy, 10/29/43, Subject: "Battleship Building Program," King Manuscript Files, October 1943, NHC.
41. Chief of Naval Operations to Secretary of the Navy, 10/26/43, Subject: "Naval Ship-building Program," ABC 561 (11-7-43), RG 165, NA.
42. Chairman, General Board, to Secretary of the Navy, 11/1/43, Subject: "Naval Shipbuilding Program," SecNav/CNO Secret File 1943, A1–3, RG 80, NA.
43. Secretary of the Navy to Admiral Brainard, JPSC, 11/2/43, SecNav/CNO Secret File 1943, A1–3, RG 80, NA.
44. Joint Production Survey Committee to Joint Chiefs of Staff, 11/7/43, Title: JCS 573, Subject: "Report on Army, Navy, and Maritime Commission Shipbuilding," ABC 561 (11-7-43), RG 165, NA.
45. Senior Navy Member, Joint Production Survey Committee, to Vice CNO, 10/7/43, Subject: "Request for Staff Assistance," CCS 334 JPSC (9-18-43), RG 218, NA.
46. Vice CNO to Director, Office of War Mobilization, 11/18/43, CCS 561.4 (9-21-43) section 1, RG 218, NA.
47. Minutes, Joint Chiefs of Staff 141st Meeting, 1/11/44, ABC 561 (11-7-43), RG 165, NA.
48. Report of Munitions Assignments Board, 12/31/43, Subject: "Naval Procurement Program," CCS 400 (12-31-43), RG 218, NA.
49. Joint Production Survey Committee to Senior Member, Joint Staff Planners, 1/26/44, Subject: "Control of the Building Program of Combatant Ships," CCS 561.4 (9-21-43) section 2, RG 218, NA.
50. Joint War Plans Committee to White Team, 1/31/44, Title: JWPC 184/D, Subject: "Control of the Building Program of Combatant Ships," CCS 561.4 (9-21-43) section 2, RG 218, NA.
51. Joint War Plans Committee to Joint Staff Planners, 3/17/44, Title: JPS 382/1, Subject: "Control of the Building Program of Combatant Ships," CCS 561.4 (9-21-43) section 2, RG 218, NA.
52. Minutes of Joint Staff Planners 140th Meeting, 3/22/44, CCS 334 JPS (1-12-44), RG 218, NA.
53. Ibid.
54. Joint War Plans Committee to Joint Staff Planners, 3/28/44, Title: JPS 382/2, Subject: "Control of the Building Program of Combatant Ships," ABC 561 (11-7-43), RG 165, NA.
55. Minutes, Joint Staff Planners 142d Meeting, 3/29/44, CCS 334 JPS (1-12-44), RG 218, NA.

56. Ibid.
57. Minutes, Joint Staff Planners 143d Meeting, 4/5/44, CCS 334 JPS (1-12-44), RG 218, NA.
58. Congress, House, Committee on Appropriations, *Navy Department Appropriation Bill for 1945,* 1 March 1944, 21–22.
59. Ibid., 31.
60. Congress, Senate, Committee on Appropriations, *Navy Department Appropriation Bill for 1945,* 17 April 1944, 5.
61. Joint War Plans Committee to Joint Staff Planners, 6/12/44, Title: JPS 382/3, Subject: "Control of the Building Program of Combatant Ships," ABC 561 (11-7-43), RG 165, NA.
62. Charter of Joint War Plans Committee, 5/11/43, Title: JCS 202/14/D, ABC 381 UN (1-23-42) section 3, RG 165, NA.
63. Charter of Joint Staff Planners, 5/11/43, Title: JCS 202/13/D, ABC 381 UN (1-23-42) section 3, RG 165, NA.
64. Minutes, Joint Staff Planners 156th Meeting, 6/14/44, CCS 334 JPS (4-19-44), RG 218, NA.
65. Ibid.
66. Joint Staff Planners to Joint War Plans Committee, 6/20/44, Subject: "Control of the Building Program of Combatant Ships," ABC 561 (11-7-43), RG 165, NA.
67. Joint War Plans Committee to Joint Staff Planners, 6/24/44, Title: JPS 382/4, Subject: "Control of the Building Program of Combatant Ships," ABC 561 (11-7-43), RG 165, NA.
68. Notes on Joint Staff Planners 157th Meeting, 6/28/44, Subject: "Control of the Building Program of Combatant Ships (JPS 382/4)," ABC 561 (11-7-43), RG 165, NA.
69. Minutes, Joint Staff Planners 162d Meeting, 8/10/44, CCS 334 JPS (4-19-44), RG 218, NA.
70. Joint War Plans Committee to Joint Staff Planners, 8/15/44, Title: JPS 382/5, Subject: "Control of the Building Program of Combatant Ships," ABC 561 (11-7-43), RG 165, NA.
71. Report by Joint War Plans Committee, 6/9/45, Title: JWPC 343/1, Subject: "Requirements in Land-Based and Carrier-Based Aircraft to Accomplish the Defeat of Japan," ABC 370.01 (7-25-42) section 6, RG 165, NA.

Chapter 6. The Fleet's Personnel Crisis, 1943–1944

1. Chief of Staff to General McNarney, 5/25/43, in *The Papers of George Catlett Marshall,* ed. Bland, 3:703.
2. Assistant Chief of Staff G-3 to Chief of Staff, 2/5/43, Subject: "Troop Basis Planning," Chief of Staff Secret Correspondence File 1942–1943, 320.2 section 3, RG 165, NA.

3. Palmer, "Mobilization of the Ground Army," in Greenfield, Palmer, and Wiley, *The Organization of Ground Combat Troops,* 222–23.
4. Congress, Senate, Committee on Military Affairs, *Married Men Exemption (Drafting of Fathers),* 20 September 1943, 251–52.
5. Minutes, Joint Chiefs of Staff 91st Meeting, 6/8/43, CCS 334 JCS Meetings (5-21-43), RG 218, NA.
6. Henry L. Stimson Diaries, Vol. 43, entry for 6/14/43, Manuscripts and Archives, Yale University Library, New Haven, Conn.
7. Deputy Chief of Staff to Maddocks, Chamberlain and Carter, 5/24/43, Subject: "Revision of the Current Military Program," ABC 400 (2-20-43), RG 165, NA.
8. Matloff, "The 90-Division Gamble," in *Command Decisions,* ed. Green-field, 373.
9. Special Army Committee to Deputy Chief of Staff, 6/5/43, Subject: "Troop Bases for All Services for 1944 and Beyond," ABC 370.01 (7-25-42) section 3, RG 165, NA.
10. Ibid.
11. Chief of Staff to Admiral King, 7/10/43, OPD 320.2 case 678, RG 165, NA.
12. Admiral King to General Marshall, 7/13/43, OPD 320.2 case 678, RG 165, NA.
13. Bureau of Naval Personnel to Commander in Chief, U.S. Fleet, 7/13/43, Subject: "Strength of the Army," COMINCH Secret File 1943, P16–1, RG 38, NA.
14. Joint Chiefs of Staff to President, 9/30/42, OPD 320.2 case 423, RG 165, NA.
15. Congress, House, Committee on Appropriations, *Navy Department Appropriation Bill for 1944,* 10 April 1943, 10, 30–31.
16. Secretary of the Navy to President via Joint Chiefs of Staff, 7/29/43, 00 Files 1942–1947, box 1, folder 12–A, NHC.
17. President to Secretary of the Navy, 8/3/43, SecNav/CNO Secret File 1943, P16–1, RG 80, NA.
18. Chief of Policy Section, Operations Division to Col. Nelson, 7/20/43, Subject: "Troop Bases for All Services for 1944 and Beyond," ABC 370.01 (7-25-42) section 3, RG 165, NA.
19. Chief, Logistics Group, Operations Division to General Handy, 11/2/43, Subject: "Troop Bases for All Services for 1944 and Beyond," OPD 320.2 case 819, RG 165, NA.
20. Chief of Naval Operations to Secretary of the Navy, 9/4/43, Subject: "Manpower Strength in the Navy, Marine Corps and Coast Guard," Ernest J. King Papers, LC.
21. Congress, Senate, Committee on Military Affairs, *Married Men Exemption (Drafting of Fathers),* 20 September 1943, 311.
22. Joint Logistics Committee to Joint Chiefs of Staff, 11/10/43, Title: JCS 154/7, Subject: "Troop Bases for All Services for 1944 and Beyond," ABC 370.01 (7-25-42) section 3, RG 165, NA.

23. Deputy Chief of Staff (Admiral Cooke) to Chief of Naval Operations, 11/6/43, Subject: "Troop Bases for All Services for 1944 and Beyond," Navy Strategic Plans Division series 3, box 68, NHC.
24. Chief of Naval Operations to All Bureaus and Offices of the Navy Department, 11/23/43, General Board 421, 1943–44, RG 80, NA.
25. Joint Logistics Committee to Joint Chiefs of Staff, 11/10/43, Title: JCS 154/7, Subject: "Troop Bases for All Services for 1944 and Beyond," ABC 370.01 (7-25-42) section 3, RG 165, NA.
26. Chief of Naval Operations to Joint Chiefs of Staff, 1/29/44, Title: JCS 154/9, Subject: "Navy Personnel Plan for Fiscal Year 1945," ABC 370.01 (7-25-42) section 3, RG 165, NA.
27. Acting Secretary of the Navy to President, 1/28/44, SecNav/CNO Secret File 1944, P16–1, RG 80, NA.
28. President to Secretary of the Navy, 2/8/44, JCS Chairman's File (Leahy), 1942–48, RG 218, NA.
29. Minutes, Joint Chiefs of Staff 144th Meeting, 2/1/44, CCS 334 JCS Meetings (12-28-43), RG 218, NA.
30. Joint Logistics Committee to Joint Chiefs of Staff, 2/12/44, Title: JCS 154/10, Subject: "Navy Personnel Plan for the Fiscal Year 1945," CCS 320.2 (7-25-42) section 4, RG 218, NA.
31. Joint Chiefs of Staff to Commander-in-Chief, U.S. Fleet, 2/23/44, Subject: "Navy Personnel Plan for the Fiscal Year 1945," ABC 370.01 (7-25-42) section 3, RG 165, NA.
32. Secretary of the Navy to Chief of Naval Personnel, 1/26/44, Subject: "Operating Force Plan, Revision of," COMINCH Secret File 1944, P 16–1, RG 38, NA.
33. Chief of Naval Personnel to Fleet and Sea Frontier Commanders, 1/28/44, Subject: "Establishment of Provisional Allowance," General Board 421, 1943–44, RG 80, NA.
34. Chief of Naval Operations to Vice CNO and Chief of Bureau of Naval Personnel, 2/14/44, Subject: "Personnel Situation," 00 Files 1941–1946, box 41, file 31, NHC.
35. Secretary of the Navy to Bureaus and Shore Establishments, 11/12/43, Subject: "Navy Manpower Survey Board," Correspondence of Secretary of the Navy Frank Knox, 1940–44, 15-2-1, RG 80, NA.
36. Senior Member, Navy Manpower Survey Board, to Secretary of the Navy, 2/29/44, Subject: "Statement to Be Made before the House Naval Appropriations Committee," Correspondence of Secretary of the Navy Frank Knox, 1940–44, 15-2-1, RG 80, NA.
37. Vice CNO to Chief of Naval Operations, 2/7/44, Subject: "Naval Personnel Situation," COMINCH Secret File 1944 P16–1, RG 38, NA.
38. L. D. McCormick to Vice Chief of Naval Operations, 2/14/44, Subject: "Navy Personnel Strength-Fiscal Year 1945," SecNav/CNO Secret File 1944 P16–1, RG 80, NA.

39. Congress, House, Committee on Appropriations, *Navy Department Appropriation Bill for 1945*, 29 February 1944, 54.
40. Bureau of Naval Personnel, "U.S. Bureau of Naval Personnel-Planning and Control Activity," 1946, 26.
41. Chief of Naval Personnel to Commander in Chief, U.S. Fleet, 1/18/44, Subject: "Final Report on Manpower Problems and Relation of Training Programs Thereto," King Manuscript Files, January 1944, NHC.
42. Chief of Naval Personnel to Listed Agencies, 5/21/45, Subject: "The Personnel Situation in the Navy and the Program for Future Months," General Board 421, 1945, RG 80, NA.
43. Bureau of Naval Personnel, "U.S. Bureau of Naval Personnel-Planning and Control Activity," 1946, 16.
44. Unsigned Memorandum to Secretary of the Navy, 3/2/44, SecNav/CNO Secret File 1944, P16–1, RG 80, NA.
45. Vice CNO to Chief of Naval Operations, 3/24/44, Subject: "Personnel Situation," COMINCH Secret File 1944, P16–1, RG 38, NA.
46. Ibid.
47. Minutes, Meeting of Joint Chiefs of Staff with Civilian Agency Heads, 3/21/44, CCS 334 JCS Meetings (3-11-44) RG 218, NA.
48. Bureau of Naval Personnel to Chief of Naval Operations, 4/8/44, Subject: "Navy Personnel Strength, June 30 1945," COMINCH Secret File 1944, P16–1, RG 38, NA.
49. Vice Chief of Naval Operations to Chief of Naval Operations, 4/19/44, Subject: "Navy Personnel Strength, June 30 1945," COMINCH Secret File 1944, P16–1, RG 38, NA.
50. Chief of Naval Operations to Vice Chief of Naval Operations, no date, Subject: "Navy Personnel Requirements, June 30 1945," COMINCH Secret File 1944, P16–1, RG 38, NA.
51. Vice Chief of Naval Operations to Committee Members, 4/6/44, Subject: "Study of Naval Personnel Requirements," COMINCH Secret File 1944, P16–1, RG 38, NA.
52. Report of Special Navy Committee, 5/3/44, Subject: "Naval Personnel Requirements for 1944–1945," COMINCH Top Secret File 1944, P16–1, RG 38, NA.
53. Ibid.
54. Chief of Naval Operations to Commander in Chief, Pacific Fleet, 5/7/44, Subject: "Naval Personnel Requirements for 1944–1945," COMINCH Top Secret File 1944, P16–1, RG 38, NA.
55. Commander in Chief, Pacific Fleet, to Chief of Naval Operations, 5/28/44, Subject: "Naval Personnel Requirements for 1944–1945," COMINCH Top Secret File 1944, P16–1, RG 38, NA.
56. Ibid., margin note.
57. F. S. Low to Admirals Horne, Edwards, and Jacobs, 6/15/44, Subject: "Personnel Problem," SecNav/CNO Top Secret File 1944, P16–1, RG 80, NA.

58. Ibid.

59. Commander in Chief, U.S. Fleet, to Joint Chiefs of Staff, 7/2/44, Title: JCS 154/11, Subject: "Naval Personnel Requirements, 30 June 1945," ABC 370.01 (7-25-42) section 3, RG 165, NA.

60. Ibid.

61. Coakley and Leighton, *Global Logistics and Strategy, 1943–1945*, 253–56.

62. Ibid., 308–9.

63. Spector, *Eagle against the Sun*, 279–80.

64. Coakley and Leighton, *Global Logistics and Strategy, 1943–45*, 407.

65. "D. Z. Z." to Colonel Lincoln, 7/12/44, Subject: "General Roberts' Note re: Navy Personnel Increase in JCS 154/11," ABC 370.01 (7-25-42) section 3, RG 165, NA.

66. Chief of Staff to the President, 8/22/44, Subject: "Strength of the Army," JCS Chairman's File (Leahy) 1942–1948, RG 218, NA.

67. Unsigned Memorandum to War Department Staff Divisions, 7/3/44, Subject: "Study of JCS 154/11," ABC 370.01 (7-25-42) section 3, RG 165, NA.

68. Deputy Director, Plans and Operations, Army Service Forces, to General Roberts, 7/4/44, Subject: "Naval Personnel Requirements 30 June 1945," ABC 370.01 (7-25-42) section 3, RG 165, NA.

69. Ibid.

70. Joint Logistics Committee to Joint Chiefs of Staff, 7/13/44, Title: JCS 154/12, Subject: "Navy Personnel Requirements, 30 June 1945," ABC 370.01 (7-25-42) section 3, RG 165, NA.

71. Chief of Staff to Justice Byrnes, 3/23/44, Subject: "Manpower," Chief of Staff Secret Correspondence File 1944–1945 320.2, case 36, RG 165, NA.

72. F. N. R. (General Roberts) to Secretary, War Department General Staff, 7/15/44, ABC 370.01 (7-25-42) section 3, RG 165, NA.

73. Joint Logistics Committee to Joint Chiefs of Staff, 11/7/44, Title: JCS 154/14, Subject: "Naval Personnel Requirements, 30 June 1945," ABC 370.01 (7-25-42) section 3, RG 165, NA.

74. Minutes of Conference at CINCPAC Headquarters, July 13–22, 1944, King Manuscript Files, series 4, NHC.

75. Chief of Naval Personnel to Chief of Naval Operations, 4/4/45, Subject: "Personnel Estimates," Navy Strategic Plans Division series 3, box 68, NHC.

76. Assistant Chief of Naval Personnel to Commander, Western Sea Frontier, 9/17/45, Subject: "Complements and Allowances," Bureau of Naval Personnel Correspondence File 1941–1945, P16–1, RG 24, NA.

CHAPTER 7. The Internal Debate, 1944

1. Davis, *Postwar Defense Policy*, 13.

2. Ibid., 23.

3. Chief of Naval Operations to Secretary of the Navy, 3/28/44, Subject: "Review of Building Program," SecNav/CNO Secret File 1944 A1–3, RG 80, NA.

4. Secretary of the Navy to the General Board, 3/29/44, Subject: "Review of Building Program," Navy Strategic Plans Division series 14, box 194, NHC.

5. Vice Chief of Naval Operations to Commander in Chief, U.S. Fleet, 3/31/44, Subject: "Future Construction of Ships," General Board 420.2, 1943–1945, RG 80, NA.

6. Chief of Naval Operations to Secretary of the Navy, 4/13/44, Subject: "Future Construction of Ships," Navy Strategic Plans Division series 14, box 194, NHC.

7. Chief of Naval Operations to Vice CNO, 4/24/44, and reply slip, 00 Files 1941–1946, box 41, file 31 (VCNO), NHC.

8. Navy General Board to Secretary of the Navy, 5/17/44, Subject: "Building Program," SecNav/CNO Secret File 1944, A1–3, RG 80, NA.

9. Navy Planning and Statistics Branch to Secretary of the Navy, 6/2/44, Subject: "Building Program, Combatant Ships," SecNav/CNO Secret File 1944, A1–3, RG 80, NA.

10. Lobdell, "Frank Knox," in *American Secretaries of the Navy,* ed. Coletta, 692.

11. Assistant Secretary of the Navy to Secretary of the Navy, 5/18/44, Correspondence of Secretary of the Navy James Forrestal, 1944–1947, 61-1-24, RG 80, NA.

12. Secretary of the Navy to Admiral Horne, 5/24/44, Correspondence of Secretary of the Navy James Forrestal, 1944–1947, 55-1-1, RG 80, NA.

13. Captain Duncan to Admiral King, 5/27/44, Subject: "Destroyer and Submarine Building Program," Navy Strategic Plans Division series 12, box 160, NHC.

14. Admiral King to Secretary of the Navy, 5/31/44, Navy Strategic Plans Division series 3, box 68, NHC.

15. Secretary of the Navy to Chief of Naval Operations, 6/2/44, Subject: "Cutbacks," SecNav/CNO Top Secret File 1945, A1–3, RG 80, NA.

16. Vice CNO to Committee Members, 6/10/44, Subject: "Committee on Cutbacks in Naval Shipbuilding Program," Navy Strategic Plans Division series 12, box 172, NHC.

17. Robert W. Love, "Ernest Joseph King," in *The Chiefs of Naval Operations,* ed. Love, 162.

18. Rogow, *James Forrestal,* 102–3.

19. Vice CNO to Admiral King, 6/17/44, Subject: "Logistics Plan—Pacific Maximum Effort—Assumptions For," Navy Strategic Plans Division series 12, box 172, NHC.

20. Chief of Naval Operations to Admiral Horne, 6/20/44, Subject: "Logistics Plan—Pacific Maximum Effort—Assumptions For," Navy Strategic Plans Division series 12, box 172, NHC.

21. Admiral King to Commander in Chief, Pacific Fleet, 6/10/44, Navy Strategic Plans Division series 12, box 172, NHC.

22. Commander in Chief, Pacific Fleet, to Admiral King, 6/19/44, Navy Strategic Plans Division series 12, box 172, NHC.

23. Chief of Naval Operations to Secretary of the Navy, 7/11/44, Subject: "Cutbacks in Naval Shipbuilding Program," Navy Strategic Plans Division series 12, box 172, NHC.

24. Chief of Naval Operations to Commander in Chief, Pacific Fleet, 7/25/44, Subject: "Submarine Building Program," Navy Strategic Plans Division series 14, box 194, NHC.

25. Chief of Naval Operations to Secretary of the Navy, 5/26/44, Subject: "Additional Cancellation of DE Construction," SecNav/CNO Top Secret File 1945, A1–3, RG 80, NA.

26. Chief of Naval Operations to Secretary of the Navy, 6/3/44, Subject: "Cancellation of Construction of Thirty-five Destroyer Escorts," Navy Strategic Plans Division series 12, box 160, NHC.

27. Staff Study, 5-28-44, Subject: "A Study of the Requirements for Naval Aviation in the Pacific with Comments and Recommendations from the Commander in Chief, U.S. Pacific Fleet," Navy Strategic Plans Division series 3, box 63, NHC.

28. Chief of Bureau of Ships to Admiral King, 6/26/44, Navy Strategic Plans Division series 12, box 160, NHC.

29. Commander in Chief, Pacific Fleet, to Chief of Naval Operations, 7/5/44, Navy Strategic Plans Division series 12, box 160, NHC.

30. Minutes of Meeting of Cut-back Committee, 7/25/44, Navy Strategic Plans Division series 12, box 172, NHC.

31. Index Cards, "Requirements," 7/6/44, Navy Strategic Plans Division series 12, box 183, NHC.

32. Ibid.

33. Assistant Chief of Staff-Plans to Admiral King, 8/7/44, Subject: "Cut-back in Destroyer Program," Navy Strategic Plans Division series 12, box 172, NHC.

34. Commander in Chief, Pacific Fleet, to Chief of Naval Operations, 8/11/44, Subject: "Ship Requirements as of 30 September 1945 for Operations in the Pacific to Defeat Japan," Navy Strategic Plans Division series 12, box 183, NHC.

35. Report of the Special Committee on Cut-backs, 11/30/44, SecNav/CNO Secret File 1944, A1–3, RG 80, NA.

36. Ibid.

37. Bureau of Ships to Admiral King, 7/19/44, Subject: "Control of Shipbuilding," Navy Strategic Plans Division series 12, box 172, NHC.

38. Chief of Naval Operations to Secretary of the Navy, 6/23/44, Subject: "Combatant Ships—Future Development Program," SecNav/CNO Secret File 1944, A1–3, RG 80, NA.

39. Chief of Naval Operations to Chiefs of Navy Bureaus, 7/28/44, Subject: "Prospective Building Program for Planning Purposes Only," General Board 420.2, 1943–1945, RG 80, NA.

40. Bureau of Ships to Chief of Naval Operations, 8/21/44, Subject: "Six-inch Light Cruiser Building Program," SecNav/CNO Top Secret File 1945, A1–3, RG 80, NA.

41. Chief of Naval Operations to Secretary of the Navy, 9/5/44, Subject: "Cutbacks in Naval Shipbuilding Program," Navy Strategic Plans Division series 12, box 172, NHC.

42. Vice CNO to Secretary of the Navy, 1/12/45, Subject: "Cut-backs in Navy Building Program," SecNav/CNO Top Secret File 1945, A1–3, RG 80, NA.

43. Chief of Naval Operations to Secretary of the Navy, 9/4/44, Subject: "Information Regarding Cutbacks in Navy Program," SecNav/CNO Secret File 1944 A1–3, RG 80, NA.

44. Chief of Naval Operations to Secretary of Navy, 9/28/44, Subject: "Combatant Shipbuilding Program," SecNav/CNO Secret File 1944 A1–3, RG 80, NA.

45. Joint War Plans Committee to Joint Staff Planners, 7/15/43, Title: JPS 193/1, Subject: "Strategic Deployment of U.S. Forces to 1 July 1944," ABC 320.2 (3-13-43) section 1, RG 165, NA.

46. Joint War Plans Committee to Joint Staff Planners, 1/23/44, Title: JPS 193/4, Subject: "Strategic Deployment of U.S. Forces to December 31, 1944," ABC 320.2 (3-13-43) section 2, RG 165, NA.

47. King, *The U.S. Navy at War, 1941–1945,* 287–88.

48. Vice CNO to Commander in Chief, U.S. Fleet, 3/31/44, Subject: "Future Construction of Ships," General Board 420.2, 1943–1945, RG 80, NA.

49. Charts, "Estimated Deployment of Ships, 30 April 1944 to 30 September 1945," Navy Strategic Plans Division series 12, box 160, NA.

50. Report of the Special Committee on Cut-backs, 12/31/44, 00 Files 1941–1946, box 37, file 144, NHC.

51. Joint Staff Planners to Joint Chiefs of Staff, 12/23/44, Title: JCS 521/9, Subject: "Strategic Deployment of U.S. Forces Following the Defeat of Germany," ABC 320.2 (3-13-43) section 6, RG 165, NA.

52. Ibid.

53. Statistical Section, Division of Naval Intelligence, 1/1/45, Subject: "Combatant Vessels of the Seven Principal Naval Powers," CINCPAC Files 1945, A8/QN, RG 313, NA.

54. Minutes, Special Joint Chiefs of Staff Meeting, 9/9/43, CCS 334 JCS Meetings (8-7-43), RG 218, NA.

55. Admiral King to Admiral Stark, 11/5/43, King Manuscript Files, November 1943, NHC.

56. Merrill Bartlett and Robert Love, Jr., "Anglo-American Naval Diplomacy and the British Pacific Fleet, 1942–1945," *American Neptune* (July 1982): 211–14.

CHAPTER 8. Forrestal's Conversion and the Endgame, 1945

1. King and Whitehall, *Fleet Admiral King,* 421.

2. Gene Duffield to Secretary of the Navy, 12/30/44, Correspondence of Secretary of the Navy James Forrestal, 1944–1947, 61-1-24, RG 80, NA.

3. Secretary of the Navy to the President, 1/2/45, Correspondence of Secretary of the Navy James Forrestal, 1944–1947, 34-2-22, RG 80, NA.

4. Ibid.

5. Rogow, *James Forrestal,* 124–25.

6. Minutes of Top Policy Group 1st Meeting, 11/13/44, Records of Secretary of the Navy James Forrestal, 1944–1947, RG 80, NA.

7. Minutes of Top Policy Group 8th Meeting, 1/1/45, Records of Secretary of the Navy James Forrestal, 1944–1947, RG 80, NA.

8. Secretary of War to Chief of Staff, n.d., Subject: "Strength of the Army," Secretary of War "Safe" File 1940–1945, "Size of the Army," RG 107, NA.

9. Memorandum of Meeting in Secretary's Office, 1/6/45, James Forrestal Papers, box 19, "Construction Program," Princeton University.

10. Ibid.

11. Secretary of the Navy to Mr. Gates, 1/6/45, Correspondence of Secretary of the Navy James Forrestal, 1944–1947, 61-1-24, RG 80, NA.

12. Chief of Naval Operations to Secretary of the Navy, 1/8/45, Subject: "Combatant Vessel Construction Program," Navy Strategic Plans Division series 14, part 3, box 206, NHC.

13. Minutes of Top Policy Group 9th Meeting, 1/8/45, Records of Secretary of the Navy James Forrestal, 1944–1947, RG 80, NA.

14. Secretary of the Navy to President, 1/8/45, SecNav/CNO Secret File 1944, A1–3, RG 80, NA.

15. President's Naval Aide to Secretary of the Navy, 1/9/45, Subject: "Combatant Vessel Construction Program," Map Room Files, box 162, A1–3, FDRL.

16. Admiral Leahy to Representative Carl Vinson, 1/16/45, Correspondence of Secretary of the Navy James Forrestal, 1944–1947, 61-1-24, RG 80, NA.

17. Somers, *Presidential Agency,* 66–67.

18. Director, Bureau of Budget, to President, 1/17/45, Subject: "Proposed Combatant Vessel Construction Program," SecNav/CNO Secret File 1944, A1–3, RG 80, NA.

19. Minutes of Top Policy Group 11th Meeting, 1/22/45, Records of Secretary of the Navy James Forrestal, 1944–1947, RG 80, NA.

20. Secretary of the Navy to the President, 1/23/45, Subject: "Proposed Reply to Director of the Budget, Prepared by Admiral King," Correspondence of Secretary of the Navy James Forrestal, 1944–1947, 61-1-24, RG 80, NA.

21. Ibid., enclosure.

22. Lewis L. Strauss to Secretary of the Navy, 1/25/45, Subject: "Proposed Combatant Shipbuilding Program (664,000 Tons)," Correspondence of Secretary of the Navy James Forrestal, 1944–1947, 61-1-24, RG 80, NA.

23. President's Naval Aide to the President, 1/31/45, Map Room Files, box 162, A1–3, FDRL.

24. Director of Bureau of the Budget to Secretary of the Navy, 2/7/45, General Board 420.2, 1943–1945, RG 80, NA.

25. Chief of Naval Operations to Bureau Chiefs, 2/12/45, Subject: "Combatant Vessel Construction Program," General Board 420.2, 1943–1945, RG 80, NA.
26. Bureau of Ships to Chief of Naval Operations, 2/24/45, Subject: "Combatant Vessel Construction Program," General Board 420.2, 1943–1945, RG 80, NA.
27. Statement of the Director of Budget and Reports, 3/1/45, Office of Budget and Reports General Correspondence 1940–1947, series 12–3, RG 80, NA.
28. Draft Testimony of Secretary of the Navy on Navy Appropriations Bill for Fiscal Year 1945–1946, 3/12/45, Office of Fiscal Director General Correspondence 1944–1945, L-1-1, RG 80, NA.
29. Congress, House, Committee on Appropriations, *Navy Department Appropriation Bill for 1946,* 14 March 1945, 30.
30. Ibid., 34.
31. Byrnes, *All in One Lifetime,* 189–90.
32. H. Struve Hensel to Secretary of the Navy, 3/16/45, Subject: "Cabinet Meeting of 3/16/45," James Forrestal Diaries, Vol. 2, Princeton University.
33. James Byrnes to Secretary of the Navy, 3/3/45, SecNav/CNO Secret File 1944, A1–3, RG 80, NA.
34. President to Secretary of the Navy, 3/22/45, SecNav/CNO Secret File 1944, A1–3, RG 80, NA.
35. Congress, House, Committee on Appropriations, *Naval Appropriations Bill, Fiscal Year 1946,* 12.
36. Report by the Office of the Chief of Naval Operations, "Combatant Shipbuilding, 1-1-42 to 7-1-46," 51.
37. Rep. Harry R. Shepard to Vice CNO, 5/7/45, SecNav/CNO Confidential File 1945, L-1-1, RG 80, NA.
38. Admiral Cochrane to Representative Carl Vinson, 3/31/45, Correspondence of Secretary of the Navy James Forrestal, 1944–1947, 61-1-42, RG 80, NA.
39. Joint Staff Planners to Joint Chiefs of Staff, 3/29/45, Title JCS 521/12, Subject: "Strategic Deployment of U.S. Forces Following the Defeat of Germany," ABC 320.2 (3-13-43) section 8, RG 165, NA.
40. Maj. Gen. R. C. Moore to Chief of Staff, 4/45, Subject: "Military Aircraft Requirements after the Defeat of Germany," ABC 320.2 (3-13-43) section 8, RG 165, NA.
41. Chief of Staff to Joint Chiefs of Staff, 4/10/45, Title: JCS 521/16, Subject: "Strategic Deployment of U.S. Forces Following the Defeat of Germany," ABC 320.2 (3-13-43) section 9, RG 165, NA.
42. Barlow, *The Revolt of the Admirals,* 44–45.
43. Hayes, *The History of the Joint Chiefs of Staff,* 659.
44. Notes on Joint Staff Planners 171st Meeting, "Tactical Air Forces Required to Accomplish the Earliest Possible Conclusive Defeat of Japan (JPS 522/1)," 9/28/44, ABC 320.2 (3-13-43) section 6, RG 165, NA.

45. Memorandum by the Chief of Naval Operations, 4/7/45, Title: JCS 521/15, Subject: "Strategic Deployment of U.S. Forces Following the Defeat of Germany," ABC 320.2 (3-13-43) section 9, RG 165, NA.

46. Joint War Plans Committee to Joint Staff Planners, 7/2/45, Title: JWPC 49/27/M, Subject: "Strategic Deployment of U.S. Forces," ABC 320.2 (3-13-43) section 10, RG 165, NA.

47. Record of Requirements Review Board 16th Meeting, 6/16/45, SecNav/CNO Secret File 1945, A–19, RG 80, NA.

48. "R. F. T." to Colonel Wood, 5/11/45, ABC 370.01 (7-25-42) section 6, RG 165, NA.

49. Joint War Plans Committee to Joint Staff Planners, 6/9/45, Title: JWPC 343/1, Subject: "Requirements in Land-Based and Carrier-Based Aircraft to Accomplish the Defeat of Japan," ABC 370.01 (7-25-42) section 6, RG 165, NA.

50. Ibid.

51. Memorandum "Discussion of JWPC 343/1," ABC 370.01 (7-25-42) section 6, RG 165, NA.

52. Report of the Special Committee on Cutbacks in the Naval Shipbuilding Program, 5/31/45, Navy Strategic Plans Division, series 12, box 172, NHC.

53. Chief of Naval Operations to Secretary of the Navy, 4/27/45, Subject: "Estimate of the Post-War Naval Establishment," COMINCH Secret File 1945, A1–1, RG 38, NA.

54. Davis, *Postwar Defense Policy,* 158.

55. Ibid., 163.

56. Admiral A. J. Hepburn to Vice Admiral R. S. Edwards, 1/17/45, Subject: "Strength of Post-War Fleet," Navy Strategic Plans Division series 14, box 197, NHC.

57. E. W. Burrough, Post-War Planning Division to Admiral Edwards, 5/22/45, Subject: "Cutback in Navy Shipbuilding Program," Navy Strategic Plans Division series 14, box 194, NHC.

58. Report by the Office of the Chief of Naval Operations, "Combatant Ship-building, 1-1-42 to 7-1-46," 45.

59. Secretary of the Navy to General Board and Bureau Chiefs, 5/10/45, Subject: "Combatant Ships—Development and Improvement of Design," Navy Strategic Plans Division series 14, box 194, NHC.

60. Secretary of the Navy to the President, 5/10/45, Subject: "Combatant Ship Development and Building Program," Navy Strategic Plans Division series 14, box 194, NHC.

61. Minutes of Top Policy Group 22d Meeting, 5/21/45, Records of Secretary of the Navy James Forrestal, 1944–1947, RG 80, NA.

62. Secretary of the Navy to Chairman, General Board, 6/29/45, Subject: "Post-War Building Program," Navy Strategic Plans Division series 14, box 194, NHC.

63. Historical Section, Commander in Chief, United States Fleet, *Commander in Chief, United States Fleet, Headquarters,* 32–44.

64. Admiral R. S. Edwards to Admiral King, 6/1/45, COMINCH Secret File 1945, A1–3, RG 38, NA.

65. Truman to Government Agency Heads, 7/6/45, quoted in Albion, *Makers of Naval Policy, 1798–1947,* 464.

66. Secretary of the Navy to Chief of Naval Operations, 7/24/45, Correspondence of Secretary of the Navy James Forrestal, 1944–1947, 61-1-24, RG 80, NA.

67. Minutes of Top Policy Group 29th Meeting, 7/30/45, Records of Secretary of the Navy James Forrestal, 1944–1947, RG 80, NA.

68. Report of Special Committee on Cut-Backs, 7/31/45, Navy Strategic Plans Division series 12, box 172, NHC.

69. Admiral King to Secretary of the Navy, 8/7/45, Subject: "The Naval Shipbuilding Program—Reduction of," CINCPAC Confidential Files 1945, A –1, box 2604, RG 313, NA.

70. Chief of Naval Operations to Bureau of Ships, 8/11/45, Subject: "Naval Shipbuilding Program—Curtailment of," CINCPAC Confidential Files 1945, A –1, box 2604, RG 313, NA.

71. Report of Special Committee on Cut Backs in the Naval Shipbuilding Program, 8/31/45, COMINCH Secret File 1945, A1-1, "Postwar Plans," RG 38, NA.

72. Director of Budget and Reports to Bureau of Ships, 9/12/45, Office of Budget and Reports, Plans for Post-War Operations, De-Mobilization, and Cut-Backs, 1945–1946, RG 80, NA.

73. Secretary of the Navy to Director of War Mobilization and Reconversion, 12/15/45, Subject: "Reduction of Naval Shipbuilding Program," Navy Strategic Plans Division series 14, box 194, NHC.

74. Bureau of Ships, *An Administrative History of the Bureau of Ships during World War II,* 4:13.

BIBLIOGRAPHY

PRIMARY SOURCES

Most of the information in this book was drawn from the official records of the individuals and organizations responsible for making the decisions that affected navy expansion. Navy sources used in the National Archives included the official correspondence of Navy Secretaries Frank Knox and James Forrestal, the records of meetings of the Top Policy Group created by Forrestal, the Secretary of the Navy/Chief of Naval Operations Correspondence File (a collection of important materials from the CNO and his staff), the COMINCH Correspondence File (a similar collection from the staff of the commander in chief, U.S. Fleet), the collection of General Board special studies, hearings, and correspondence, the records of the Bureau of Personnel and the Bureau of Ships, the records of the commander in chief, Pacific Fleet, the records of the Navy Department Office of Budget and Reports, and the records of the Office of Fiscal Director.

Army sources in the National Archives included the correspondence of the army chief of staff, the correspondence of the secretary of war, the records of the American-British Conversations File kept by the Strategy and Policy Group of the Operations Division of the War Department General Staff, the records of the Operations Division and the Personnel Division (G-3) of the War Department, and the records of the War Plans Division (predecessor of the Operations Division).

Joint Sources in the National Archives included the Joint Chiefs of Staff Chairman's File of Adm. William D. Leahy, reports and hearings of the Joint

Bibliography

Board, and the correspondence and meeting minutes of joint organizations affiliated with the Combined Chiefs of Staff, especially the Joint Staff Planners and Joint Logistics Committee and their subordinate organizations.

Navy materials in the collection of the Naval Historical Center, Washington, D.C., included the official correspondence of Admirals Ernest J. King and Harold R. Stark, the Double Zero Files from Admiral King's office, and the records of the Navy Strategic Plans Division (formerly the Plans Division of the COMINCH staff).

The Library of Congress Manuscript Collection contained papers of Admiral King and Gen. H. H. Arnold of the Army Air Forces, as well as microfilm copies of the papers of Secretary of War Henry L. Stimson, of Secretary Stimson's diary, and of Admiral Leahy's diary.

Other collections consulted included the James Forrestal Papers and Diaries at Princeton University, the George C. Marshall Papers at the George C. Marshall Library, and the holdings of the Franklin D. Roosevelt Library in Hyde Park, New York.

CONGRESSIONAL HEARINGS, DEBATES, AND REPORTS

HEARINGS

U.S. Congress. House. Committee on Appropriations. *Navy Department Appropriation Bill for 1941, Hearings before the Committee on Appropriations.* 76th Cong., 3d sess., May 1940.

———. *Navy Department Appropriation Bill for 1942: Hearings before the Subcommittee of the Committee on Appropriations.* 77th Cong., 1st sess., February 1941.

———. *Navy Department Appropriation Bill for 1943, Hearings before the Committee on Appropriations.* 77th Cong., 2d sess., January 1942.

———. *Supplemental Navy Department Appropriation Bill for 1943: Hearings before the Committee on Appropriations.* 78th Cong., 1st sess., February 1943.

———. *Navy Department Appropriation Bill for 1944: Hearings before the Subcommittee of the Committee on Appropriations.* 78th Cong., 1st sess., April 1943.

———. *Navy Department Appropriation Bill for 1945: Hearings before the Committee on Appropriations.* 78th Cong., 2d sess., February-March 1944.

———. *Navy Department Appropriation Bill for 1946: Hearings before the Committee on Appropriations.* 79th Cong., 1st sess., March 1945.

U.S. Congress. House. Committee on Military Affairs. *Lowering the Draft Age to Eighteen Years: Hearings before the Committee on Military Affairs.* 77th Cong., 2d sess., October 1942.

U.S. Congress. House. Committee on Naval Affairs. *Bill to Establish the Composition of the United States Navy: Hearings before the Committee on Naval Affairs.* 76th Cong., 3d sess., January 1940.

————. *Hearing on HR 10100, to Establish the Composition of the U.S. Navy, to Authorize the Construction of Certain Naval Vessels.* 76th Cong., 3d sess., June 1940.

U.S. Congress. Senate. *Investigation of the National Defense Program: Hearings before the Special Committee Investigating the National Defense Program.* Part 5. 77th Cong., 1st sess., July 1941.

U.S. Congress. Senate. Committee on Appropriations. *Second Supplemental Defense Appropriation Bill for 1941: Hearings before the Committee on Appropriations.* 76th Cong., 3d sess., August 1940.

————. *Investigation of Manpower: Hearings before the Committee on Appropriations.* 78th Cong., 1st sess., February 1943.

————. *Navy Department Appropriation Bill for 1945: Hearings before the Subcommittee of the Committee on Appropriations.* 78th Cong., 2d sess., April 1944.

U.S. Congress. Senate. Committee on Military Affairs. *Lowering the Draft Age to Eighteen Years: Hearings before the Committee on Military Affairs.* 77th Cong., 2d sess., October 1942.

————. *Married Men Exemption (Drafting of Fathers): Hearing before the Committee on Military Affairs.* 78th Cong., 1st sess., September 1943.

U.S. Congress. Senate. Committee on Naval Affairs. *Construction of Certain Naval Vessels: Hearings before the Committee on Naval Affairs.* 76th Cong., 3d sess., April 1940.

————. *Hearing before the Committee on Naval Affairs on HR 8026.* 76th Cong., 3d sess., May 1940.

————. *Authorizing Major Alterations to Certain Naval Vessels and Additional Shipbuilding Facilities and Equipment for the Navy: Hearing before the Committee on Naval Affairs.* 77th Cong., 1st sess., January 1941.

————. *Additional Shipbuilding, Ship Repair, and Ordnance Manufacturing Facilities: Hearing before the Committee on Naval Affairs.* 77th Cong., 1st sess., July 1941.

DEBATES

U.S. Congress. House. Debate on HR 8026. 76th Cong., 3d sess. *Congressional Record,* 12 March 1940.

————. Debate on HR 10100. 76th Cong., 3d sess. *Congressional Record,* 22 June 1940.

————. Representative Vinson Speaking for HR 7184. 77th Cong., 2d sess. *Congressional Record,* 18 June 1942.

U.S. Congress. Senate. Debate on HR 10100. 76th Cong., 3d sess. *Congressional Record,* 10 July 1940.

REPORTS

U.S. Congress. House. Committee on Appropriations. *Naval Appropriations Bill, Fiscal Year 1946.* 79th Cong., 1st sess., 1945, H.R. 424.

U.S. Congress. House. Committee on Naval Affairs. *To Establish the Composition of the U.S. Navy, to Authorize the Construction of Certain*

Bibliography

Naval Vessels, and for Other Purposes. House Report 2252. 77th Cong., 2d sess., June 1942.

————. *Investigation of the Progress of the War Effort.* House Report. 78th Cong., 2d sess., 1944.

SECONDARY SOURCES

BOOKS

Albion, Robert G. *Makers of Naval Policy, 1798–1947.* Annapolis, Md.: Naval Institute Press, 1980.

Barlow, Jeffrey G. *The Revolt of the Admirals: The Fight for Naval Aviation, 1945–1950.* Washington, D.C.: Department of the Navy, 1994.

Bland, Larry I. ed. *The Papers of George Catlett Marshall,* volume 3: *The Right Man for the Job: December 7, 1941–May 31, 1943.* Baltimore: Johns Hopkins University Press, 1991.

Buell, Thomas. *Master of Sea Power: A Biography of Fleet Admiral Ernest J. King.* Boston: Little, Brown, 1980.

Byrnes, James F. *All in One Lifetime.* New York: Harper and Brothers, 1958.

Chaikin, William, and Charles Coleman. *Shipbuilding Policies of the War Production Board, January 1942–November 1945.* Historical Reports on War Administration: War Production Board Special Study no. 26. April 15, 1947.

Cline, Ray S. *U.S. Army in World War II, the War Department, Washington Command Post: The Operations Division.* Washington, D.C.: Department of the Army, 1951.

Coakley, Robert, and Richard Leighton. *U. S. Army in World War II, the War Department, Global Logistics and Strategy, 1943–1945.* Washington, D.C.: U.S. Army, 1968.

Connery, Robert H. *The Navy and the Industrial Mobilization in World War II.* Princeton: Princeton University Press, 1951.

Davis, George T. *A Navy Second to None: The Development of Modern American Naval Policy.* New York: Harcourt, Brace, 1940.

Davis, Vernon E. *The History of the Joint Chiefs of Staff in World War II: Organizational Development,* volume 2: *Development of the JCS Committee Structure.* Washington, D.C.: Historical Division, Joint Chiefs of Staff, 1972.

Davis, Vincent. *Postwar Defense Policy and the U.S. Navy, 1943–1946.* Chapel Hill: University of North Carolina Press, 1966.

Farr, Gail E., and Brett F. Bostwick. *Shipbuilding at Cramp & Sons.* Philadelphia: Philadelphia Maritime Museum, 1991.

Fifty Years: New York Shipbuilding Corporation. Camden: New York Shipbuilding Corporation, 1949.

Flynn, George. *The Mess in Washington: Manpower Mobilization in World War II.* Westport, Conn.: Greenwood Press, 1979.

Bibliography

Friedman, Norman. *U.S. Destroyers: An Illustrated Design History.* Annapolis, Md.: Naval Institute Press, 1982.

Furer, Julius A. *Administration of the Navy Department in World War II.* Washington, D.C.: Department of the Navy, 1959.

Futrell, Robert. *Ideas, Concepts, Doctrine: A History of Basic Thinking in the United States Air Force, 1907–1964.* New York: Arno Press, 1980.

Hayes, Grace P. *The History of the Joint Chiefs of Staff in World War II: The War against Japan.* Annapolis, Md.: Naval Institute Press, 1982.

Heiner, Albert P. *Henry J. Kaiser, Western Colossus.* San Francisco: Halo Books, 1991.

Hewes, James Jr. *From Root to McNamara: Army Organization and Administration, 1900–1963.* Washington, D.C.: U.S. Army Center of Military History, 1975.

Hooks, Gregory. *Forging the Military-Industrial Complex: World War II's Battle of the Potomac.* Urbana: University of Illinois Press, 1991.

Hoopes, Townsend, and Douglas Brinkley. *Driven Patriot: The Life and Times of James Forrestal.* New York: Alfred Knopf, 1992.

King, Ernest J. *The U.S. Navy at War, 1941–1945.* Washington, D.C.: United States Navy Department, 1946.

King, Ernest J., and Walter M. Whitehall. *Fleet Admiral King: A Naval Record.* New York: W. W. Norton, 1952.

Kirkpatrick, Charles E. *An Unknown Future and a Doubtful Present: Writing the Victory Plan of 1941.* Washington, D.C.: U.S. Army Center of Military History, 1990.

Lane, Fredric C. *Ships for Victory: A History of Shipbuilding under the U.S. Maritime Commission in World War II.* Baltimore: Johns Hopkins University Press, 1951.

Leutze, James R. *Bargaining for Supremacy: Anglo-American Naval Collaboration, 1937–1941.* Chapel Hill: University of North Carolina Press, 1977.

Lott, Arnold S. *A Long Line of Ships: Mare Island's Century of Naval Activity in California.* Annapolis, Md.: U.S. Naval Institute, 1954.

Lowenthal, Mark M. *Leadership and Indecision: American War Planning and Policy Process, 1937–1942.* New York: Garland Publishing, 1988.

Mansfield, George. *Historical Review: Boston Naval Shipyard, 1938–1957.* Boston: Department of the Navy, 1957.

Matloff, Maurice, and Edwin M. Snell. *The U.S. Army in World War II, the War Department: Strategic Planning for Coalition Warfare, 1941–1942.* Washington, D.C.: Department of the Army, 1953.

Miller, Edward S. *War Plan Orange.* Annapolis, Md.: Naval Institute Press, 1991.

Richardson, James O. *On the Treadmill to Pearl Harbor: The Memoirs of Admiral James O. Richardson.* Washington, D.C.: Department of the Navy, 1973.

Robertson, David. *Sly and Able: A Political Biography of James F. Byrnes.* New York: W. W. Norton, 1994.

Bibliography

Rogow, Arnold A. *James Forrestal: A Study of Personality, Politics and Policy.* New York: Macmillan, 1963.

Silverstone, Paul H. *U.S. Warships of World War II.* New York: Doubleday, 1965.

Smith, R. Elberton. *United States Army in World War II: The Army and Economic Mobilization.* Washington, D.C.: Department of the Army, 1959.

Snow, Ralph L. *Bath Iron Works: The First Hundred Years.* Bath: Maine Maritime Museum, 1987.

Somers, Herman M. *Presidential Agency: The Office of War Mobilization and Conversion.* Cambridge: Harvard University Press, 1950. Reprint. New York: Greenwood Press, 1969.

Spector, Ronald H. *Eagle against the Sun.* New York: Free Press, 1985.

Watson, Mark S. *U.S. Army in World War II, the War Department, Chief of Staff: Prewar Plans and Preparations.* Washington, D.C.: Department of the Army, 1950.

Wedemeyer, Albert C. *Wedemeyer Reports!* New York: Henry Holt, 1958.

Weinberg, Gerhard L. *A World at Arms: A Global History of World War II.* Cambridge: Cambridge University Press, 1994.

Weir, Gary E. *Forged in War: The Naval-Industrial Complex and American Submarine Construction, 1940–1961.* Washington, D.C.: Department of the Navy, 1993.

White, Gerald T. *Billions for Defense: Government Financing by the Defense Plant Corporation during World War II.* University: University of Alabama Press, 1980.

Winslow, Richard E. III. *Portsmouth Built: Submarines of the Portsmouth Naval Shipyard.* Portsmouth: Portsmouth Marine Society, 1985.

ADMINISTRATIVE HISTORIES

Bureau of the Budget. *The United States at War: Development and Administration of the War Program by the Federal Government.* Washington, D.C.: USGPO, 1947.

Historical Section, Commander in Chief, U.S. Fleet. 1st draft narrative. *Commander in Chief, United States Fleet, Headquarters.* United States Naval Administration in World War II Series. Washington, D.C.: Department of the Navy, 1946.

U.S. Navy Bureau of Ships. *An Administrative History of the Bureau of Ships during World War II.* Washington, D.C.: Department of the Navy, 1952.

U.S. Navy Bureau of Yards and Docks. *Building the Navy's Bases in World War II: History of the Bureau of Yards and Docks and the Civil Engineer Corps, 1940–1946.* Washington, D.C.: USGPO, 1947.

ARTICLES AND ESSAYS

Bartlett, Merrill, and Robert Love, Jr. "Anglo-American Naval Diplomacy and the British Pacific Fleet, 1942–1945." *American Neptune* (July 1982).

Bibliography

Gemery, Henry, and Jan Hogendorn. "The Microeconomic Bases of Short-Run Learning Curves: Destroyer Production in World War II." In *The Sinews of War: Essays on the Economic History of World War II*. Edited by Geofrey T. Mills and Hugh Rockoff. Ames: Iowa State University, 1993.

Goldberg, Alfred. "Production Planning and Organization." In *The Army Air Forces in World War II*, volume 6: *Men and Planes*. Edited by Wesley F. Craven and James L. Cate. Chicago: University of Chicago Press, 1955. Reprint. Washington, D.C.: Office of Air Force History, 1982.

Lobdell, George H. "Frank Knox." In *American Secretaries of the Navy*, volume 1: *1913–1972*. Edited by Paolo E. Coletta. Annapolis, Md.: Naval Institute Press, 1980.

Love, Robert W. "Ernest Joseph King." In *The Chiefs of Naval Operations*. Edited by Robert W. Love. Annapolis, Md.: Naval Institute Press, 1980.

Matloff, Maurice. "The Ninety-Division Gamble." In *Command Decisions*. Edited by Kent R. Greenfield. Washington, D.C.: Department of the Army, 1960.

McVoy, James, Virgil Rinehart, and Prescott Palmer. "The Roosevelt Resurgence." In *Naval Engineering and American Seapower*. Edited by Randolph W. King. Baltimore: Nautical and Aviation Publishing Company of America, 1989.

Palmer, Robert R. "Mobilization of the Ground Army." In Kent Greenfield, Robert Palmer, and Bell Wiley, *The Organization of Ground Combat Troops*. Washington, D.C.: Department of the Army, 1947.

Simpson, B. Mitchell III. "Harold Raynsford Stark." In *The Chiefs of Naval Operations*. Edited by Robert W. Love. Annapolis, Md.: Naval Institute Press, 1980.

Smith, H. Gerrish, and L. C. Brown. "Shipyard Statistics." In *The Ship-building Business in the United States of America*. Edited by F. G. Fasset, Jr. New York: Society of Naval Architects and Marine Engineers, 1948.

Walter, John C. "Congressman Carl Vinson and Franklin D. Roosevelt: Naval Preparedness and the Coming of World War II, 1932–1940." *Georgia Historical Quarterly* 65 (Summer 1980): 303.

UNPUBLISHED REPORTS AND HISTORICAL MANUSCRIPTS

Annual Report of the Secretary of the Navy to the President, Fiscal Year 1945.

Barksdale, Arthur S., Jr. "History of the Norfolk Navy Yard in World War II." Unpublished manuscript, Navy Department Library, Washington, D.C.

Bureau of Naval Personnel. "U.S. Bureau of Naval Personnel: Planning and Control Activity," 1946.

Enders, Calvin W. "The Vinson Navy." Ph.D. dissertation, Michigan State University, 1970.

Office of the Chief of Naval Operations. "Combatant Shipbuilding, 1-1-42 to 7-1-46." Office of the Chief of Naval Operations, 1946.

Bibliography

Reynolds, Charles V., Jr. "America and a Two-Ocean Navy, 1933–1941." Ph.D. dissertation, Boston University, 1978.

INTERVIEWS

Carter, Lt. Gen. Marshall S. (Ret.). Interview by Col. Geo S. Pappas. 26 March 1973. U.S. Army Center of Military History, Washington, D.C.

Duncan, Adm. Donald B. Interview by History Research Office, Columbia University, 1964–67, Naval Historical Center, Washington, D.C.

INDEX

Note: Numbers set in italic type indicate tables within the text.

aircraft carriers: accelerated production of, 148; Army Air Forces criticize, 175; escort type, *59*, 149, 163; favored in wartime expansion bill, 35–36; King prefers over battleships, 34; navy's lack of experience with, 15; Roosevelt disapproves of large type, 35; total building program of, 95–96, 163; total requirements for, 149–50

aircraft program: dispute over size of, 72; effects on navy program, 73–75; King criticizes, 175; reductions in, 76–77; required for invasion of Japan, 173–74

Air War Plans Division (AWPD). *See* Army Air Forces

amphibious shipping program, 135–38

armor plate. *See* battleships

Army Air Forces (AAF): criticize aircraft carrier program, 175; manpower shortages in, 77; postwar considerations of, 174; prewar plans of, 28–29; as primary rival of navy, 173; units released by defeat of Germany, 172

army deployment: after defeat of Germany, 172; cargo ship losses and, 93; estimates of, 48; increased merchant shipbuilding and, 77–78; lags behind projections, 120; limits mobilization levels, 83–84; political repercussions of, 174

army mobilization: civilian control over, 86; effects of shipping limitations on, 46, 83–85; manpower limitations and, 90; navy views on, 48–49, 89–90, 92, 122; plan for, in 1943, 45; potential increases to, 115; prewar plans for, 25, 27–28; reduction in, for 1943, 120–22, 124; strategic rationale for, 84, 87–88

army personnel strength: average age in army, 137; frozen at 1943 levels, 90–91; over authorized limit, 137; projected for 1943, 45–46; projected for 1948, 83–84; reductions in, for 1943, 120–22, 124

Index

Index

Index

The **Naval Institute Press** is the book-publishing arm of the U.S. Naval Institute, a private, nonprofit, membership society for sea service professionals and others who share an interest in naval and maritime affairs. Established in 1873 at the U.S. Naval Academy in Annapolis, Maryland, where its offices remain today, the Naval Institute has almost 85,000 members worldwide.

Members of the Naval Institute support the education programs of the society and receive the influential monthly magazine *Proceedings* and discounts on fine nautical prints and on ship and aircraft photos. They also have access to the transcripts of the Institute's Oral History Program and get discounted admission to any of the Institute-sponsored seminars offered around the country.

The Naval Institute also publishes *Naval History* magazine. This colorful bimonthly is filled with entertaining and thought-provoking articles, first-person reminiscences, and dramatic art and photography. Mem-bers receive a discount on *Naval History* subscriptions.

The Naval Institute's book-publishing program, begun in 1898 with basic guides to naval practices, has broadened its scope in recent years to include books of more general interest. Now the Naval Institute Press publishes about 100 titles each year, ranging from how-to books on boating and navigation to battle histories, biographies, ship and aircraft guides, and novels. Institute members receive discounts of 20 to 50 percent on the Press's nearly 600 books in print.

Full-time students are eligible for special half-price membership rates. Life memberships are also available.

For a free catalog describing Naval Institute Press books currently available, and for further information about subscribing to *Naval History* magazine or about joining the U.S. Naval Institute, please write to:

Membership Department
U.S. Naval Institute
118 Maryland Avenue
Annapolis, Maryland 21402-5035

Telephone: (800) 233-8764
Fax: (410) 269-7940